Preface

This book is mainly targeted for BCA exam of Theory of Computer Science. It has been introduced in market after seeing the huge demand of ready to grasp material for exams with high level of quality, and its un-availability in market. We the GullyBaba Publishing House took a step ahead to publish the quality material focusing on exams at the same time giving you indepth knowledge about the subject.

GPH Book is the pioneer effort that provides a unique methodology so as to perform better in exams. If your goal is to attain higher grade use this powerful study tool independently or along with your text.

*On the Web : **www.gullybaba.com** is the vital resource for your exams acting as catalyst to boost up your preparation. Gullybaba.com has been Listed **no.1** in www.google.com and www.yahoo.com when you search "IGNOU MCA BCA MBA". Now you can access us on the net through **www.doctorignou.com, www.doeacconline.com, www.gphindia.com, and www.gullybabapublishinghouse.com.***

Feedback about the book can be sent at **cs72writers@gullybaba.com.**

Acknowledgments :

We appreciate the staff and facility support provided by GullyBaba Publishing House. In particular, we appreciate the encouragement and professional advises received from Mr. Ajay Saini, Mr. Tarun Sharma, B. K. Krishna and many more.

Also we would like to thank typesetting and designing team Mrs. Bhawna Verma, Mr. Shravan Vats, Mr. Parveen Kumar, and Mr. Mukesh.

We gratefully acknowledges the significant contributions of Mr. Mahesh Chand, Mrs. Bimla Devi, Mrs. Bhawna Verma and our experts in bringing out this publication.

New Delhi ***Publisher***

Contents

Question Papers

C++ AND OBJECT ORIENTED PROGRAMMING

CS-72

For

Bachelor of Computer Applications [BCA]

By

Dr. A.K. Saini

Ph.d., M.PHIL., MCS, M.Sc., MBA

IGNOU Course Writer

Arun Tanwar

B.Tech.

CLOSER TO NATURE

WE USE RECYCLED PAPER

Useful For

IGNOU, Nalanda University, Kurushetra University, Lalit Narayan Mithila University, Andhra University, Pt. Sunderlal Sharma (Open) University (Bilaspur), Annamalai University, Bangalore University, Bharathiar University, Bharathidasan University, HP University, Jamia Millia Islamia, Kakatiya University (Andhra Pradesh), KSOU (Karnataka), KOU (Rajasthan), MPBOU (MP), MDU (Haryana), Punjab University, Tamilnadu Open University, Sri Padmavati Mahila Visvavidyalayam (Andhra Pradesh), Sri Venkateswara University (Andhra Pradesh), UCSDE (Kerala), University of Jammu, YCMOU, Rajasthan University, UPRTOU (UP) and all other Indian Universities.

GULLYBABA PUBLISHING HOUSE (P) LTD.

AN ISO 9001:2008 CERTIFIED CO.

Developed and Produced by:
GullyBaba Publishing House (P) Ltd.

Regd. Office:
2525/193, 1st Floor,
Onkar Nagar-A, Tri Nagar,
New Delhi-110035
Landmark: Kanhaiya Nagar Metro Station

Branch Office:
1A/2A, 20, Hari Sadan,
Ansari Road, Daryaganj,
New Delhi-110002

E-mail: info@gullybaba.com, Website: GullyBaba.com

Edition: 2013
Price: ₹410/-

ISBN: 978-81-89086-29-9

Feedback is the breakfast of Champions.

Ken Blanchard

You can Help other students.
"Inform any error or mistake in this book."

We and Universe
will reward you for Your Kind act.

Email at : feedback@gullybaba.com
or
WhatsApp on 9350849407

CHAPTER-1

BASIC FOUNDATION

PROCEDURAL LANGUAGES & OOP

Q1 What is Object Oriented Programming? How is it different from procedural programming? Does object oriented programming paradigm not use procedural programming at all? Justify your answer. [JUN02, Q1(a)]

 # What are the advantages of object oriented programming? How is it different from procedural programming? What are the disadvantages of object oriented systems? [JUN01]

Object Oriented Programming : is a programming methodology where the main emphasis is given on the object or the data and not on the functions or operations that operate on data. Data is undervalued in procedural programming. Here, the design puts data upfront & organization of data is significant area. Access rights are reserved as well to protect data from accidental changes by an intruder.

Advantages :

(i) Promotes organization in programming style.

(ii) Offers reusability i.e. the work done in the past can be put into use as such in future.

(iii) One function can have many forms that permits widening of area of application.

Disadvantages :

(i) OOP is a high level concept so takes more time to execute as many routines run behind at the time of execution

(ii) Offers less number of functions as compared to low level programming which interacts directly with hardware.

(iii) Increased burden on part of OOP developer.

Difference : Procedural languages are the languages where each statement in the language tells the computer to do something. Get some input add these numbers, divided by 6, display that output. A program in a procedural language is a list of instructions. For very small programs no other organizing principle (often called a paradigm) is needed. The programmer creates the list of instructions, and the computer caries them out. Pascal, C, BASIC, Fortran, and similar languages are procedural languages.

OOP does use procedural programming but only for small internal code. Actually the whole organisation of data finds its base at procedural steps. The structure that we call OOP has its foundation in procedural languages. E.g. data & function put together to form an object, but data & functions follow sequential or procedural steps of programming.

DIVISION INTO FUNCTIONS

When programs become larger, a single list of instructions becomes unwieldy. Few programmers can comprehend a program of more than a few hundred statements unless it is broken down into smaller units. For this reason the function was adopted as a way to make programs more comprehensible to their human creators. (The term function is used in C++ and C. In other languages the same concept may be referred to as a subroutine, a subprogram, or a procedure)

PROBLEMS WITH STRUCTURED PROGRAMMING

The principal idea behind structured programming was as simple as the idea of "divide and conquer." A computer program could be regarded as consisting of a set of tasks. Any task that was too complex to be simply described would be broken into a set of smaller component tasks, until the tasks were sufficiently small and self-contained to be easily understood. As programs grow ever larger and more complex, even the structured programming approach beings to show signs of strain. You may have heard about, or been involved in, horror stories of program development. The project is too complex, the schedule slips, more programmers are added, complexity increases, cost skyrocket, the schedule slips further, and finally disaster.

Analyzing the reasons for these failures reveals that there are weakness in the procedural paradigm itself. No matter how well the structured programming approach is implemented, large programs become excessively complex.

What are the reason for this failure of procedural languages? One of the most crucial is the role played by data.

DATA IS UNDERVALUED

In a procedural language, the emphasis is on doing things--read the keyboard, add the values, check for error, and so on. The subdivision of a program into functions continues this emphasis. Functions do thing as single program statements do. What they do may be more complex or abstract, but the emphasis is still on the action.

WHAT HAPPENS TO THE DATA IN THIS PARADIGM?

Data is, after all, the reason for a program's existence. Data is given second-class status in the organization of procedural languages.

For example, in an inventory program, the data that makes up the inventory is probably read from a disk file into memory, where it is treated as a global variable. By global we mean that the variables that constitute the data are declared outside of any function, so they are accessible to all functions. These functions perform various operations on the data. They read it, analyze it, update it, rearrange it, display it, write it back to the disk, and so on.

We should note that most languages, such as pascal and C, also support local variables, which are hidden within a single function. But local variables are not useful for important data that must be accessed by many different functions. Figure below shows the relationship between global and local variables.

Global and Local Variables

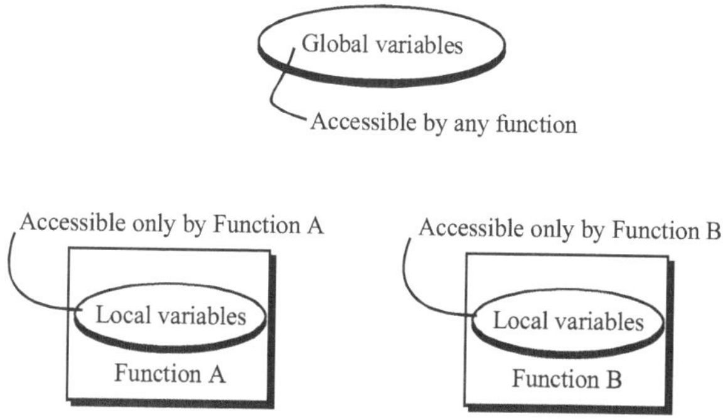

The Procedural Paradigm

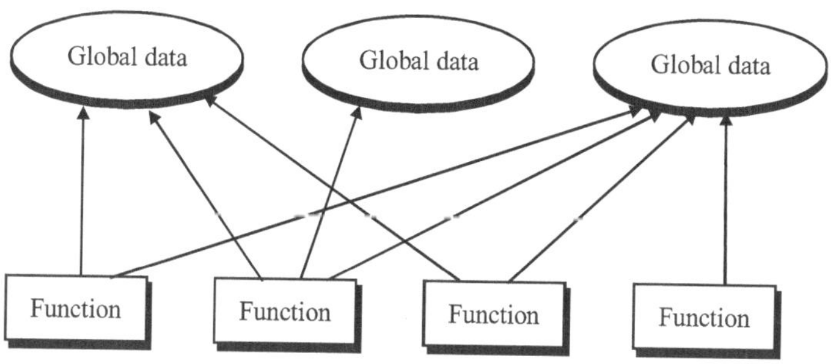

Now suppose a new programmer is hired to write a function to analyze this inventory data in a certain way. Unfamiliar with the subtitles of the program, the programmer creates a function which has complete access to the data. It's like leaving your personal papers in the lobby of your apartment building: Anyone can change or destroy them. In the same way. Global data can be corrupted by functions that have no authorization to change it. What is needed is a way to restrict access to the data, to hide it from all but a few critical functions. This will Protect the data, simplify maintenance, and offer other benefits as well.

TRADITIONAL LANGUAGES DOES NOT PROVIDE EXTENSIBILITY.

One is the difficulty of creating new data types. Computer languages typically have several built-in data types: your own data type? Perhaps you want to work with complex numbers, or two-dimensional coordinates or dates-quantities the built-in-data types don't handle easily. Being able to create your own types is called extensibility; you can extend the capabilities of the language. Traditional languages are not usually extensible. Without unnatural convolutions, you can't bundle together both X and Y coordinates into a single variable called point, and then add subtract values of this type. The result is that traditional programs are more complex to write and maintain.

The object-oriented approach : Solution to above problems.

The fundamental idea behind object-oriented languages is to combine both data and the functions that operate on that data into a single unit called ***an object***. An object's functions, called member functions in C++ typically provide the only way to access its data. If you want to read a data item in an object, you call only way to access its data. If you want to read a data item in an object, you call a member function in the object. It will read the item and return the value to you it can't access the data directly. The data is hidden, so it is safe to accidental alterations. Data and its functions are said to be encapsulated into a single entity, ***data encapsulation and data hiding*** are key terms in the description of object-oriented languages.

No other functions can access the data. This simplifies writing, debugging, and maintaining the program.

A C++ program typically consist of a number of objects, which communicates with each other by calling one another's member functions.

We should mention that what are called member functions in C++ are called methods in some other-oriented (OO) languages (such as Smalltalk, one of the first OO languages). Also data items are referred to as ***instance variables***. Calling an object's member function is referred to as ***sending a message to the object***. These terms are not usually used in C++.

AN ANALOGY

You might want to think of objects as departments such as sales accounting personnel, and so on in company. The people in each department control and operate on that department's data. Dividing the company into departments makes it easier to comprehend and control the company's activities, and helps to maintain the integrity of the information used by the company.

The Object-oriented Paradigm

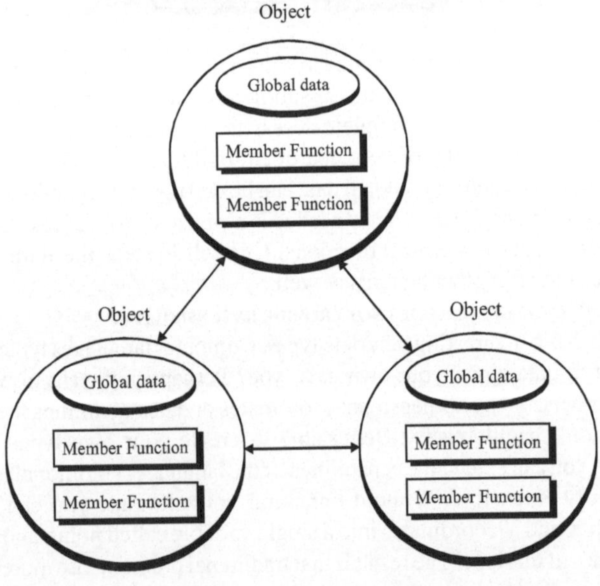

KNOW OBJECT-ORIENTED LANGUAGES IN DETAIL

Let's briefly examine a few of the major elements of object-oriented languages or C++.

OBJECTS

When you approach a programming problem in an object-oriented language you are no longer ask how the problem will be divided into functions, but how it will be divided into object. Thinking in terms of object, rather than functions has a surprisingly helpful effect on how easily programs can be designed. This results from the close match between objects in the programming sense and objects in the real world.

What kinds of things become objects in object-oriented programs? The answer to this is limited only by your imagination, but below are some examples :

PHYSICAL OBJECTS

Automobiles in a traffic-flow simulation
Electrical components in a circuit-design program
Countries in an economics model
Aircraft in an-traffic-control system

ELEMENTS OF THE COMPUTER-USER ENVIRONMENT

The mouse and the keyboard
Windows
Menus
Graphics object (lines, rectangles, circles)

The match between programming objects and real-world object is the happy results of combining data and functions: The resulting objects offer a revolution in program design. No such close match between programing constructs and the items being modeled exists in a procedural language.

CLASSES

In OOP we say that objects are members of classes. What does this mean? Let's look at an analogy. Almost all computer languages have built-in data types. For instance a data type int. Meaning integer, is predefined in C++ . You can declare as many variables of types int as you need in your program:

```
int marks;
int no_of_assignments;
int no_of_papers;
```

In a similar way you can make objects of the same class, as shown in the following figure.

A Class and Its Objects

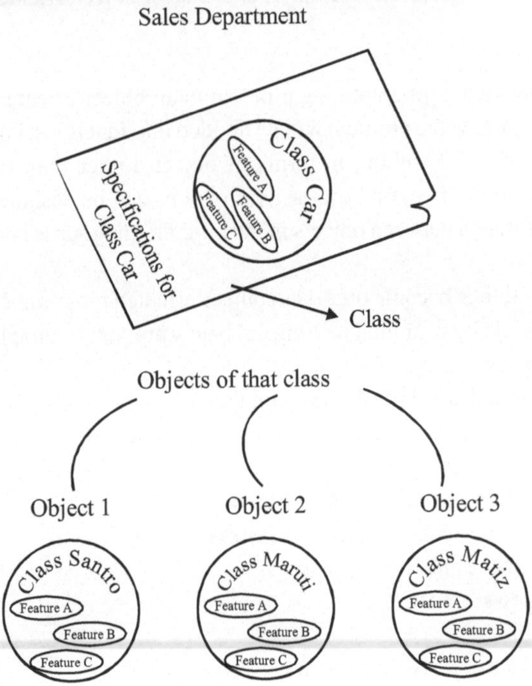

A class serves as a plan, or template. It specifies what data and what functions will be included in object of that class. Defining the class doesn't create any abject, just as the mere existence of a type int doesn't create any variables.
A class is thus a collection of similar objects. This fits our nontechnical understanding of the class of mountaineers. There is no one person called "mountaineers" but specific people with specific names are members of this class if they posses certain characteristics.

INHERITANCE

The idea of classes leads to the idea of inheritance. In our daily lives, we use the concept of classes being divided into subclasses. We know that the class of animals is divided into mammals, amphibians, insects, bird, and so on. The class of vehicles is divided into cars, truck, buses, and motorcycles.
Principle in this sort of division is that each subclass shares common characteristics with the class from which it's derived. Cars, truck, buses, and motorcycles all have wheels and a motor; these are the defining characteristics of vehicles. In addition to the characteristics: buses, for instance, have seats for many people, while trucks have space for large loads.
This ideas shown in the following figure notice in the figure that features A and B, which are part of the base class, are common to all derived classes, but that each

deriver class also has features of its own.

In a similar way, an OOP class can be divided into subclass. In C++ the original class is called the base class: other classes can be defined to share characteristics, but add their own as well. These are called derived classes.

Inheritance is somewhat analogous to using functions to simplify a traditional procedural program. If we find that three different sections of a procedural program do almost exactly the same thing, we recognize an opportunity to extract the common elements of these three sections and put them into a single function. As functions do in a procedural program, inheritance shortens an object-oriented program and clarifies the relationship among program elements.

Inheritance

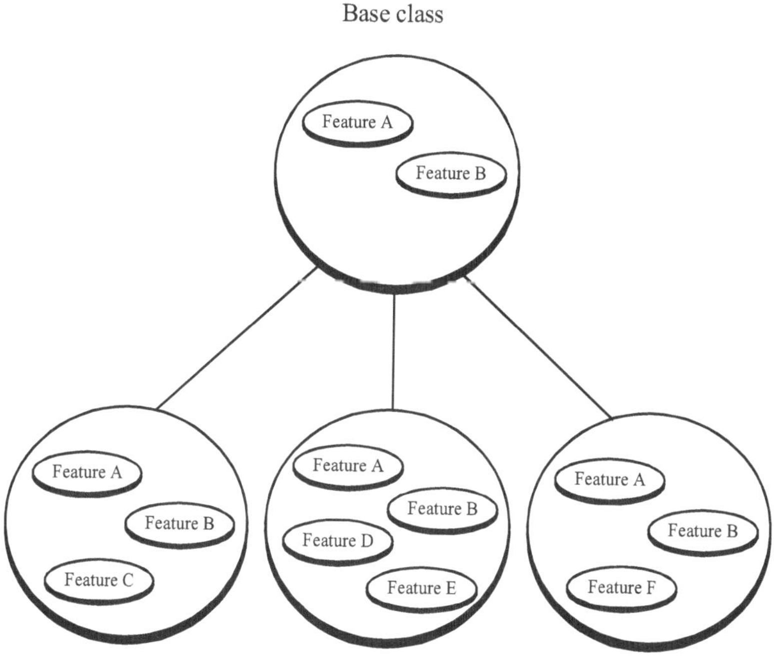

Derived Classes

REUSABILITY

Once a class has been written, created, and debugged, it can be distributed to other programmers for use in their own programs. This is called reusability. It is similar to the way a library of functions in a procedural language can be incorporate into different programs.

In OOP the concept of inheritance provides an important extension to the idea of reusability. A programmer can take an existing class without modifying and can use to develop any new application. This is done by deriving a new class from the existing one. The new class will inherit the capabilities of the old one but is free to add new features of its own.

For example, you might have written (or purchased from someone else) a class that creates a menu system, such as used in the Turbo C++ integrated development system (IDE). This class works fine, and you don't want to change it but you want to add the capability to make some menu entries flash on and off. To do this you simply create a new class that inherits all the capability of the existing one but adds flashing menu entries.

CREATING NEW DATA TYPES

One of the benefits of objects is that it give the programmer a convenient way to construct new data types. Suppose you work with two-dimensional positions (such as X and Y coordinates, or latitude and longitude) in your program. You would like to express operations on these positional values with normal arithmetic operations, such as

Position1 = position2 + origin;

Where the variables position1, position2 and origin each represent a pair of independent numerical quantities. By creating a class that incorporates these two values, and declaring position1, position2 and origin to be objects of this class, we can, in effect, create a new data type. Many features of C++ are intended to facilitate the creation of new data types in this manner.

POLYMORPHISM & OVERLOADING

Note that the = (equal) and + (plus) operators, used above don't act the same way they do in operations on built-in types like int. The object position1 and so on are not predefined in C++, but are programmer-defined objects of class position. How do the = and + operations know how to operate on objects? The answer is that we can define new operations for these operators. These operators will be member functions of the position class.

Using operators or functions in different ways, depending on what they are operating on, is called polymorphism. One thing with several distinct forms. When an existing operator, such as + or = is given the capability to operate on a new data type, it is said to be overloaded. Overloading is a kind of polymorphism; it is also an important features of OOP.

CHAPTER-2

OOPS FEATURES

- Introduction
- Advantages
- C++ & OOPS
- Encapsulation & Data Hiding
- Inheritance & Reuse
- Polymorphism
- Difference Between C & C++
- Scope Resolution Operator (::)
- Default Arguments
- New & Delete
- Cin, Cout as Objects

INTRODUCTION TO C++

C++ was developed by Bjarne Stroustrup at Bell Laboratories in 1983. Originally, it was called as " C with class". C+ as an enhancement to the C language was developed primarily to facilitate managing, programming and maintaining large software projects.

The most important aspect of the C language is, probably, the flexibility to do whatever the programmer wants. The limits of the language are defined by the programmer's imagination. Unfortunately, with very large projects in which many programmers use shared routines, this liberty can lead to what are called as 'side effects'. This is one problem, which C++ attempts to resolve by restricting indiscriminate access. At the same time, C++, also attempts to keep the freedom and flexibility given by the language. All the keywords of C are keywords of C++ also. In addition we have some new one's too.

However, C++ is not merely an extension of the C language, where some new symbols have been added. The basic purpose of C++ language is to add features to the C language that supports the concepts of OOP.

What are the advantages of C++?

- **The Learning Curve for C Programmers is very fast:** Most of the companies already have C programmers. They do not want that their programmer become ineffective in a day. C++ is an extension of C, thus, reduces the learning time. In addition, C++ compiler accepts C code.
- **Efficiency:** C++ allows greater control of program performance and also allows programmers to interact with assembly code as the case with C language. Thus, C++ is quite a performance-oriented language. It sacrifices some flexibility in order to remain efficient, however, C++ uses compile-time binding, which means that the

programmer must specify the specific class of an object, or at the very least, the most general class that an object can belong to. This makes for high run-time efficiency and small code size.

- **Systems are Easier to Express and Understand:** Since, C++ supports object oriented paradigm, thus, demonstrates the compatibility of good solution expression as it deals with higher-level concept like objects and classes rather than functions and data. It also produces maintainable code. The programs that are easier to understand are easier to maintain.
- **Good Library Support:** One of the fastest ways to create a program is to use already written code from the library. C++ libraries are easy to use and can be used in creating new classes, C++ guarantees proper initialization, and call to library functions/classes, you can use the libraries.
- **Source code Reuse using Templates:** Template feature reuses same source code with automatic modification for different classes. It is a very powerful tool that allows reuse of library code. Templates hide complexity of the code reuse for different classes on the user.
- **Error Handling:** C++ supports error-handling capabilities that catches the errors and reports them too. This feature provides control of error handling to the programmers in a similar way as being done for the libraries.
- **Programming in Large:** Many programming languages have their own limitation; some have limitations of line of code, some on recursion etc. However, C++ provides many features that support the programming. Some of these features are:

(i) Templates, namespaces and exception handling,
(ii) Strongly typed easy to use compiler,
(iii) Small or large programs are allowed,
(iv) Objects help in reducing complex program to manageable one.

C++ AND OBJECT-ORIENTED PROGRAMMING

The most important term is '***Abstraction***'. Abstraction means ignoring those aspects of a subject that are not revealed to the current purpose in order to concentrate more fully on those that are relevant. To an analyst who is as good as a subject expert it means choosing certain things or aspects of the system over others at a time. Most of the things in the real world are intrinsically complex, far more complex than one can comprehend at a time. By using abstraction one selects only a part of the whole complex instead of working with the whole thing. It does not mean ignoring the details altogether but only temporarily, the details are embedded inside and are dealt with at a later stage. Abstraction is used by OOP as a primary method of managing complexity.

Association is the principle by which ideas are connected together or united. Association is used to tie together certain things that happen at some point in time or under similar conditions.

Communicating with messages is the principle for managing complexity, which is used when interfaces are involved to communicate between the entities. OOP uses classes and objects have attributes, which can be exclusively accessed by services of the objects. To change the attributes of the object (a data member of the object), a message has to be sent to the object to invoke the service. This mechanism helps in implementing encapsulation and data abstraction.

Encapsulation and Data Hiding

The property of being a self-contained unit is called encapsulation. The idea that the encapsulated unit can be used without knowing how it works is called data hiding.

Encapsulation is the principle by which related contents of a system are kept together. It minimizes traffic between different parts of the work and it separates certain specific requirements from other parts of specification, which use those requirements. The important advantage of using encapsulation is that it helps to minimize rework when developing a new system. The part of the work, which is prone to change, can be encapsulated together. Thus any changes can be made without affecting the overall system and hence changes can be easily incorporated.

As noted before, when an engineer needs to add resistor to the device she is creating, she doesn't typically build a new one from the scratch. She walks over to a bin of resistors, examines the bin of resistors, examines the colored bands that indicate the properties, and picks the one she needs. The resistor is a "black box" as far as the engineer is concerned - that is, she doesn't care how it does its work as long as it conforms to her specifications.

All the resistor's properties are encapsulated in the resistor object - they are not spread out through the circuitry. It is not necessary to understand how the resistor works to use it effectively, because its data is hidden inside the resistor covering.

C++ supports the properties of encapsulation and data hiding through the creation of user-defined types, called classes. Once created, a well-defined class acts as a fully encapsulated entity and can be used as a whole unit. The actual inner workings of the class should be hidden; users of well-defined class do not need to know how the class works, only how to use it.

Inheritance and Reuse

Consider a car manufacturing company. When they want to build a new car, they have two choices. They can start from the scratch, or they can modify an existing model. Perhaps their former model is nearly perfect (say CAR1), but they would like to add a turbocharger and a six-speed transmission. The chief engineers would prefer to use the earlier model and make some changes to it than creating a new one (CAR2).

C++ supports the idea of reuse through inheritance. Through this concept, a new type can be declared that is an extension of the existing type. This new subclass is said to derive from the existing type and is sometimes called a derived type.

Polymorphism

The CAR2 in the above example may respond differently than the CAR1 when the car accelerates. The CAR2 might engage fuel injection and a turbocharger, for example, whereas the CAR1 simply get petrol into its carburetor. A user, however, does not have to know about these differences; the user simply presses the accelerator and the car responds with the correct function.

C++ supports this idea - that different objects do "the right thing" - through function polymorphism and class polymorphism. ***Poly*** means many, whereas ***morph*** means form. Thus, ***polymorphism*** refers to the same name taking many forms.

SOME DIFFERENCES BETWEEN C AND C++

There are several differences between the C language and C++, which have nothing to do with OOP. Some of them are highlighted below.

ADDITIONAL KEYWORDS IN C++

class	friend	virtual	inline
private	public	protected	const
this	new	delete	operator

The actual use and description of these additional keywords will be covered in their specific contexts.

COMMENTS

Comments are integral part of any program. Comments help in coding, debugging and maintaining a program. The compiler ignores them. They should be used liberally in the program .

In C++, a comment starts with two forward slashes (//) and ends with the end of that line. A comment can start at the beginning of the line or on a line following the program statement. This form of giving comments is particularly useful for the short line comments. If a comment continues on more than a line, the two forward slashes should be given on every line.

The C style of giving a comment is also available in C++. This style (/*....*/) is particularly useful when the comment spans more than a line.

e.g.

```
void main()
{
  /* this is a good old style of giving
  a comment. It can be continued to
next line and has to be ended with */


    clrscr();   // Clears the Screen
    init();     // Initialize variables.
      :
    :
}
```

VARIABLE DECLARATION

This declaration of variables in the C language is allowed only in the beginning of their block, prior to executable program statements. In C++ declaration of variables can be interspread with executable program statements. The scope of variables, however, remains the same - the block in which they are declared.

e.g.

```
void main()
{
 int x = 10;
  printf (" the value of x= % d\n",x);
 int y = 0;
  for( int z= 0; z < 10; ; z++)      // variable declared here.
    {
 y ++;
 x ++;
    }
}
```

Although, a deviation from the old style of declaring all variables in the beginning of the block, this does save some amount of memory, i.e., a variable is not given a memory until the declaration statement. Also, since a variable can be declared just before using it is suppose to give a better control over variables.

THE SCOPE RESOLUTION OPERATOR(::)

Global variables are defined outside any functions and thus can be used by all the functions defined thereafter. However, if a global variable is declared with the same name as that of a local variable of a function, the local variable is the one in the scope when the program executes that function. The C++ language provides the scope resolution operator (::) to access the global variable thus overriding a local variable with the same name. This operator is prefixed to the name of the global variable. The following example shows its usage.

```
int global = 10;

void main()
{
  int global = 20;

  printf(" Just writing global prints : %d\n", global);
  printf(" Writing ::global prints : %d\n", ::global);
}
```

The ***output*** of this program will be:

```
Just writing global prints : 20
Writing ::global prints   : 10
```

DEFAULT ARGUMENTS

A default argument is a value that is automatically assigned to a formal variable, if the actual argument from the function call is omitted.

e.g.

```
void drawbox( int x1=1, int y1=1, int x2=25, int y2=80, int color=7);
                                              // Prototype

void main ( void )
 {
  drawbox(10,1,25,80,14);                    // parameters passed
  drawbox();                                 // uses default arguments
 }

void drawbox( int x1, int y1, int x2, int y2, int color)
 {
      // Body of the function
 }
```

Function drawbox() draws a box around the edges of the coordinates passed as parameters. If these parameters are omitted, then the default values, as given in the declaration are passed.

When a function is declared, default values must be added from right to left. In other words, a default value for a particular argument cannot be given unless all default values for the arguments to its right are given. This is quite logical, since, if there are some arguments missing in the middle then the compiler would not know as to which arguments have been specified and which should be taken as default.

e.g.

```
void drawbox( int x1=1, int y1=1, int x2=25, int y2=80, int color = 7);
// Valid

void drawbox( int x1, int y1, int x2, int y2, int color = 7);
// Valid

void drawbox( int x1=1, int y1=1, int x2=25, int y2=80, int color );
// Not Valid
```

Default arguments are useful when the arguments almost have the same value. They are also useful to increase the number of arguments to a function in an already working program. In this case, using default arguments mean that existing function calls need not be modified, whereas, new function calls pass more number of arguments.

THE NEW AND DELETE OPERATORS

The C language has defined library functions- malloc() and free() for dynamic allocation and de-allocation of memory. C++ provides yet another approach to allocate blocks of memory - the ***new operator***. This operator allocates memory for a given size and returns a pointer to its starting point. C++ also provides delete, to release the memory allocated by new. The pointer returned by the new operator need not be typecasted.

e.g.

```
char arr[100];            // Compile_time allocation of an array
char *arr;                // Character pointer
arr = new char[size];     //Run time allocation of an
                          //array. Size can be a
                          //constant or a variable.
```

In the above example, new returns a pointer to a block of size bytes. It is synonymous with declaring a character array. However, declaring an array is an example of static binding - the array is built at the compile time. This array remains in existence right from the beginning of the program to its end, even if not in use. Whereas, the array declared by new operator can be allocated memory only when required and can be released when over with, using the delete operator. This is an example of dynamic binding.

It is possible that the system may not have enough memory available to satisfy a request by the new operator. In this case, new returns a null pointer. Thus, the returned value from the new should always be checked before performing any operations on it, which otherwise may lead to a sudden system crashes.

Once the new operator allocates memory, it can be accessed using the indirection operator (*) or the array subscripts.

e.g.

```
int *some = new int [10];        // A block of 10 integers
double *d5 = new  double[5];     // A block of 5 doubles
char *cp;
  cp = new char;                 // One character only.
  delete some;                   // Release memory.
  delete d5;

char *ptr , *str = “the shy is blue“;

  ptr = new char [strlen(str)+1];     // Character array

  if( ptr != 0)
  {
    strcpy(ptr,str);
  }
  else
  {
    printf(“ not enough memory “);
  }

struct date
{
int dd,mm,yy;
};
```

```
    date *dp = new date;  // This allocated a new structure
                          // to the pointer variable dp

        printf(" enter day ");
        scanf("%d",&dp->dd);
        :
}
```

THE CIN AND COUT OBJECTS

In C++ the keyword *cin* with the extraction operator " >>" is used to accept the input from the keyword. *cout* with the insertion operator " << " is used to display string literals and values, in place of scanf() and printf() functions of C. However, here we do not need any type specifiers like %d , %f etc., to denote the variables, cin and cout can be used in context with any basic data types.

e.g.

```
int ivar;
float fvar;
char cvar;
char name[10];

cin >> ivar ;
cin >> fvar >> cvar >> name;

cout<< " ivar = " << ivar << endl;
cout<< " fvar = " <<fvar << " cvar= " << cvar << name;
```

Q1. What is the Different between object base and Object Oriented ?

The main different between the object oriented and object base is that. In object oriented you use build in class, template class and also define your own class according to our need. While in case of object base we can only use build in class. User cannot create his own class.

Q2. What is the meaning of data abstraction? What is encapsulation? How does C++ achieve these two concepts? Describe with the help of an example.

[DEC01;Q1(a)]

Abstraction refers to the act of representing essential features without including the background details or explanations. Classes use the concept of abstraction and are defined as a list of abstract attributes such as size, weight and cost, and functions to operate on these attributes. They encapsulate all the essential properties of the objects that are to be created. Since the classes use the concept of data abstraction, they are known as Abstract Data Types (ADT).

E.g float a;

int b;

Here, background details of how is number stored in float or int data type is not a matter of programmer's concern.

The wrapping up of data and functions into a single union (called class) is known as encapsulation. Data **encapsulation** is the most striking feature of a class. The data is not accessible to the outside world and only those functions which are wrapped in the class can access it. These functions provide the interface between the object's data and the program. This insulation of the data from direct access by the program is called ***data hiding***.

E.g.

```
class A {
int a;
public :
void getData() {}
        };

void main()
{
A a1;
a1.getData();
}
```

The data 'a' & function getData() are encapsulated in object a1.

CHAPTER-3

STRUCTURE AND CLASS

- Overview
- Structures
- Classes
- Constructors
- Destructors

OVERVIEW

Object-oriented programming (OOP) is a conceptual approach to design programs. This session will continue our discussion on OOP and C++. Some of the features of OOP are Data encapsulation and data hiding, and possible because of data abstraction. All these features have one thing in common - the vehicle to implement them. This vehicle is class. It is a new data type similar to structures. Since, the structure data type is a stepping-stone to this singular important concept of C++, let us take another look at it.

STRUCTURES

A structure is a user-defined data type, which may contain different data types as its members. Creating a structure is a two-part process. First, a structure template is defined. This template gives a lot of information to the compiler. For instance, How it is stored in the memory? How many member variables are there in this composite data element? What are the types of its member variables? For data types like int, float, double, char this information is built into the compiler. But for the user-defined data types like structures, it has to be provided to the compiler. This is given in the definition of the structure template. This template creates a new data type. Variables of this new data type can then be declared and used like basic data types.

e.g.

```
struct Student
{
int Rollno;
char Name[15];
int Marks[6];
float percent;
};
```

The above example depicts structure called Student with enclosed data variables. The keyword struct is used to define a structure template. Student is a name or tag. The variables of this type can be declared as follows :

```
struct Student s1,s2;
```

[or]

In C++ you can even omit the struct tag and declare the variables as,

```
Student s1 = {100, "Sanket" , 20,10,30,40,50,60, 35.0};
Student s2,jack;
Student *sptr = &s1;
Student s[100];
```

In C++, functions also can be declared in a structure template. These functions are called as member functions.
E.g.

```
struct Student
{
  int Rollno;
  char Name[15];
  int Marks[6];
  float percent;

  void Getdetails();
  void Putdetails();
  int ClacPercent();
};
```

There are three functions in the template given above. These functions have been incorporated in the structure definition to make it a fundamental unit. The binding of data and the functions that operate on that data is called as data encapsulation. But the problem is that the member variables of this structure can be accessed by functions other than the ones declared in the structure template. This direct access of member variables of a structure by functions outside the structure is not what OOP has to offer. The actual OOP methodology in this regard is implemented in C++ not by the structure data type, but by the data type class. The data type class is just like structures, but with a difference. It also has some access specifier, which controls the access to member variables of a class.

INTRODUCTION TO CLASSES

Object-oriented programming (OOP) is a conceptual approach to design programs. It can be implemented in many languages, whether they directly support OOP concepts or not. The C language also can be used to implement many of the object-oriented principles. However, C++ supports the object-oriented features directly. All these features like Data abstraction, Data encapsulation, Information hiding etc have one thing in common - the vehicle that is used to implement them. The vehicle is " class."

Class is a user defined data type just like structures, but with a difference. It also has three sections namely private, public and protected. Using these, access to member variables of a class can be strictly controlled.

CLASS DEFINITION

The following is the general format of defining a class template:

```
class tag_name
{
 public :                                      // Must
    type member_variable_name;
    :
    type member_function_name();
    :

 private:                                      // Optional
    type member_variable_name;
    :
    type member_function_name();
    :
};
```

The keyword class is used to define a class template. The private and public sections of a class are given by the keywords 'private' and 'public' respectively. They determine the accessibility of the members. All the variables declared in the class, whether in the private or the public section, are the members of the class. Since the class scope is private by default, you can also omit the keyword private. In such cases you must declare the variables before public, as writing public overrides the private scope of the class.

E.g.

```
class tag_name
{
    type member_variable_name;   // private
    :
    type member_function_name(); // private
    :
 public :                                      // Must
    type member_variable_name;
    :
    type member_function_name();
    :
};
```

The variables and functions from the public section are accessible to any function of the program. However, a program can access the private members of a class only by using the public member functions of the class. This insulation of data members from direct access in a program is called ***information hiding***.

E.g.

```
class player
```

```
{
public :
    void getstats(void);
    void showstats(void);
    int no_player;

private :
    char name[40];
    int  age;
    int  runs;
    int  tests;
    float average;
    float calcaverage(void);
};
```

The above example models a cricket player. The variables in the private section - name, age, runs, highest, tests, and average - can be accessed only by member functions of the class calcaverage(), getstats() and showstats(). The functions in the public section - getstats() and showstats() can be called from the program directly, but function calcaverage() can be called only from the member functions of the class - getstats() and showstats().
With information hiding one need not know how actually the data is represented or functions implemented. The program need not to know about the changes in the private data and functions. The interface(public) functions take care of this. The OOP methodology is to hide the implementation specific details, thus reducing the complexities involved.

CLASSES AND OBJECTS

As seen earlier, a class is a vehicle to implement the OOP features in the C++ language. Once a class is declared, an object of that type can be defined. An object is said to be a specific instance of a class just like Maruti car is an instance of a vehicle or Pigeon is the instance of a bird. Once a class has been defined several objects of that type can be declared. For instance, an object of the class defined above can be declared with the following statement:

```
player Sachin, Dravid, Mohan;
  [Or]
class player Sachin, Dravid, Mohan;
```

where Sachin and Dravid are two objects of the class player. Both the objects have their own set of member variables. Once the object is declared, its public members can be accessed using the dot operator with the name of the object. We can also use the variable no_player in the public section with a dot operator in functions other than the functions declared in the public section of the class.

E.g.

```
Sachin.getstats();
Dravid.showstats();
Mohan.no_player = 10;
```

PUBLIC, PRIVATE AND PROTECTED MEMBERS

Class members can either be declared in `public','protected' or in the 'private' sections of the class. But as one of the features of OOP is to prevent data from unrestricted access, the data members of the class are normally declared in the private section. The member functions that form the interface between the object and the program are declared in ***public*** section (otherwise these functions can not be called from the program). The member functions which may have been broken down further or those, which do not form a part of the interface, are declared in the ***private*** section of the class. By default all the members of the class are private. The third access specifier '***protected***' that is not used in the above example, pertains to the member functions of some new class that will be inherited from the base class. As far as non-member functions are concerned, private and protected are one and the same.

CONSTRUCTORS

Example:

```
#include <iostream.h>
class integer
{
private :
int i ;
public :
void getdata( )
{
cout<<endl<<"Enter any integer";
cin>>i;
}
void setdata(intj)
{
i=j;
}
integer() // zero argument constructor
{
}
integer(intj) // one argument constructor
{
i=j;
}
void displaydata()
{
```

```
cout<<endl<<"value of i="<<i;
}
};
void main()
{
integer i1(100), i2, i3;
i1.displaydata();
i2.setdata(200);
i2.displaydata();
i3.getdata();
i3.displaydata();
}
```

The constructor is a special member function that allows us to set up values while defining the object, without the need to make a separate call to a member function. They have exactly the same name as the class of which they are members. No return type is used for constructors. Why not? Since the constructor is called automatically when an object is created, returning a value would not make sense.

In our program the statement

integer i1(100), i2, i3;

creates three objects of the type integer.

If you notice carefully you would find that there are two constructors with the same name integer(). Hence we call these constructors as overloaded constructors.

```
integer i2;            //calls zero-argument constructor
integer i1(100);       //calls one-argument constructor
```

DESTRUCTORS

We've seen that a special member function-the constructor-is called automatically when an object is first created. Similarly, when an object is destroyed a function called destructor automatically gets called. A destructor has the same name as the constructor (which is same as the class name) but is preceded by a tilde. The following program shows destructor at work.

```
#include <iostream.h>
class example
{
private :
int data ;
public:
example( ) // constructor (same name as class)
{
cout << endl << "inside the constructor" ;
}
~example( ) // destructor (same name with tilde)
{
cout << endl << "Inside the destructor";
```

```
}
};
void main()
{
example e;
}
```

When the object e gets created the constructor gets called when control goes outside main( ) the object e gets destroyed.

Q1. Design and implement a class student_list having the following requirements: [JUN03;Q1(d)]

· It stores details of two types of students "residential" and "non-residential".
· Different fee structures are stored for different types of students.
· Fee of the student is calculated on the basis of types and are vastly different.
· You need to define the class hierarchy of the student supporting above.
· The classes should include necessary constructors, destructors and fee calculation functions (make suitable assumptions.)
· The student name should be represented using pointers.
Write the appropriate main( ) function. Make suitable assumptions, if any.

```
#include<iostream.h>
#include<conio.h>
class std_list
{
public :
char *name;
int length;
char res_type;
int total;
                                        //default constructor
std_list()
{
length=20;
name=new char[length+1];
total=0;
}
                                        //destructor
~std_list()
{
delete name;
}
        void accept();                  //function for accepting the detail of
student
        void display();                 // function to display the student
details
```

```
void fee();                                  // function to accept fee;
};                                           //end of class
void std_list::fee()
{
if((res_type=='y')||(res_type=='Y'))
{
total=5000+5000+2000;
}
else
{
total=5000;
}
cout<<"total ==> "<<total;
}
void std_list::display()
{
cout<<"\n\n\n\nThe name of the student is \t";
cout<<name;
cout<<"\nThe residential type\t";
cout<<res_type;
cout<<"\nyour total fees \t";
cout<<total;
getch();
}

void std_list::accept()
{
cout<<"\nEnter your name =>\t";
cin>>name;
cout.flush();
cout<< "Choose The residential type "<<endl;
cout<<" 1 Residential include Room rent+Food Cost+tutionfees cost==>12000"<<endl;
cout<<" 2 Non Residential include Tutionfees cost ==>5000 "<<endl;
cout<<"press 1 for Residential   \n";
cout<<"press 2 for non Residential\t";
cin>>res_type;

    if((res_type=='y')||(res_type=='Y'))
    {
      cout<<"\n\n\nyou choose Residential option so your charges are as ";
      cout<<"\nyour Room  Rent is  5000 \t";
      cout<<"\nyour tuition Fees is 5000 \t";
      cout<<"\nyour Food cost is   2000 \t";
    }
    else
```

```
{
cout<<"Your Tuition fee is 5000 \t";
}
}
void main()
{
clrscr();
std_list ob;
ob.accept();
ob.fee();
ob.display();
}
```

Q2. Design and implement a class point stack using pointers. (The data representation must not be an array). Implement constructor(s), destructor and other suitable functions. [JUN03;Q3]

```
#include<iostream.h>
#include<conio.h>
#define max 100
class point_stack
{
int *arr;
int tos;
public:
public_stack()
{
tos=0;
cout<<"stack Initialized\n";
}
~point_stack()
{
cout<<"stack destroyed\n";
getch();
}
void push(int i)
{
if(tos==max)
{
cout<<"Stack is full\n";
return;
}
*arr=i;
tos++;
arr++;
}
```

```
int pop()
{
if(tos==0)
{
cout<<"stack overflow\n";
return 1;
}
arr--;
return *arr;
}
};
void main()
{
clrscr();
point_stack a,b;
a.push(1);
b.push(2);
a.push(3);
b.push(4);
cout<<a.pop()<<"\n";
cout<<a.pop()<<"\n";
cout<<b.pop()<<"\n";
cout<<b.pop()<<"\n";
getch();
}
```

Q3. Design and implement the class stack implement constructor, destructor and other suitable function.

```
#include<iostream.h>
#include<stdio.h>
#include<conio.h>
#include<process.h>

class st
{
public :
int stack[30],top;
st()
{   top=-1;
}
int pop(int stack[],int &top);
void push(int stack[],int &top,int val,int n);
void display(int stack[],int top);
};
//Insert in stack
```

```
void st::push(int stack[],int &top,int val,int n)
{
if(top < n)
{
top++;
stack[top]=val;
}
else
cout<<"Stack is full";
}
//deletion in stack
int st::pop(int stack[],int &top)
{
int delvalue;
if(top>=0)
{
delvalue=stack[top];
top--;
return delvalue;
}
else
{
cout<<"\n Stack is empty";
return(-9999);
}
}

//Display in stack
void st::display(int stack[],int top)
{
int i;
if(top>=0)
{
cout<<"\n";
for(i=top;i>=0;i--)
{
cout<<stack[i]<<" ";
}
getch();
fflush(stdin);
}
}
void main()
{
st obj;
```

```
int val,choice;
do
{
//clrscr();
cout<<"\n        Menu     ";
cout<<"\n 1 ==> Push   2 ==> Pop";
cout<<"\n 3 ==> Display 4 ==>Quit ";
cout<<"Enter your choice";
cin>>choice;
switch(choice)
{
case 1: cout<<"Enter the value to pushed";
cin>>val;
obj.push(obj.stack,obj.top,val,30);
break;
case 2: val=obj.pop(obj.stack,obj.top);
if(val!=-9999)
cout<<"\n the popped last value of stack  is "<<val;
break;
case 3: obj.display(obj.stack,obj.top);
break;
casc 4: cxit(0);
default:
cout<<"wrong value ";
}
}while(choice!=4);
}
```

Q4. Design and implement a class matrix having the following requirements:

[DEC02;Q1(d)]

- **It represents matrix in two dimensional arrays. The maximum size of array can be 100 × 100.**
- **There is a constructor that allocates the array of maximum size to the matrix object.**
- **You can store any matrix of size m × n (m £ 100 and n £ 100) in this class. There is an additional initialisation function to do so.**
- **It prints the stored matrix in row/column format.**
- **It adds and subtracts two matrices of same size.**
- **It multiplies two given matrices after checking the necessary time constraints.**
- **The class has provision for copy constructor and overloaded assignment operation.**

Write the appropriate main( ) function. Make suitable assumptions, if any.

```
#include<conio.h>
#include<stdio.h>
#include<iostream.h>
#include<iomanip.h>
```

```
class matrix
{
private:
int maxrow,maxcol;
int *ptr;
public:

matrix(int r, int c)
{
maxrow=r;
maxcol=c;
ptr=new int[r *c];
}

void getmat()
{
int i,j,mat_off,temp;
cout<<endl<<"Enter Elements matrix : "<<endl;
for(i=0;i<maxrow;i++)
{
for(j=0;j<maxcol;j++)
{
mat_off=i*maxcol+j;
cin>>ptr[mat_off];
}
}
}

void printmat()
{
int i,j,mat_off;
for(i=0;i<maxrow;i++)
{
cout<<endl;
for(j=0;j<maxcol;j++)
{
mat_off=i*maxcol+j;
cout<<setw(3)<<ptr[mat_off];
}
}
}

int detmat()
{
matrix q(maxrow-1,maxcol-1);
```

```
int sign=1,sum=0,i,j,k,count;
int newsize,newpos,pos,order;

order=maxrow;
if(order==1)
return(ptr[0]);
for(i=0;i<order;i++,sign*=-1)
{
for(j=1;j<order;j++)
{
for(k=0,count=0;k<order;k++)
{
if(k==i)
continue;

pos=j*order+k;
newpos=(j-1)*(order-1)+count;
q.ptr[newpos]=ptr[pos];
count++;
}
}
sum=sum+ptr[i]*sign*q.detmat();
}
return (sum);
}

matrix operator + (matrix b)
{
matrix c(maxrow,maxcol);
int i,j,mat_off;

for(i=0;i<maxrow;i++)
{
for(j=0;j<maxcol;j++)
{
mat_off=i*maxcol+j;
c.ptr[mat_off]=ptr[mat_off]+b.ptr[mat_off];
}
}
return(c);
}

matrix operator * (matrix b)
{
matrix c(b.maxcol,maxrow);
```

```
int i,j,k,mat_off1,mat_off2,mat_off3;

for(i=0;i<c.maxrow;i++)
{
for(j=0;j<c.maxcol;j++)
{
mat_off3=i*c.maxcol+j;
c.ptr[mat_off3]=0;
for(k=0;k<b.maxrow;k++)
{
mat_off2=k*b.maxcol+j;
mat_off1=i*maxcol+k;
c.ptr[mat_off3]+=ptr[mat_off1]*b.ptr[mat_off2];
}
}
}
return(c);
}

int operator ==(matrix b)
{
int i,j,mat_off;
if(maxrow!=b.maxrow||maxcol!=b.maxcol)
return(0);

for(i=0;i<maxrow;i++)
{
for(j=0;j<maxcol;j++)
{
mat_off=i*maxcol+j;
if(ptr[mat_off]!=b.ptr[mat_off])
return 0;
}
return(0);
}
return(1);
}
};

void main()
{
int rowa,cola,rowb,colb;

cout<<endl<<"Enter dimensions of A";
cin>>rowa>>cola;
```

```
matrix a(rowa,cola);
a.getmat();

cout<<endl<<"Enter dimensions of matrix B";
cin>>rowb>>colb;
matrix b(rowb,colb);
b.getmat();

matrix c(rowa,cola);
c=a+b;
cout<<endl<<"The sum of two matrix = ";
c.printmat();

matrix d(rowa,colb);
d=a*b;
cout<<endl<<"The product of two matrices = ";
d.printmat();

cout<<endl<<"Determinant of matrix a = "<<a.detmat();
if(a==b)
cout<<endl<<"a & b are equal ";
else
cout<<endl<<"a & b are equal ";
}
```

Q5. Design and implement a class linked-queue which is implemented using pointers. The class includes AddQ, DeleteQ and Empty operations (standard operations of Data Structure Queue). Make suitable assumptions, if any.

[DEC02;Q2]

```
#include<iostream.h>
#include <stdio.h>
#include<ctype.h>
#define FALSE 0
#define NULL 0
struct listelement
{
int    dataitem;
struct listelement *link;
};
class queue :public listelement
{
public:
listelement * lp,* tempp;
void Menu (int *choice);
listelement * AddQ (listelement * listpointer, int data);
```

```
listelement * DeleteQ (listelement * listpointer);
void PrintQueue (listelement * listpointer);
void ClearQueue (listelement * listpointer);
};
void main ()
{
listelement *listpointer;
queue x;
int data,choice;
listpointer = NULL;
do {
x.Menu (&choice);
switch (choice) {
case 1:
cout<< ("Enter data item value to add ");
cin>>data;
listpointer = x.AddQ (listpointer, data);
break;
case 2:
if (listpointer == NULL)
cout<<"Queue empty!\n";
else
listpointer = x.DeleteQ (listpointer);
break;
case 3:
x.PrintQueue (listpointer);
break;
default:
cout<<"Invalid menu choice - try again\n";
break;
}
} while (choice != 4);
x.ClearQueue (listpointer);
}
/* main */
void queue::Menu (int *choice)
{
char local;
cout<<"\nEnter\t1 to add item,\n\t2 to remove item\n\
\t3 to print queue\n\t4 to quit\n";
do {
local = getchar ();
if ((isdigit (local) == FALSE) && (local != '\n'))
{
```

```
cout<< "\nyou must enter an integer.\n";
cout<< "Enter 1 to add, 2 to remove, 3 to print, 4 to quit\n";
}
} while (isdigit ((unsigned char) local) == FALSE);
*choice = (int) local - '0';
}
listelement * queue:: AddQ (listelement * listpointer, int data)
{
lp = listpointer;
if (listpointer != NULL)
{
while (listpointer -> link != NULL)
listpointer = listpointer -> link;
listpointer -> link = new listelement;
listpointer = listpointer -> link;
listpointer -> link = NULL;
listpointer -> dataitem = data;
return lp;
}
else {
listpointer = new listelement;
listpointer -> link - NULL;
listpointer -> dataitem = data;
return listpointer;
}
}
istelement * queue ::DeleteQ (listelement * listpointer)
{
cout<<"Element removed is"<<listpointer -> dataitem;
tempp = listpointer -> link;
free (listpointer);
return tempp;
}
void queue ::PrintQueue (listelement * listpointer)
{
if (listpointer == NULL)
cout<<"queue is empty!\n";
else
while (listpointer != NULL) {
cout<<listpointer -> dataitem;
listpointer = listpointer -> link;
}
cout<<"\n";
}
```

```
void queue::ClearQueue (listelement * listpointer)
{
while (listpointer != NULL) {
listpointer = DeleteQ (listpointer);
}
}
```

Q6. Design and implement a class linked having constructors/destructors and operations of adding an item for searching a value and inserting a value after a searched item. (Please assume singly link list). Make suitable assumptions, if any.

```
.#include<iostream.h>
#include<conio.h>
class Linked
{
public:
int info;
Linked *next;
Linked *first;
Linked()
{
first=0;
next='\0';
}
~Linked()
{
delete next;
delete first;
}
void addnode(void);
void insnode(void);
void display(void);
};
void Linked::addnode()
{
Linked *curr;
static Linked *last=0;
curr=new Linked();
cout<<"Enter number:";
cin>>curr->info;
curr->next='\0';
if (last)
last->next=curr;
else
first=curr;
```

```
last=curr;
}
void Linked::display()
{
Linked *l;
l=first;
do
{
cout<<l->info<<"";
l=l->next;
}
while(l!='\0');
}
void Linked::insnode()
{
Linked *curr,*last,*l,*n;
int no,val,flag=0;
l=first;
cout<<"Enter value which you want to search :";
cin>>no;
cout<<"Enter value which you want to insert :";
cin>>val;
}
while(l!= "\0")
if(l->info==no)
{
curr=l;
flag=1;
break;
}
else
{
l=l->next;
}
}
if(flag==0)
{
cout<<"not found";
getch();
return ;
}
else
{
n=new Linked();
n->info=val;
n->next='\0';
```

```
last=l->next;
curr->next=n;
n->next=last;
}
}
void main()
{
clrscr();
Linked ob;
int ch,f;
do
{
clrscr();
cout<<"1.Add Node\n";
cout<<"2.Insert Node\n";
cout<<"3.Display and Exit\n";
cout<<"Enter choice:";
cin>>ch;
switch(ch)
{
case 1:ob.addnode();
break;
case 2:ob.insnode();
break;
case 3:ob.display();
getch();
break;
}
}while(ch!=3);
}
```

Q7. Design and implement a table class in C++ having the following requirements. [DEC01;Q5]

The table may have only floating point values.

· The sum of a row or a column can be calculated with the help of overloaded sum function.

· There is a copy constructor and other constructor for the table.

· There are functions to find largest and the smallest values from the table and its positions in the table.

· It allows addition and subtraction of two tables having similar size.

ANS :

```
#include<iostream.h>
#include<conio.h>
class table
{
public:
```

```
float a[10];
int size,i;
float sum();
void accept();
float min();
float max();
void display();
friend table operator +(table x, table y);
table()
{
size=0;
i=0;
}
table(table &x)                    //copy constructor
{
for(i=0;i<x.size;i++)
{
a[i]=x.a[i];
}
}
};

//function to overload the operator
table operator +(table x,table y)
{
table temp;
if(x.size==y.size)
{
for(int i=0;i<x.size;i++)
temp.a[i]=x.a[i] + y.a[i];
return temp;
}
else
cout<<"size doesn't match";
}
//function to accept the array
void table ::accept()
{
cout<<"\nEnter the number of element you want to enter";
cin>>size;
for(int i=0;i<size;i++)
cin>>a[i];
}
//function for sum of row
float table::sum()
```

```
{
float sum=0.0;
for(int i=0;i<size;i++)
{
sum+=a[i];
}
return sum;
}

//function to find minimum in row
float table::min()
{
float m=a[i-1],temp;
for(int j=0;j<size;j++)
{
if(m>a[j])
{
temp=m;
m=a[j];
a[j]=temp;
}
}
return m;
}
//function to find maximum in row
float table::max()
{
float m=a[i-1],temp;
for(int j=0;j<size;j++)
{
if(m<a[j])
{
temp=m;
m=a[j];
a[j]=temp;
}
}
return m;
}

void table::display()
{
for(int i=0;i<size;i++)
cout<<a[i];
}
```

```
void main()
{
float w;
char ch;
table x,y,z;
clrscr();

x.accept ();
w=x.min();
cout<<"\nMinimum value i"<<w;

w=x.max();
cout<<"\nMaximum value i"<<w;
w=x.sum();
cout<<"\nAfter the row addition value is "<<w;

cout<<"\nDo you want to add another vector to this vector";
cin>>ch;
if(ch=='y'||ch=='Y')
{
y.accept();
z=x+y;
}
cout<<"\nAfter the table row addition value is ";
//"after the  table addition value is store in z";
z.display();
}
```

Q8. Write a program in C++ for merging two strings into one. You must design the program using pointers. Strings should be represented using pointers.

[JUN01;Q2]

#: Write a C++ program having the following functionality: [DEC01;Q1(c)]

- **The program have a class string in it.**
- **The string class have the data member as pointer to character.**
- **The class has overloaded constructor and copy constructor.**
- **The class have overloaded + operator which concatenates two strings.**
- **The class have a destructor.**
- **The class have functions for string comparison.**

Also write the appropriate main function that demonstrate the complete functionality of the class string.

```
# include<string.h>
# include<iostream.h>
class string
```

```
{
char *p;
int len;
public :
string( ) {len = 0; p = 0 ;}                    ///create null string
string ( const char * s) ;                      /// create string from array s
string (const string & s) ;                     ///copy constructor
~string ( ) {delete p ;}                        /// destructor
friend string operator + (const string & s, const string & t);
friend int operator <= (const string & s, const string & t);
friend void show (const string s) ;
string &operator=(string &c)
{strcpy(p,c.p);
return *this; }
};

string :: string (const char * s)
{
len = strlen (s);
p = new char [len + 1];
strcpy (p,s);
}
string :: string (const string & s)
{
len = s.len;
p = new char[len + 1];
strcpy (p, s.p);
{
//...............OVERLOADING+operator............................
string operator + (const string & s, const string & t)
{
string temp;
temp.len = s.len + t.len;
temp.p = new char [temp . len + 1];
strcpy (temp.p, s.p);
strcat (temp.p, t.p);
return (temp);
}
//..................OVERLOADING<= operator..........................
Int operator <= (const string & s, const string & t)
{
int m = strlen (s . p);
int n = strlen (t.p);
if (m <= n) return (1);
else return (0);
```

```
}
void show (const string s)
{
cout << s.p;
}
main ( )
{
string s1 = "New";
string s2 = "York";
string s3 = "Delhi"
string t1, t2, t3, t4;

t1 = s1;
t2 = s2;
t3 = s1+s2;
t4 = s1 + s3 ;

cout << "\nt1 = "; show (t1);
cout << "\nt2 = "; show (t2);
cout << "\n";
cout << "\nt3 = "; show (t3);
cout << "\nt4 = "; show (t4);
cout << "\n\n";

if (t3 <= t4)
{
show (t3);
cout << " smaller than";
show (t4);
cout << "\n";
}
else
{
show (t4);
cout << "smaller than";
show (t3) ;
cout << "\n";
}
}
/////////////////////////////////////////////// < PROGRAM >/////////////////////////////////////////
//
```

The following is the output of Program

t1 = New

t2 = York

t3 = New York

t4 = New Delhi
New York smaller than New Delhi.

Q9. Design and implement a class 'Itemlist' having following requirements:
- It is a linear array of size N
- Each element has Itemcode, Item Price and Quantity
- Item to be appended to the list
- Delete item from the list with the help of item code
- Print total value of stock

```
#include<iostream.h>
#include<conio.h>
class Itemlist
{
private:
struct node
{
int itemcode;
float itemprice;
int quantity;
node*link;
}*p;
public:
Itemlist();
void append(int,float,int);
void del(int);
void total();
//~Itemlist();
};

Itemlist::Itemlist()
{
p=NULL;
}
void Itemlist::append(int code,float price,int qua)
{
node*q,*t;
if(p==NULL)
{
//create first node
p=new node;
p->itemcode=code;
p->itemprice=price;
p->quantity=qua;
p->link=NULL;
```

```
}
else
{
//go to last node
q=p;
while(q->link!=NULL)
q=q->link;
//add node at the end
t=new node;
t->itemcode=code;
t->itemprice=price;
t->quantity=qua;
q->link=t;
t->link=NULL;
}
}
void Itemlist::del(int code)
{
node*q,*r;
q=p;
//if node to be deleted is first node
if(q->itemcode==code)
{
p=q->link;
delete q;
return;
}
//traverse
r=q;
while(q!=NULL)
{
if(q->itemcode==code)
{r->link=q->link;
delete q;
return;
}
r=q;
q=q->link;
}
cout<<"\n\nElement "<<code<< "not found\n";
}
void Itemlist::total()
{
node*q;
float t=0;
```

```
for(q=p;q!=NULL;q=q->link)
t=t+q->itemprice*q->quantity;
cout<<"\n total value of stock is:"<<t;}
void main()
{
clrscr();
Itemlist l;
cout<<"\n Value of stock :\n";
l.total();
l.append(001,1200.5,50);
l.append(002,1400.2,20);
l.append(003,1500.5,100);
cout<<"\n Value of stock :\n";
l.total();
l.del(002);
l.del(004);//Element 004 not present message
cout<<"\n Value of stock now";
l.total();
getch();
}
```

Q10. Design and implement a class 'binsearch' for a binary search tree. It includes search, remove and add options. Make suitable assumption [DEC03;Q2]

```
#include<iostream.h>
#include<conio.h>
#define TRUE 1
#define FALSE 0
class binsearch
{
private:
struct node
{
node*left;
int item;
node*right;
}*start;
public:
binsearch();
~binsearch();
void traverse();
void search(int,int&,node*&,node*&);
void add(int);void delend(node*);
void del(int);void inorder(node*);
};
```

```
binsearch::binsearch()
{
start=NULL;
}
binsearch::~binsearch()
{
delend(start);
}


void binsearch::search(int n,int&found,node*&parent,node*&x)
{
node*q;
found=FALSE;
parent=NULL;
if(start==NULL)
return;
q=start;
while(q!=NULL)
{
if(q->item==n)
{
found=TRUE;
x=q;
return;
}
if(q->item>n)
{
parent=q;
q=q->left;}
else
{
parent=q;
q=q->right;
}
}
}
void binsearch::add(int n)
{
int found;
node*t,*parent,*x;
search(n,found,parent,x);
if(found==TRUE)
cout<<"\n"<<"such a node already exists";
else
```

```
{
t=new node;
t->item=n;
t->left=NULL;
t->right=NULL;
if(parent==NULL)
start=t;
else
parent->item>n?parent->left=t:parent->right=t;
}
}
void binsearch::delend(node*q)
{
if(q!=NULL)
{
delend(q->left);
del(q->item);
delend(q->right);
}
}
void binsearch::del(int num)
{
int found;
node*parent,*x,*xsucc;
/* if tree is empty*/
if(start==NULL)
{
cout<<endl<<"Tree is empty";
return;
}
parent=x=NULL;
//call search function to find node to be deleted
search(num,found,parent,x);
//if not found
if(found==FALSE)
{
cout<<endl<<"Node not found";
return;
}
//if node to be deleted has two children
if(x->left!=NULL&&x->right!=NULL)
{
parent=x;
xsucc=x->right;
while(xsucc->left!=NULL)
```

```
{
parent=xsucc;
xsucc=xsucc->left;
}
x->item=xsucc->item;
x=xsucc;
}
//if node to be deleted has no child
if(x->left==NULL&&x->right==NULL)
{
if(parent->right==x)
parent->right=NULL;
else
parent->left=NULL;
delete x;
return;
}
//if it has left child only
if(x->left!=NULL&&x->right==NULL)
{
if(parent->left==x)
parent->left=x->left;
else
parent->right=x->left;
delete x;
return;
}
//if it has right child only
if(x->left==NULL && x->right!=NULL)
{
if(parent->left==x)
parent->left=x->right;
else
parent->right=x->right;
delete x;
return;
}
}
void binsearch::traverse()
{
inorder(start);
}
void binsearch::inorder(node*q)
{
if(q!=NULL)
```

```
{
inorder(q->left);
cout<<endl<<q->item;
inorder(q->right);
}
}
void main()
{
binsearch t;
int i,num;
for(i=0;i<=6;i++)
{
cout<<"\n"<<"Enter data to be inserted";
cin>>num;
t.add(num);
}
t.traverse();
cout<<endl<<"Enter value to be deleted";
cin>>num;
t.del(num);
cout<<endl;
t.traverse();
getch();
}
```

CHAPTER-4

INTRODUCTION TO FUNCTIONS

- Function Prototype
- Call by Reference & Call by Value
- Static Member,Static Function
- Friend Function & Friend Classes
- Inline Functions

We have already seen the powerful features of OOP that make C++ such a strong language. In this session we will continue exploring some other features, which make this language more powerful.

Function Prototypes

A function prototype is a declaration that defines both: the argument passed to the function and the type of value returned by the function. If we were to call a function fool() which receives a float and an int as arguments and returns a double value its prototype would look like this:

```
double fool (float, int);
```

The C++ compiler uses this prototype to ensure that the types of the arguments you pass in a function call are same as those mentioned in the prototype. If there is a mismatch the compiler points it out immediately. This is known as ***strong type checking***; something which C lacks.

Without strong type checking, it is easier to pass illegal values to functions. For example, a non-prototype function would allow you to pass an int to a pointer variable, or a float to a long int. The C++ compiler would immediately report such types of errors. In C++ prototypes do more than making sure that actual arguments (those used in calling function) and formal arguments (those used in called function) match in number, order and type. C++ internally generates names for functions, including the argument type information. This information is used when several functions have same names.

Remember that all function in C++ must be prototyped. This means every function must have its argument list declared, and the actual definition of a function must exactly match its prototypes in the number, order and types of parameters.

CALL BY REFERENCE, CALL BY VALUE

Call by reference - A reference provides an alias i.e. alternate name for the variable. It is useful when the values of the original variables are to be changed using a function Reference arguments are indicated by an ampersand preceeding the argument e.g. int & a;

Example

```
#include<iostream.h>
#include<Conio.h>
void Swap (int &, int &)
void main ()
{
int a,b;
Cout<<"Enter any two values for a and b" <<end l;
Cin>>a;
Cin>>b;
Swap(a,b);
Cout<<"The two entered numbers are"<<"a"<<a<<" "<<",-and"<<"b"<<b<<end l.;
}
void Swap (int & a, int & b)
{
int c:
c = a;
a = b
b = c;
}
```

The above program uses ***call by reference*** method for invoking a function.

Call by value : In this method the called function creates a new set of variables and copies the value of arguments into them. The function does not have access to the original variable(actual parameters) and can only work on the copies of values it created. It is useful when the original values are not to be modified. In fact, call by value method offers insurance that the function cannot harm the original value.

The following example explain this:-

```
        Calling()
        { int passit = 90;
        Called (Passit) ;
Cout<<passit;     //there will be no change in passit value, remains 90.
}
void Called (int receiveit)
{
receiveit = 0;
}
```

In call by references arguments that are objects, are passed by references to the called method. Any change made to the object by the called method is reflected in the calling method

```
Calling ()
{
int passit=90;
Cout<<passit     //passit changes here to 0.
}
Called (int &receiveit)
```

```
}
receiveit=0;
}
```

In a call by reference, the memory address i.e. reference of the argument's variable is passed to the called method.

When the called ()method changes the value of the argument, the change is reflected in the calling() method.

The output-generated from the above program is "changed".

STATIC CLASS MEMBERS

As we already know all the objects of the class have different data members but invoke the same member functions. However, there is an exception to this rule. If the data member is declared with the keyword *static,* then only one such data item is created for the entire class, no matter how many objects it has. Static data members are useful, if all objects of a class must share a common data item. Whereas, the visibility of this data item remains same, the duration of this variable is for entire lifetime of the program.

For example, such a variable can be particularly useful if an object requires to know how many objects of its kind exist.

```
class counter
{
public :
counter ();
int getcount();
private:
static int count;
};
counter::counter ()
{
count++;
}

int counter::getcount()
{
return ( count );
}
int counter :: count = 0;                    // INITIALIZATION OF STATIC MEMBER.

void main()
{
counter c1,c2;
cout << " Count = " << c1.getcount() << endl;
cout << " Count = " << c2.getcount() << endl;
```

```
counter c3;

cout << " Count = " << c3.getcount() << endl;

counter c4,c5;

cout << " Count = " << c4.getcount() << endl;
cout << " Count = " << c5.getcount() << endl;
}
```

Output:

```
Count=2          //not 1 because 2 objects are already created.
Count=2
Count=3
Count=5
Count=5
```

In the above example, the class counter demonstrates the use of static data members. It contains just one data member count. *Notice the initialization of this static class member*. For some compilers it is mandatory. Even though the data member is in the private section it can be accessed in this case as a global variable directly, but has to be preceded by the name of the class and the scope resolution operator. This example contains a constructor to increment this variable. Similarly, there can be a destructor to decrement it.

You can use these to generate register numbers for student objects from a student class. Whenever an object is created, it will be automatically assigned a register number if the register number is a static variable and a constructor is used to write an equation to generate separate register numbers in some order. You could initialize the variable to give the first register number and then use this in the constructor for further operations.

STATIC MEMBER FUNCTIONS

All the objects of the class share static data members of a class. The example above demonstrates how to keep track of all the objects of a class which are in existence. However, this function uses existing objects to invoke a member function getcount(), which returns the value of the static data member. *What if the programme does not want to use objects to invoke this function and still the programme would like to know how many objects have been created? If there is no object how the member function is invoked?* Further, as can be seen from the previous output, the number of objects (count) remains same at a given instance no matter which object is used to invoke the member function. In fact, the use of existing objects, like in the above example, is not an effective way to access the value of the static data member. A specific object should not be used to refer to this member, since it does not belong to that object; it belongs to the entire class. C++ gives a facility to define static function members, for the same. That is, to invoke such a function, an object is not required. It can be invoked with the name of the class. The programme given below illustrates its use.

```
class counter
{
public :
counter ();
static int getcount();

private:
static int count;
};

counter::counter ()
{
count++;
}

int counter::getcount()
{
return ( count );
}
int counter :: count = 0;      // INITIALIZATION OF STATIC MEMBER.

void main()
{
counter c1,c2;

cout << " Count = " << counter :: getcount() << endl;
cout << " Count = " << counter :: getcount() << endl;

counter c3;

cout << " Count = " << counter :: getcount() << endl;

counter c4,c5;

cout << " Count = " << counter :: getcount() << endl;
cout << " Count = " << counter :: getcount() << endl;
}
```

Output:

Count = 2
Count = 2
Count = 3
Count = 5
Count = 5

FRIEND FUNCTIONS

Q5. What is the need of friend functions? Describe the usage of friend functions with the help of an example. [JUN03;Q6(a)]

 # What is the purpose of using friend functions? Describe with an example. Can a class be made friend of other class? Justify your answer.

One of the main features of OOP is information hiding. A class encapsulates data and methods to operate on that data in a single unit. The data from the class can be accessed only through member functions of the class. This restricted access not only hides the implementation details of the methods and the data structure, it also saves the data from any possible misuse, accidental or otherwise. However, the concept of data encapsulation sometimes takes information hiding too far. There are situations where a rigid and controlled access leads to inconvenience and hardships.

For instance, consider a case where a function is required to operate on object of two different classes. This function cannot be made a member of both the classes. What can be done is that a function can be defined outside both the classes and made to operate on both. That is, a function not belonging to either, but able to access both. Such a function is called as a **friend function**. In other words, a friend function is a nonmember function, which has access to a class's private members. It is like allowing access to one's personal belongings to a friend.

USING A FRIEND

Using a friend function is quite simple. The following example defines a friend function to access members of two classes.

```
class Bclass;                              // Forward Declaration
class Aclass
{
public :
Aclass(int v)
{
Avar = v;
}

friend int addup(Aclass &ac, Bclass &bc);
private :
int Avar;
};

class Bclass
{
public :
Bclass(int v)
{
Bvar = v;
```

```
}

friend int addup(Aclass &ac, Bclass &bc);
private :
int Bvar;
};

int addup(Aclass &ac, Bclass &bc)
{
return( ac.Avar + bc.Bvar);
}

void main()
{
Aclass aobj;
Bclass bobj;

int total;
total = addup(aobj,bobj);
}
```

The program defines two classes - Aclass and Bclass. It also has constructors for these classes. A friend function, addup(), is declared in the definition of both the classes, although it does not belong to either. This friend function returns the sum of the two private members of the classes. Notice, that this function can directly access the private members of the classes. To access the private members, the name of the member has to be prefixed with the name of the object, along with the dot operator.

The first line in the program is called forward declaration. This is required to inform the compiler that the definition for class Bclass comes after class Aclass and therefore it will not show any error on encountering the object of Bclass in the declaration of the friend function. Since it does not belong to both the classes, while defining it outside we do not give any scope resolution and we do not invoke it with the help of any object. Also, the keyword friend is just written before the declaration and not used while defining.

Sometimes friend functions can be avoided using inheritance and they are preferred. Excessive use of friend over many classes suggests a poorly designed program structure. But sometimes they are unavoidable.

Granting friendship to another class

Yes, a class can be made friend of other class. To grant friendship to another class, write the keyword followed by the class name. The keyword class is optional. Note that this declaration also implies a forward declaration of the class to which the friendship is being granted. The implication of this declaration is that all of the member functions of the friend class are friend functions of the class that bestows the friendship.

```
class Aclass
```

```
{
public :
    :
    :
    :

friend class Bclass;                    // Friend declaration.
private :
int Avar;
};

class Bclass
{
public :
    :
    :
void fn1(Aclass ac)
{
Bvar = ac. Avar;                        //Avar can be accessed.
}
private :
int Bvar;
};

void main()
{
Aclass aobj;
Bclass bobj;
bobj.fn1(aobj);
}
```

The program declares class Bclass to be a friend of Aclass. It means that all member functions of Bclass have been granted direct access to all member functions of Aclass.

INLINE FUNCTIONS

Imagine a C language program, which reads disk records containing employee information. If this is a payroll application each employee record data is probably processed via a series of function calls. These function calls could be to print the entity data, to compute the salary, to compute the taxes to be withheld etc,. Each one of these calls inherently contains overhead that must be part of your overall program. In other words it takes code, space and time to push actual arguments onto the stack, call the function, push some return value onto the stack and finally pop all of those values .

C++ provides the ***inline functions***, a mechanism by which these explicit function calls can be avoided.

"An inline function by definition is a function whose code gets substituted in place of the actual call to that function."

Whenever the compiler encounters a call to that function it merely replaces it with the code itself thereby saving you all of the overhead. Such a function can be either a member of a class or a global function. Inline functions work best when they are small, straightforward bodies of code that are not called from too many different places within your program. The time saved will increase with the increase in number of calls.

Even if you request that the compiler make a function into an inline function, the compiler may or may not honor that request. It depends on the code of the function. For example, the compiler will not inline any function that contains a loop, static data member, or aggregate initializer list. In such cases, a warning message will be issued.

The disadvantage with inline functions is that if the code itself ever needs to be modified, then all programs using these functions would then have to be recompiled. Furthermore, an inline function is a violation of implementation hiding.

HOW TO WRITE A GLOBAL INLINE FUNCTION

First, let's get away from member functions for a moment and consider a global function. To make a request that this function be inline :

* Precede the return type of the function with the keyword inline.
* Write the function body (the definition, not just the declaration) before any calls to that function.

Here is a program that uses an inline function to compute and return the absolute value of its input argument.

```
# include <stdio.h>
inline int abs(int x)
{
return x <0? -x : x ;
}

void main( )
{
for (int i=-2 ; i<2 ; ++i)
{
int value = abs(i) ;
printf ("Absolute value of %+d = %+d\n",i, value);
}
}
```

The output is:

Absolute value of -2 =+2
Absolute value of -1 =+1
Absolute value of +0 =+0
Absolute value of +1 =+1

When the call to the abs( ) function is encountered, the compiler, instead of making a function call, generates this assembly code.

Q1. What are the usages of "const" keyword in functions and arguments? Describe with the help of example. [JUN03;Q2(a)]

 # What is the meaning of having "const and classname" as a parameter in a function? Describe. [DEC01;Q6(a)]

ANS : We have met the const keyword already as a way of defining a constant value which can be used in place of a raw number within your program. The const keyword has several other uses in C++, particularly in relation to function definitions. Consider the function definition:

```
int ConstArgs(const int &Arg1, const float &Arg2) {….}
```

The const keyword before each argument tells the compiler that although these arguments are being passed by reference, they are not allowed to be modified within the function body. They become, in essence, 'read-only objects: their values may be accessed but not altered. Thus, the following function definition would give rise to a compile-time error:

```
int ConstArgs(const int &Arg1, const float &Arg2)
{
Arg1 *= 2;
}
```

A general rule is: if you agree with those people who tell you to pass arguments by reference whenever possible, you should carefully consider whether each variable should be changed within the function to which it is being passed. If not, you should ensure that it is declared as a const parameter in the function definition. Thus is purely a safeguard against subtle errors; if your program is written correctly, it won't make any difference whether the const is there or not, but if you make a mistake and attempt to alter a variable within a function where it shouldn't be altered, the prefix const just might save you hours or debugging. Another use of the const keyword is *after* a function declaration in a class.

Constant member functions are used in classes to protect changes to class's data. For example, in the class definition:

```
Class ConstClass
{
private:
declarations
public:
int ConstFunc(args) cosnt;
};
```

the const after the declaration of ConstFunc( ) states that ConstFunc( ) is not allowed to change any fields of the object that calls it. For example, with the code fragment:

```
ConstClass Object;
Object.ConstFunc( );
```

The call to ConstFunc ( ) must not alter any of the values of any of the data fields of Object. This is another safety feature in C++ designed to help you catch programming errors early. If you declare a function as const in this fashion and then inadvertently insert some statements into the definition of that function that alter some of the fields of the object calling the function, the compiler will flag an error. It is therefore a good idea to think carefully about whether or not a function should be allowed to alter data fields and, if not, declare it as const.

Q2. What is a "Reference" in C++?

ANS : A reference is an alternate name of object, and you can use it just as you would use the object itself. You can think of a reference as the address of an item except that unlike a pointer, a reference is not a real variable- a reference is initialized when it is defined, and you cannot modify its value later on.

Q3. Where are they used ? Explain with the help of examples.

ANS : The syntax of a reference mimics that of a pointer except that a reference needs an ampersand (&) where that pointer declaration has an asterisk (*). Thus,

```
int *ptr;                //An uninitialized pointer to integer
```

Defines an int pointer, whereas the following is a reference to an int variable named I:

```
int &r=I;          //Reference to I (an int variable)
```

As a practical example of the use of reference, here is the swap_int function with arguments passed by reference:

```
void swap_int(int &a, int &b)
{
int temp;
temp=a;
a=b;
b=temp;
}
```

Compare this version of the function with the one that used pointer. You can see that version that uses references looks cleaner. You no longer have to dereference pointer in each expression. It is also simple to use the new version of the function, because you do not have to provide as arguments, the address of the integers being swapped. Instead, you call the function as if the arguments were being passed by value:

```
void swap_int( int&, int& );                  // prototype of function
int x=2; y=3;
swap_int(x, y);                              // Now x=3 and y=2
```

The compiler knows from the function's prototype that it has to pass references to the variables x and y.

Q4. Why do you need references in C++? How can a reference be used in parameter passing? Describe with the help of an example. [JUN02;Q6(b)]

 # What is a reference variable? What is the usage of references in parameter passing? Why are references needed when call by value exists? What is the purpose of "const" keyword with respect to references? [DEC02,Q3(b)]

Need /Usage of Passing By Reference : This sounds like a good reason to always pass by reference, but if you are awake you should spot a danger here. Remember that one difference between that two methods of passing a variable is that in one case, any changes made on the variable within the function have no effect on the calling routine, while in the other case, the changes *do* affect the variable in the calling routine. If you pass a variable by reference and inadvertently make changes to it within the function that you don't. Fortunately, C++ has a mechanism that allows you to protect against such an error, even if you pass the variable by reference.

Use of Reference in parameter passing

C++ provides a second way of passing a variable to a function called *passing by reference*. The syntax for this is:

```
int RefFunction (int &Arg1, float &Arg2);
```

Note that each argument is prefixed by an ampersand. Such a function is called in exactly the same way as one where the arguments are passed by value:

```
ReturnedInt = RefFunction (Int, Float2);
```

The difference between IntFunction and RefFunction is that the *addresses* of the arguments are passed in RefFunction, and not the actual values. As such, no extra memory is reserved within the function, since no copy of the arguments need to be made. This variable Arg1 within the function and the variable Int1 passed to it are identical: they share the same address in memory. In this case, any change made to Arg1 within the function will also affect Int1 the calling routine.

Example:

```
#include<iostream.h>
void main()
{
void change(int&);
int a=10;
cout<<"Starting value of a is "<<a;
change(a);
cout<<"The changed value of a is "<<a;
getch();
}
void change(int &x)
{
x=x+2;
}
```

Need of references when call by value exists:

1) Passing By Value

Dynamic memory allocation using the new operator, as in the last section, is only one instance in which dynamic allocation occurs. The other instance is more suitable, and happens more often than you might expect. This occurs when data are passed to functions as arguments. Let us review what happens when a function is called. A function such as:

int IntFunction (int Arg1, float Arg2) {.....}

expects two arguments, one int and on float, and returns int. Such a function is called from another function with a statement like:

eturnedInt = IntFunction (Int1, Float2);

where int1 and ReturnedInt have been declared previously and ints, and Float2 as a float. The arguments Arg1 and Arg2 in the function's argument list are variable *local* to the function. The space for them is allocated when the function is called and released when the function returns. The space for the argument Arg1, for example, is allocated *dynamically* when the function is called, the value passed to that argument (Int1) is copied to the space just allocated, the variable is used within the function in whatever manner the function's statements dictate, and that the memory is deallocated (freed up for later use by the same program or any other program running on the same machine) when the function terminates, and control passes back to the routine that called the function in the first place. This method of passing arguments to a function is known as *passing by value*, because only the *value* of the variable is passed to the function, not the address of the variable. Any changes made to the local copy of the value within the function do not affect the original variable in the calling routine.

2)Passing by reference

As we have seen in the previous section that when we pass a variable to a function as such i.e. by value we do not see the changes in the variable's value.That is why we must use & symbol i.e. pass by reference.See example presented before.

Purpose of "const" keyword with respect to references:

We use const keyword with reference whenever we want to avoid passing variable to a function by value i.e. avoid making copy and we want that the called function should not change the value of variable & only use it.

Example:

```
#include<iostream.h>
void main()
{
int change(const int&);
int a=10;
cout<<"Starting value of a is "<<a;
int x=change(a);
cout<<"The changed value of a is "<<x;
```

```
getch();
}
int change(const int &x)
{
int r=x+2; //cannot use x=x+2
return r;
}
```

Q5. "The access rules violated by friend functions and pointers." Comment on the above statement. Give reasons in support or against the above statement. [DEC02;Q5(b)]

Friend function has ability that can access the private data of the class. Pointer can access the address of any part of data. Again where is the security. So by both pointer and function ***access rules violation*** is done in C++. For example,

```
class x
{
int data;
void add( );
public:
friend void add( x obj; y obj2);
}

void add(x obj; obj2)
{
int sum;
sum = obj.data + obj.2data;
}

{
class y
int 2data;
public:
friend void add( x obj; y obj2);
}

main( )
{
x obj2;
y obj3;
obj2.data = 10;
obj3.2data = 20;
data (obj2, obj3)
}
```

Q6. Explain how pointer to functions can be declared in C++. Under what conditions can two pointer variables be added, subtracted and compared?

[DEC03;Q3(b)]

Pointer to a function is made (like pointer to an array is) by using name of function.
if we have int a[10];
pointer to it is

int*p=a;

For a function as int display()
we will have pointer fn as
int(*fn)();
fn-display;
now we can call function display by using pointer fn.
as
(*fn(();
Note: pointer to function is used in manipulators like
endl .

1) Pointers can never be added.
2) They can be subtracted if both pointers point to same array

```
eg.,    int arr[]={10,20,30,45,67,56,44};
int*i,*j;
i=&arr[1];
j=&arr[5];
cout<<j-i
```

3) They can be compared if both pointers point to objects of same type

```
eg.:-   int arr[]={10,20,36,72,45,36};
int*j,*k;
j=&arr[4];
k=(arr+4);
if(j==k)
cout<<"Pointer point to same location.";
else
cout<<"Pointer point to different location";
```

Output :
Pointers point to same location.

Q7. What is meant by call by value and call by reference? Under what conditions is call by reference preferred over call by value? [DEC03;Q5(c)]

Call by reference - A reference provides an alias i.e. alternate name for the variable. It is useful when the values of the original variables are to be changed using a function reference arguments which are indicated by an ampersand (&) proceeding the argument e.g. int & a;

Example

```
#include<iostream.h>
#include<conio.h>
void Swap (int &, int &)
void main ()
{
```

```
int a,b;
Cout<<"Enter any two values for a and b" <<end l;
Cin>>a;
Cin>>b;
Swap(a,b);
Cout<<"The two entered numbers are"<<"a"<<a<<" "<<",-and"<<"b"<<b<<end
l.;
}
void Swap (int & a, int & b)
{
int c:
c = a;
a = b
b = c;
}
```

The above program uses call by reference method for invoking a function.

Call by value : In this method the called function creates a new set of variables and copies the value of arguments into them. The function does not have access to the original variable(actual parameters) can only work on the copies of values it created. It is useful when the original values are not to be modified. In fact, call by value method offers insurance that the function cannot harm the original value. The following example explains this:-

```
Calling ()
{ int passit = 90;
Called (Passit) ;
Cout<<passit;     //there will be no change in passit value, remains 90.
}
void Called (int receiveit)
{
receiveit = 0;
}
```

In call by references arguments that are objects, are passed by references to the called method. Any change made to the object by the called method is reflected in the calling method

```
Calling ()
{
int passit=90;
Cout<<passit     //passit changes here to 0.
}
Called (int &receiveit)
}
receiveit=0;
}
```

In a call by reference, the memory address i.e. reference of the argument's variable is passed to the called method.

When the called() method changes the value of the argument, the change is reflected in the calling() method.

The output-generated from the above program is "changed".

Conditions in which call by reference is preferred over call by value:

1)We want to avoid making copy of variables to a function.

2)We want to reflect changes in real value of variable.

Q8. Describe Macro and Inline functions? [DEC03;Q6(i)]

Macros and Inline functions

Macro

We can define **Macro** by using #define directive. Each time the macro is encountered, the arguments used in its defition are replaced by the actual arguments found in the program. This form of a macro is called a function-like macro. For example.

```
#include<iostream.h>
#define ABS( a )                    (a ) < 0 ? – (a ) : ( a )
int main( )
{
cont<<"abs of 1 and 1 ; "<<ABS (-1 ) <<ABS ( 1 );
return 0;
}
```

When this program is compiled, a in the macro definition will be substituted with the values 1 and 1.

The use of a function-like macro in place of real functions has one major benefit: it increases the execution speed of the code because there is no function call overhead. However, if the size of the function-like macro is very large, this increased speed may be paid for with an increase in the size of the program because of duplicate code.

Although parameterized macros are a valuable features, C++ has a way of creating inline code which uses the inline keyword.

Inline functions

In C++, we can create short functions that are not actually called; rather, their code is expanded in line at the point of each invocation. This process is similar to using a function like macro. To cause a function to be expanded in line rather than called, precede its definition with the inline instead of called :

```
#include<iostream.h>
inline int max( int a, int b)
{
return a>b.? a : b;
}
void main ( )
{
cout << max(10, 20);
cout<< " "<<max(99,88 );
}
```

Q9. What is bridge function ? [JUNE01;Q5(c)]

Bridge function is other name of friend function.

The concept of data encapsulation sometimes takes information hiding too far. There are situations where a rigid and controlled access leads to inconvenience and hardships.

For instance, consider a case where a function is required to operate on object of two different classes. This function cannot be made a member of both the classes. What can be done is that a function can be defined outside both the classes and made to operate on both. That is, a function not belonging to either, but able to access both. Such a function is called as a friend function. In other words, a friend function is a nonmember function, which has access to a class's private members.

Using a Friend

Using a friend function is quite simple. The following example defines a friend function to access members of two classes.

```
class Bclass;                    // Forward Declaration
class Aclass
{
public :
Aclass(int v)
{
Avar = v;
}

friend int addup(Aclass &ac, Bclass &bc);
private :
int Avar;
};

class Bclass
{
public :
Bclass(int v)
{
Bvar = v;
}

friend int addup(Aclass &ac, Bclass &bc);
private :
int Bvar;
};

int addup(Aclass &ac, Bclass &bc)
{
return( ac.Avar + bc.Bvar);
```

```
}

void main()
{
Aclass aobj;
Bclass bobj;

int total;
total = addup(aobj,bobj);
}
```

The program defines two classes - Aclass and Bclass. It also has constructors for these classes. A friend function, addup(), is declared in the definition of both the classes, although it does not belong to either. This friend function returns the sum of the two private members of the classes.

Sometimes friend functions can be avoided using inheritance and they are preferred. Excessive use of friend over many classes suggests a poorly designed program structure. But sometimes they are unavoidable.

CHAPTER-5

POLYMORPHISM

- Function overloading
- Operator overloading

Operator overloading is nothing but defining a member function, for a particular operator, which will be invoked when the operator is used with objects of that class. This is also called ***operational polymorphism***. The second form of polymorphism in C++ is ***functional polymorphism*** also called ***function overloading***.

FUNCTION OVERLOADING

Function overloading is a form of polymorphism. Function overloading facilitates defining one function having many forms. In other words it facilitates defining several functions with the same name, thus overloading the function names. Like in operator overloading, even here, the compiler uses context to determine which definition of an overloaded function is to be invoked.

Function overloading is used to define a set of functions that essentially, do the same thing, but use different argument lists. The argument list of the function is also called as the function's signature. You can overload the function only if their signatures are different.

The differences can be

1. In number of arguments,

2. Data types of the arguments,

3. Order of arguments, if the number and data types of the arguments are same.

E.g.

```
int add( int, int );
int add( int, int, int );
float add( float, float );
float add( int, float, int );
float add(int,int,float);
```

The compiler cannot distinguish if the signature is same and only return type is different. Hence, it is a must, that their signature is different. The following functions therefore raise a compilation error.

E.g.

```
float add( int, float, int );
int add( int, float, int );
```

Consider the following example, which raises a given number to a given power and returns the result.

```
long long_raise_to(int num, int power)
{
long lp = 1;

for( int i = 1; i <= power ; i++ )
{
lp = lp * num ;
}
return lp;
}

double double_raise_to( double num, int power)
{
double dp = 1;

for( int i = 1; i <= power ; i++ )
{
dp = dp * num ;
}
return dp;
}

void main(void)
{
cout<<"2 raise to 8 is <<long_raise_to(2,8);
cout<<"2.5 raise to 4 is <<double_raise_to(2.5,4);
}
```

PRECAUTIONS WITH FUNCTION OVERLOADING

Function overloading is a boon to designers, since different names for similar functions need not be thought of, which often is a cumbersome process, many times people run out of names. But, this facility should not be overused, it becomes an overhead in terms of readability and maintenance. ***Only those functions, which basically do the same task, on different sets of data, should be overloaded.***

OPERATOR OVERLOADING

Operator overloading is one of the most fascinating features of C++. It can transform complex, obscure program listings into intuitively obvious ones. By overloading operators we can give additional meaning to operators like +, *, -, <=, >=, etc. which by default are supposed to work only on standard data types like ints, floats etc. For example, if strl and str2 are two character arrays holding strings "Bombay" and "Nagpur" in them then to store "BombayNagpur" in a third string str3, in C the following operations need to be performed :

```
char str1[20] = 'Nagpur" ;
char str2[] = "Bombay";
char str3[20];
strcpy ( str3, str1);
strcat ( str3, str2 );
```

no doubt this does the desired task but don't you think that the following form would have made more sense:

```
str3 = str1 + str2 ;
```

Such a form obviously would not work with C, since we are attempting to apply the +operator on non-standard data types (strings) for which addition operation is not defined. *That's the place where C++ scores over C*, because it permits the + operator to be overloaded such that it knows how to add two strings.

Let us take another example where operator overloading would make the programming logic more convenient to handle. Suppose we want to perform complex number arithmetic

```
# include <iostream.h>
struct complex
{
double real, imag ;
};
complex complex_set (double r, double i ) ;
void complex_print (complex c);
complex operator + (complex c1, complex c2) ;
complex operator - (complex c1, complex c2) ;

void main ( )
{
complex a, b, c, d ;
a = complex_set (1.0, 1.0) ;
b = complex_set (2.0, 2.0) ;
c = a +b ;
d = b +c- a ;
cout << end| << "c = " ;
complex_print (c) ;
cout << end| << "d" ;
complex_print (d) ;
}
complex complex_set (double r, double i )
{
complex temp ;
```

```
temp.real = r ;
temp.imag=i ;
return temp ;
}
void complex_print (complex t)
{
cout << "(" << t.real <<',' << t.image <<")"
}
complex operator + (complex c1, complex c2)
{
complex temp ;
temp.real = c1.real + c2.real ;
temp.image = c1.image + c2.image ;
return temp ;
}
complex operator - (complex c1, complex c2)
{
complex temp ;
temp.real = c1.real-c2.real :
temp.imag= c1.image - c2.imag ;
return temp ;
}
```

Operator overloading really speaking teaches a normal C++ operator to act on a user-defined operand. In our case the operator + and - are taught to operate on a user-defined data type "complex". This is achieved by declaring a function that defines the actions to be performed on the arguments passed to it. This function is declared using the keyword operator to be overloaded.

Q1. How can you overload the input operator in C++? Describe with the help of example. [DEC02;Q5(a)]

 # How can the operators << be overloaded in C++? [DEC01;Q6(b)]

 # How can you overload the output operator in C++? Describe with the help of an example.

We can overload input /output operator using references of istream and ostream objects along with friend function to permit normal representation even for user defined objects.

```
#include<iostream.h>
class de
{
public:
int a,b,c;
friend istream & operator >>(istream & os ,de &obj);
friend ostream & operator <<(ostream & os , de &obj);
};
```

```
//overloading output operator
ostream& operator <<(ostream & os,de &obj)
{
os<<obj.a<<obj.b<<obj.c;
return os;
}
//overloading input operator
istream& operator >>(istream & os,de &obj)
{
os>>obj.a>>obj.b>>obj.c;
return os;
}
void main()
{
de w ,e;
cin>>w;
cout<<w;
cin.get();
}
```

CHAPTER-6

INHERITANCE

OVERVIEW

Object-oriented programming as seen in the preceding sessions emphasizes the data, rather than emphasizing algorithms. The previous sessions covered OOP features like extensibility, data encapsulation, information hiding, functional polymorphism and operational polymorphism. OOP, however, has more jargon associated to it, like reusability, inheritance. This session covers reusability and inheritance.

REUSABILITY

Reusability means reusing code written earlier, may be from some previous project or from the library. Reusing old code not only saves development time, but also saves the testing and debugging time. It is better to use existing code, which has been time-tested rather than reinvent it. Moreover, writing new code may introduce bugs in the program. Code, written and tested earlier, may relieve a programmer of the nitty-gritty. Details about the hardware, user-interface, files and so on. It leaves the programmer more time to concentrate on the overall logistics of the program.

INHERITANCE

The new dimension of OOP uses a method called inheritance to modify a class to suit one's needs. Inheritance means deriving new classes from the old ones. The old class is called the *base class* or *parent class or super class* and the class which is derived from this base class is called as *derived class* or *child class or sub class.* Deriving a new class from an existing one, allows redefining a member function of the base class and also adding new members to the derived class and this is possible without having the source also. In other words, a derived class not only inherits all properties of the base class but also has some refinements of its own. The base class remains unchanged in the process. In other words, the derived class "is a " type of base class, but with more details added.

Derived class

A singly inherited derived class id defined by writing :

1) The keyword *class*.
2) The name of the derived class.
3) A single colon (:).
4) The type of derivation (private, protected, or public).
5) The name of the base, or parent class.
6) The remainder of the class definition.

E.g.

```
class A
{
public :
int public_A;
void public_function_A();

private :
int pri_A;
void private_function_A();

protected :
int protected_A;
void protected_function_A();
};

class B : private A
{
public :
int public_B;
void public_function_B();

private :
int pri_B;
void private_function_B();
};
class C : public A
{
public :
int public_C;
void public_function_C();

private :
```

```
int pri_C;
void private_function_C();
};
class D : protected A
{
public :
int public_D;
void public_function_D();

private :
int pri_D;
void private_function_D();
};
```

A derived class always contains all of the members from its base class. You cannot "subtract" anything from a base class. However, accessing the inherited variables is a different matter. Just because you happen to derive a class does not mean that you are automatically granted complete and unlimited access privileges to the members of the base class. To understand this you must look at the different types of derivation and the effect of each one.

PRIVATE DERIVATION

If no specific derivation is listed, then a private derivation is assumed. If a new class is derived privately from its parent class , then :

* The private members inherited from its base class are inaccessible to new member functions in the derived class. This means that the creator of the base class has absolute control over the accessibility of these members, and there is no way that you can override this.
* The public members inherited from the base class have private access privilege. In other words, they are treated as though they were declared as new private members of the derived class, so that new member functions can access them. However, if another private derivation occurs from this derived class, then these members are inaccessible to new member functions.

E.g.

```
class base
{
private :
int number;
};
class derived : private base
{
public :
void f()
{
++number;                // Private base member not accessible
}
```

```
};
```

The compiler *error* message is

‘ base :: number ‘ is not accessible in the function derived :: f();

E.g.

```
class base
{
public :
int number;
};

class derived : private base
{
public :
void f()
{
++number;                    // Access to number O.K.
}
};

class derived2 : private derived
{
public :
void g()
{
++number;                         // Access to number is
                                        // Prohibited.
}
};
```

The compiler *error* message is

‘ base :: number ‘ is not accessible in the function derived2 :: g();

Since public members of a base class are inherited as private in the derived class, the function derived :: f() has no problem accessing it. However, when another class is derived from the class derived, this new class inherits number but cannot access it. Of course, if derived1::g() were to call upon derived::f(), there is no problem since derived::f() is public and inherited into derived2 as private.

i.e. In derived2 we can write,

```
void g()
{
f();
}
```

PUBLIC DERIVATION

Public derivations are much more common than private derivations. In this situation:

* The private members inherited from the base class are inaccessible to new member functions in the derived class.
* The public members inherited from the base class may be accessed by new member functions in the derived class and by instances of the derived class.

E.g.

```
class base
{
private :
int number;
};


class derived : public base
{
public :
void f()
{
++number;    // Private base member not accessible
}
};
```

The compiler *error* message is

' base :: number ' is not accessible in the function derived::f();

Here, only if the number is public then you can access it.

Note : *However example 2 and 3 in the above section works here if you derive them as "public".*

PROTECTED DERIVATION

In addition to doing private and public derivations, you may also do a protected derivation. In this situation:

- The private members inherited from the base class are inaccessible to new member functions in the derived class.(this is exactly same as if a private or public derivation has occurred.)
- The protected members inherited from the base class have protected access privilege.
- The public members inherited from the base class have protected access.

Thus, the only difference between a public and a protected derivation is how the public members of the parent class are inherited. It is unlikely that you will ever have occasion to do this type of derivation.

SUMMARY OF ACCESS PRIVILEGES

1. If the designer of the base class wants no one, not even a derived class to

access a member, then that member should be made private.

2. If the designer wants any derived class function to have access to it, then that member must be protected.

3. If the designer wants to let everyone, including the instances, have access to that member, then that member should be made public.

SUMMARY OF DERIVATIONS

1. Regardless of the type of derivation, private members are inherited by the derived class, but cannot be accessed by the new member function of the derived class, and certainly not by the instances of the derived class.

2. In a private derivation, the derived class inherits public and protected members as private. A new member function can access these members, but instances of the derived class may not. Also any member of subsequently derived classes may not gain access to these members because of the first rule.

3. In public derivation, the derived class inherits public members as public, and protected as protected. A new member function of the derived class may access the public and protected members of the base class,but instances of the derived class may access only the public members.

4. In a protected derivation, the derived class inherits public and protected members as protected. A new member function of the derived class may access the public and protected members of the base class, both instances of the derived class may access only the public members.

MULTILEVEL INHERITANCE

In multilevel inheritance there is a parent class, from whom we derive another class. Now from this derived class we can derive another class and so on.

Multilevel Inheritance

```
class  Aclass
{
        :
        :
}

class  Bclass : public Aclass
{
        :
        :
}

class  Cclass : public Bclass
{
class equation              :
        :
}
```

Multiple Inheritance : Multiple inheritance, as the name suggests, is deriving a class from more than one class. The derived class inherits all the properties of all its base classes. Consider the following example:

Class A Class B

Class C

Multiple Inheritance

```
class Aclass
{
:
:
};

class  Bclass
{
:
:
};

class Cclass : public Aclass , public Bclass
{

private :
:
:
public  :

Cclass(...) : Aclass (...), Bclass(...)
{
};
};
```

The class Cclass in the above example is derived from two classes - Aclass and Bclass - therefore the first line of its class definition contains the name of two classes, both publicly inherited. Like with normal inheritance, constructors have to be defined for initializing the data members of all classes. The constructor in Cclass calls constructors for base classes. The constructor calls are separated by commas.

Problems With Multiple Inheritance

The following example presents a problem with multiple inheritance.

```
class  Aclass
{
public :
void put()
```

```
{
:
}
};


class Bclass
{
 public :
void put()
{
:
}
};

class Cclass : public Aclass , public Bclass
{
public :
:
:

};

void main()
{
A objA;
B objB;
C objC;

objA.put();                  // From Class A
objB.put();                         // From class B
objC.put();                         // AMBIGUOUS -RESULTS IN ERROR
}
```

The above example has a class C derived from two classes A and B. Both these classes have a function with the same name - put(), which assume, the derived class does not have. The class C inherits the put() function from both the classes. When a call to this function is made using the object of the derived class, the compiler does not know which class it is referring to. In this case, the scope resolution operator has to be used to specify the correct object. Its usage is very simple. The statement giving an error from the above example has to be replaced with the following:

```
objC.A::put();      // for class A
objC.B::put();      // for class B
```

Multiple inheritance with a common base (Hybrid Inheritance)

Inheritance is an important and powerful feature of OOP. Only the imagination of the person concerned is the limit. There are many combinations in which inheritance can be put to use. For instance, inheriting a class from two different classes, which in turn have been derived from the same base class .

Hybrid Inheritance

```
class base
{
:
:
};

class  Aclass : public base
{
:
:
};

class  Bclass : public base
{
:
:
};

class  derived : public Aclass, public Bclass
{
:
:
};
```

Aclass and Bclass are two classes derived from the same base class. The class derived has a common ancestor - class base. This is multiple inheritance with a common base class. However, this type of inheritance is not all that simple. One potential problem here is that both, Aclass and Bclass, are derived from base and therefore both of them, contain a copy of the data members of base class. The class derived is derived from these two classes. That means it contains two copies of base class members - one from Aclass and the other from Bclass. This gives rise to ambiguity between the base data members. Another problem is that declaring an object of class derived will invoke the base class constructor twice. The solution to this problem is provided by virtual base classes.

Virtual Base Classes

This ambiguity can be resolved if the class derived contains only one copy of the class base. This can be done by making the base class a virtual class. This keyword makes the two classes share a single copy of their base class. It can be done as follows :

```
class base
{
:
:
};

class Aclass : virtual public base
{
:
:
};

class Bclass : virtual public base
{
:
:
};

class derived : public Aclass, public Bclass
{
:
:
};
```

This will resolve the ambiguity involved.

ABSTRACT CLASSES

Abstract classes are the classes, which are written just to act as base class. Consider the following classes.

```
class base
{
:
:
};
class Aclass : public base
{
:
:
};

class Bclass : public base
{
:
:
};
```

```
class  Cclass : public base
{
:
:
};

void main()
{
Aclass objA;
Bclass objB;
 Cclass objC;

:
:
}
```

There are three classes - Aclass, Bclass, Cclass - each of which is derived from the class base. The main () function declares three objects of each of these three classes. However, it does not declare any object of the class base. This class is a general class whose sole purpose is to serve as a base class for the other three. Classes used only for the purpose of deriving other classes from them are called as *abstract classes*. They simply serve as base class, and no objects for such classes are created.

VIRTUAL FUNCTIONS

The keyword virtual was earlier used to resolve ambiguity for a class derived from two classes, both having a common ancestor. These classes are called virtual base classes. This time it helps in implementing the idea of polymorphism with class inheritance. The function of the base class can be declared with the keyword *virtual.* The program with this change and its output is given below.

```
class Shape
{
public :

virtual void print()
{
cout << " I am a Shape " << endl;
}
};

class Triangle : public Shape
{
public :
void print()
{
cout << " I am a Triangle " << endl;
```

```
}
};

class Circle : public Shape
{
public :
void print()
{
cout << " I am a Circle " << endl;
}
};

void main()
{
Shape S;
Triangle T;
Circle C;
S.print();
T.print();
C.print();

Shape *ptr;

ptr = &S;
ptr -> print();
ptr = &T;
ptr -> print();

ptr = &C;
ptr -> print();
}
```

The **output** of the program is given below:

```
I am a Shape
I am a Triangle
I am a Circle

I am a Shape
I am a Triangle
I am a Circle
```

PURE VIRTUAL FUNCTIONS

As discussed earlier, an abstract class is one, which is used just for deriving some other classes. No object of this class is declared and used in the program. Similarly, there are pure virtual functions which themselves won't be used. Consider the above example with some changes.

```
class Shape
{
public :
virtual void print() = 0;                    // Pure virtual function
};

class Triangle : public Shape
{
public :
void print()
{
cout << " I am a Triangle " << endl;
}
};

class Circle : public Shape
{
public :
void print()
{
cout << " I am a Circle " << endl;
}
};
void main()
{
Shape S;
Triangle T;
Circle C;

Shape *ptr;

ptr = &T;
ptr -> print();

ptr = &C;
ptr -> print();
}
```

The **output** of the program is given below:

I am a Triangle
I am a Circle

Q1. What are the access control violation in the following program fragment :

```
Class X {
private :
int i;
void pvt_X();
protected :
int j;
void prot_X();
public :
int k;
void pub_X(int, int);
};
Class Y :: public X
{
Char c;
};
void main() {
X x;
Y y;
x.i=10;
x.k=15;
y.prot_X();
y.pub_X(5, 10);
};
```

```
Class X {
private :
int i;
void pvt_X();
protected :
int j;
void prot_X();
public :
int k;
void pub_X(int, int);
};
```

Class Y :: public X →**(MISTAKE). Here "*Class Y :: public X statement should be Class Y : public X*".**

```
{
Char c;
};
void main() {
X x;
Y y;
```

x.i=10; →**(WRONG) . "Here *'i' is a private variable hence cannot be accessed outside the class definition*".**

x.k=15; →**(Correct). Here "*k' is a public variable and can be accessed with an object of X*".**

y.prot_X(); →**(WRONG). Here "*protected members are only accessible within the derived class definition*".**

y.pub_X(5, 10);
}; →**(Correct). Here"pub_X() is a public member of class X"**

Q2. What are the access control violations in the following program segment: [JUN03;Q1(c)]

```
class test_protected {
private:
int pri;
protected:
int pro:
public:
int pub;
test_protected () { }
void print (); };
class test_pro : private test_protected
private:
int sub_pri;
public:
int read ();
void print () {
cout << pri << pro << pub << sub_pri;
} };
void main () {
test_protected t;
t.print ();
}
```

```
#include<iostream.h>
#include<conio.h>

class test_protected
{
private :
int pri;                        //private data member of the class
protected :
int pro;
public:
int pub;
test_protected(){};
```

```
void print();
};

class test_pro:private test_protected
{
private : int sub_pri;

public:
int read();
void print()
{
cout<<pri<<pro<<pub<<sub_pri;   // pri cannot access private member
                                //declare in class test_protected
      }
};
void main()
{
test_protected t;
t.print();
}
```

Q3. Design and Implement a class hierarchy for the following requirements: [JUN03;Q5]

- **The class should represent complex numbers.**
- **It should have overloaded operator for addition and multiplication of complex numbers**
- **If an attempt is made to divide one complex number with another it generates an error message.**
- **The class should have suitable constructors, destructors, copy constructor and assignment operator.**

Write appropriate main ( ). Make and state suitable assumptions, if any.

```
#include<iostream.h>
#include<conio.h>
class Complex {
double real;
double imag;
public:
class divide(){};
//constructors
Complex();          //default
Complex(float);     //real given
Complex(float, float); //both given
Complex(Complex &s); //copy constructor
//other methods
void show()
```

```
{
cout<<"real= ="<<real<<
"imaginary= ="<<imag<<endl;
}
//operator methods
Complex operator+(Complex);
Complex operator-(Complex);
Complex operator*(Complex);
Complex operator/(Complex);
void operator=(Complex);
};
//default constructor
Complex::Complex()
{
real= imag=0.0;
}
//constructor--real given but not imag
Complex::Complex(float)
{
real=r;imag-0.0;
}
Complex::Complex(Complex &s)
{
real=s.real;imag=s.imag;
}
//constructor--real and imag given
Complex::Complex(float r. float)
{
real=r;imag=i;
}
//complex+as binary operator
Complex Comjplex::operator+(Complex c)
{
return Complex(real+c.real,
imag+c.imag);
}
//Complex-as binary operator
Complex Complex::operator-(Complex c)
{
return Complex(real-c.real,imag-c.imag);
}
Complex Complex::operator*(Complex c)
{
return Complex(real*c.real-imag*c.imag,imag*c.real+real*c.imag);
}
```

```
Complex Complex::opeator/(Complex c)
{
throw divide();
void Complex::operator=(Complex c)
}
{
Complex temp;
this.real=c.real;
this.imag=c.imag;
}
void main()
{
clrscr();
Complex c1(2.0,5.2),c2(2.3,5.9),c3;
Complex c4(c3);
try{
c4=c1+c2;
c4.show();
c4=c1*c2;
c4.show();
c4=c1/c2;
}
catch(Complex::divide)
{
cout<<"can't divide".
}
getch();
}
```

Q4. What are the access control violation in the following program segment:

[DEC02;Q1(c)]

```
class All_public {
public :
int all_pub ;
All_public ( ) { };
void print ( )
}
class Inherited : Private All_public {
private:
int some_private_data;
public:
int read( );
void print( );
}
```

Thefollowing access violations are there:

1) All_public::all_pub is not accessible

Because in this example our subclass inherited is privately inherited not publicly.
2) All_public is not member of inherited subclass.
3) Inherited::Second.some_private_data=200; is not accessible because it is defined private in subclass inherited.

Q5 What are the access control violations in the following program segment:
[JUN02;Q1(c)]

```
Class A {
int x;
protected:
int y
public:
A() {x = 5, y = 10};
print( ).; //prints A.
};

Class B : public A {
int z;
public:
B() {
z = 5;
x = 1;
y = 2;
};

main() {
A a;
B b;
a.z = 5;
b.print();
b.x = 10;
};
void main ()
{
All_public first;
inherited second ;
second.all_pub = 10;
second.all_public.print( );
first.all_pub = 50;
second. some_private _ data = 200;
}.
```

CLASS B	
(1)	Private member int z
(2)	Protected member intY
(3)	Public member A(),B(),Print()

i) a.z=5 not possible a is not accessible to object of class A.
ii) b.x=10 wrong because X is private member of class A. So not inheritable.

Q6. What are the access control violations in the following program segment:
[DEC01;Q1(d)]

```
class X {
int one ;
protected :
int two ;
public :
int three;
void x1() {
one=1;
two=2;
three=3;
};
}
class Y : public x{
int four;
public:
void y2 ()
{
one=2;
two=3;
three=4;
four=5;
}
};
```

```
void main () {
X a;
Y b;
a.x1() ;
a.one=5;
b.one=10;
b.y2 ();
};
```

Class y	
(1)	Private member
	int four
(2)	protected member
	int two
(3)	public member
	int three
	void X1 ( )
	void Y2 ( )

i) a.one=5 is inaccessible because one is private member of class X.
ii) b.one is wrong because one is not a member of class Y.

Q7. What is meant by the term information violate information hiding? Describe with the help of an example. Does friend function violate information hiding? Justify your answer. [JUN01;Q1(c)]

The term information hiding differs from the term information violate. The word information violate means that you are using the Public, Private, Protected access specifier. It means that you are restricting its limit or defining its area or specifying its boundary. If any function is breaking its limit or boundary that means it violates its rules. The term information hiding refers that some part of data is hiding from user. It restrict user to access unauthorized data.

Example : Oracle database user is authorised by Database Administrator to see some of the tables and not all the company details.

Yes, friend function violate information hiding because with help of friend function you are able to access the private part or data of the class .

Q8. What is single and multiple inheritance? Explain with the help of an example. What are the problems relating to multiple inheritance? [JUN01;Q1(d)]

Reusability is yet another important feature of OOP. It is always nice if we could reuse something that already exists rather than trying to create the same all over again. It would not only save time and money but also reduce frustration and increase reliability. For example the reuse of a class that has already been tested, debugged and used many times can save us the effort of developing and testing the same again.

Fortunately, C++ strongly supports the concept of reusability. The C++ classes can be reused in several ways. Once a class has been written and tested, it can be adapted by other programmers to suit their requirements. This is basically done by creating new classes, reusing the properties of the existing ones. The mechanism of deriving a new class from an old one is called *inheritance* (*or derivation*). The old class is referred to as the base class and the new one is called the *derived class.* The derived class inherits some or all of the traits from the base class. A class can also inherit properties from more than one class or from more than one level. A derived class with only one base class is called *single inheritance* and one with several base classes is called *multiple inheritance.* On the other hand, the traits of one class may be inherited by more than one class. This process is known as hierarchical inheritance. The mechanism of deriving a class from another 'derived class' is known as *multilevel inheritance.* Following figure shows various forms of inheritance that could be used for writing extensible programs. The direction of arrow indicates the direction of inheritance.

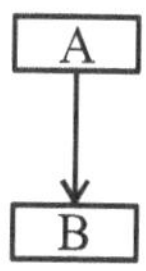

a) Single inheritance

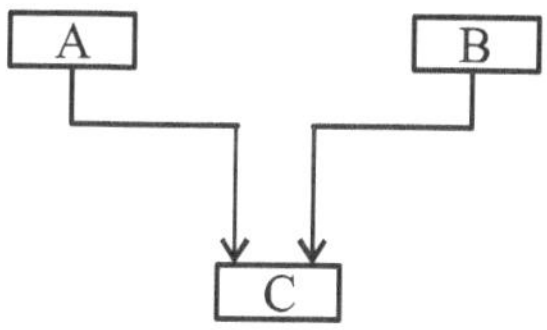

b) Multiple inheritance

Q9. Design a class hierarchy in C++ for employees of a company. Employees can be of two types, full time and part-time, all employees are employed for a particular department. One of the employees in the department is designated as manager. In your design you may include the data members, constructor, destructor and one polymorphic function for printing the details. [JUN01;Q4]

```
#include<iostream.h>
#include<conio.h>
#include<string.h>
class employee
{
protected:
int no;
char name[15];
char deptname[25];
char desig[25];
```

```
public:
void getdata()
{
cout<<"Enter No:";
cin>>no;
cout<<"\nEnter Name:";
cin>>name;
cout<<"\nEnter Department name:";
cin>>deptname;
}
void putdata()
{
cout<<"No="<<no;
cout<<"\nName="<<name<< "\n";
cout<<"Dept Name="<<deptname<<"\n";
}
};
class Fulltimeemp:public employee
{
protected:
float salary;
public:
void getdata()
{
employee::getdata();
cout<<"\nEnter salary:";
cin>>salary;
}
void putdata(void)
{
employee::putdata();
cout<<"Salary ="<<salary<<"\n";
}
};
class parttime:public employee
{
protected:
float salary;
public:
void getdata()
{
employee::getdata();
cout<<"\nEnter fees:";
cin>>salary;
}
```

```
void putdata(void)
{
employee::putdata();
cout<<"Salary ="<<salary<<"\n";
}
};
int main()
{
int ch,i=0,j=0,n,k;
do
{
clrscr();
cout<<"1.FullTimeEmployee\n";
cout<<"2.PartTimeEmployee\n";
cout<<"3.Exit\n";
cout<<"Enter choice(1/2/3):";
cin>>ch;
switch(ch)
{
case 1: Fulltimeemp ob1[10];
ob1[i++].getdata();
break;
case 2:parttime ob2[10];
ob2[j++].getdata();
break;
case 3:if(i!=0||j!=0)
{
n= i;
int k=0;
for(;k<n;k++)
ob1[k].putdata();
n=j;
k=0;
for(;k<n;k++)
ob2[k].putdata();
getch();
}
}
}while(ch!=3);
return 0;
}
```

Q10. Design and develop a polymorphic class to solve a general quadratic equation $ax^2 + bx + c = 0$.

```
#include<iostream.h>
#include<conio.h>
#include<math.h>
class equation
{
protected:
float a,b,c;


public:
void getdata()
{
cout<<"Enter value if a,b,c ";
cin>>a>>b>>c;
}
int returna(){return a;}
int returnb(){return b;}
int returnc(){return c;}

equation(){a=0;b=0;c=0;
}
equation(int x,int y,int z)
{ a=x;b=y;c=z;}
virtual void showdata(float a,float b,float c){}
};

class imaginary:public equation
{
public:
void showdata(float a,float b,float c)
{
if(b*b-4*a*c<0)
cout<<"Roots are imaginary";

}
};

class real:public equation
{
float r1 ,r2;
public:
void showdata(float a,float b,float c)
```

```
{
if(b*b-4*a*c>0)
{
r1=(-b+sqrt(b*b-4*a*c))/2*a;
r2=(-b-sqrt(b*b-4*a*c))/2*a;

cout<<"Roots are :"<<r1<<":"<<r2;
}
}
};

class equal:public equation
{
float r;
public:
void showdata(float a,float b,float c)
{
if(b*b-4*a*c==0)
{
r=-b/(2*a);

cout<<"Roots are :"<<r<<" each ";
}
}
};

void main()
{
clrscr();

equation*r[3];
imaginary m;
real re;
equal eq;
equation e;
e.getdata();
r[0]=&m;
r[1]=&re;
r[2]=&eq;
for(int i=0;i<3;i++)
r[i]->showdata(e.returna(),e.returnb(),e.returnc());
//check all functions to decide roots
getch();
}
```

Q11. What is late binding? How is it same/different from dynamic binding? [JUN03;Q6(c)]

 # What is late binding? Is it different from dynamic binding? Justify your answer with the help of an example. [DEC02;Q5(c)]

 # What is Dynamic binding? How is it useful in implementing polymorphism in object orient systems? Explain with the help of an example. [JUN01;Q1(e)]

At the design level, when a software engineer is deciding what type of action is appropriate for a given object, he or she should not be concerned about how the object interprets the action (message) and implements the methods but only what the effect of the action is on the object. Object-oriented languages like C++ and Smalltalk allow a programmer to send identical messages to dissimilar but related objects and achieve identical actions while letting the software system decide how to achieve the required action for the given object. A key issue associated with polymorphism is the timing of the software system's implementations decision. If the system decides how to implement an action at compile time, this is called early binding. If the decision is made dynamically at run-time, it is called **late binding**. *Generally late binding offers the advantages of flexibility and a high level of problem abstraction.*

Example

```
#include<iostream.h>
class x                                 //base class
{
public:
virtual void show()                     //virtual function
{
cout<<"x";
}
};

class y: public x                       //derived class
{
public:
void show()
{
cout<<"y";
}
};

class z:public y                        //super class
{
public:
void show()
{
cout<<"z";
}
```

```
};
// In this we call a function of derived class using base class pointer. One important
//point is that you must declare base function by using virtual keyword.
void main()
{
x *xb;
x xobj;
y yobj;
z zobj;

xb=&xobj;
xb->show();                    //only x class function is called
xb=&yobj;
xb->show();                    // only y class function is called
xb=&zobj;
xb->show();                    // only z class function is called
}
```

Q12. Design a polymorphic class hierarchy for the Windows based software. Assume that a window consist of Menu, Tools, Buttons and Iteraction area. Your class should include necessary data members, constructor/destructor and at least one polymorphic function. Make and state suitable assumptions, if any.

[DEC02;Q6]

```
#include<iostream.h>
#include<conio.h>
#include<stdio.h>
class windows
{
protected:
int length;
int width;
public:
void getwindowdimensions()
{
cout<<"Enter window length in pixels";
cin>>length;
cout<<"Enter window breadth in pixels";
cin>>width;
}
virtual void getdata()=0;
};


class Menu:public windows
```

```
{
char name[20][20];
int no_menu;
public:
Menu()
{
no_menu=0;
}
~Menu(){}
void getdata()
{
cout<<"Enter length & width of menu in pixels";
cin>>length>>width;
cout<<"Enter no: of menus";
cin>>no_menu;
cout<<"Enter menu names\n";
for(int i=0;i<no_menu;i++)
{
cout<<"\nMenu:"<<i+1<<":";
gets(name[i]);
}
}
};


class Tools:public windows
{
char name[20][20];
int no_tools;
public:
Tools()
{
no_tools=0;
}
~Tools(){}
void getdata()
{
cout<<"Enter no: of tools";
cin>>no_tools;
cout<<"Enter tool names\n";
for(int i=0;i<no_tools;i++)
{
cout<<"\nTool:"<<i+1<<":";
gets(name[i]);
}
```

```
}
};
class Buttons:public windows
{
char text[20][20];
int no_buttons;
public:
Buttons()
{
no_buttons=0;
}
~Buttons(){}
void getdata()
{
cout<<"Enter length & width of button in pixels";
cin>>length>>width;
cout<<"Enter no: of buttons";
cin>>no_buttons;
cout<<"Enter button names\n";
for(int i=0;i<no_buttons;i++)
{
cout<<"\nButton:"<<i+1<<":";
gets(text[i]);
}
}
};


class Interaction_Area:public windows
{
char message[50];
public:
Interaction_Area()
{
length=639;
width=479;
}
~Interaction_Area(){}
void getdata()
{
cout<<"Enter length & width of interaction area in pixels";
cin>>length>>width;
cout<<"Enter the message to appear by default";
gets(message);
}
```

```
};
void main()
{
clrscr();
windows *w[4];

Menu m1;
w[0]=&m1;
w[0]->getwindowdimensions();

Tools t1;
w[1]=&t1;

Buttons b1;
w[2]=&b1;

Interaction_Area a1;
w[3]=&a1;

cout<<"Enter data for windows & other elements\n";

for(int i=1;i<4;i++)
{
w[i]->getdata();
cout<<"\n\n";
}

getch();
}
```

Q13. Design a polymorphic class hierarchy for four-side objects. The four-side objects which may be included in this class may be square, rectangle or rombus. The class should have explicit constructors. The class should have polymorphic functions for area calculations and printing. Write the appropriate main() function that have 10 such objects and find the area of these objects /print those objects using polymorphic function. [DEC01;Q4][JUN02;Q2]

```
#include<iostream.h>
#include<conio.h>
#include<stdio.h>
class four_sided_objects
{
protected:
int length;
int width;
int height;
```

```
int area;

public:
virtual void getdata()=0;
virtual void calcarea()=0;
virtual void printarea()=0;
};

class square:public four_sided_objects
{
public:
square()
{
length=10;
}
~square(){}
void getdata()
{
cout<<"Enter side of square in pixel";
cin>>length;
}
void calcarea()
{
area=length*length;
}
void printarea()
{
cout<<"Area of square is"<<area;
}
};

class rectangle:public four_sided_objects
{
public:
rectangle()
{
length=10;
width=5;
}
~rectangle(){}
void getdata()
{
cout<<"Enter length and breadth of rectangle in pixel";
cin>>length>>width;
}
```

```
void calcarea()
{
area=length*width;
}
void printarea()
{
cout<<"Area of rectangle is"<<area;
}
};

class rhombus:public four_sided_objects
{
public:
rhombus()
{
length=10;
height=5;
}
~rhombus(){}
void getdata()
{
cout<<"Enter longer side & distance between longer sides in pixel";
cin>>length>>height;
}
void calcarea()
{
area=length*height;
}
void printarea()
{
cout<<"Area of rhombus is"<<area;
}
};

void main()
{
clrscr();
four_sided_objects *fs[3];
square s1;
rectangle r1;
rhombus h1;
fs[0]=&s1;
fs[1]=&r1;
fs[2]=&h1;
```

```
cout<<"Enter the data:\n";

for(int i=0;i<10;i++)
for(int j=0;j<3;j++)
if(j==0)
{
cout<<"\n\nEnter data for square:"<<i+1<<"\n";
fs[j]->getdata();
cout<<"\n";
fs[j]->calcarea();
fs[j]->printarea();
}
else
if(j==1)
{
cout<<"\n\nEnter data for rectangle:"<<i+1<<"\n";
fs[j]->getdata();
cout<<"\n";
fs[j]->calcarea();
fs[j]->printarea();
}
else

{
cout<<"\n\nEnter data for rhombus:"<<i+1<<"\n";
fs[j]->getdata();
cout<<"\n";
fs[j]->calcarea();
fs[j]->printarea();
}
getch();
}
```

Q14. Design a polymorphic class hierarchy for the students of a university. Each student is attached to a department. However, there are two types of students: day scholars and hostelers. Day scholars get a 30% concession in fee as they are not availing hostel fee. Design the suitable constructors/destructors and polymorphic function for fee calculation. Implement the classes. Write appropriate main( ) function which calculates the fee of the students of a batch of 100 belonging to two departments. Make and state suitable assumptions. [JUN02;Q2]

```
.#include<iostream.h>
#include<conio.h>
#include<string.h>
class student
{
```

```
protected:
int no;
char name[15];
char deptname[25];
public:
void getdata()
{
cout<<"Enter No:";
cin>>no;
cout<<"\nEnter Name:";
cin>>name;
cout<< "\nEnter Department name:";
cin>>deptname;
}
void putdata()
{
cout<<"\nNo="<<no;
cout<<"\nName="<<name;
cout<< "\nDepartment name:"<<deptname;

}
};
class daysscholar:public student
{
protected:
float fees;
public:
void getdata()
{
student::getdata();
cout<<"\nEnter fees:";
cin>>fees;
}
void putdata(void)
{
student::putdata();
cout<<"\nFees ="<<(fees-(fees*.30))<<"\n";
}
};
class hostlar:public student
{
protected:
float fees;
public:
void getdata(void)
{
student::getdata();
cout<<"\nEnter fees:";
```

```
cin>>fees;
}
void putdata(void)
{
student::putdata();
cout<<"\nFees ="<<fees<<"\n";
}
};
void main()
{
int ch,i=0,j=0,n,k;
do
{
clrscr();
cout<<"1.days scholar\n";
cout<<"2.Hostler\n";
cout<<"3.Exit\n";
cout<<"Enter choice(1/2/3):";

cin>>ch;

switch(ch)
{
case 1:daysscholar ob1[100];
ob1[i++].getdata();
break;
case 2:hostlar ob2[100];
ob2[j++].getdata();
break;
case 3:if(i!=0||j!=0)
{
n=i;
int k=0;
for(;k<n;k++)
ob1[k].putdata();
n=j;
k=0;
for(;k<n;k++)
ob2[k].putdata();
getch();
}
}
}
while(ch!=3);
}
```

CHAPTER-7

TEMPLATE AND STREAMS

- Function Templates
- Stream Class Hierarchy
- Class Template

FUNCTION TEMPLATES

Function templates provide you with the capability to write a single function that is a skeleton, or template, for a family of similar functions.

Function overloading technique it relieves someone who is using your functions from having to know about different names for various functions that essentially do the same task. Unfortunately, overloaded functions are not the ultimate solution to the problem.

Consider the following example:

```
int max(int x, int y)
{
return ( x > y) ? x : y ;
}

float max(float x, float y)
{
return ( x > y) ? x : y ;
}

long max( long x,  long y)
{
return ( x > y) ? x : y ;
}

char max(char x, char y)
{
return ( x > y) ? x : y ;
}
void main()
{
cout << max( 1,2) << endl;
cout << max( 4L,3L) << endl;
cout << max( 5.62,3.48) << endl;
cout << max('A','a') << endl;
}
```

The **output** is :

2
4
5.62
a

Even though function overloading is used, the problem with this example is that there is still too much repetitious coding. In other words, each function is essentially doing the same task. Now, instead of writing many functions, it would be nice if we were to write only one function and which can accommodate almost any type of input argument.

✓ **HOW A FUNCTION TEMPLATE SOLVES THIS PROBLEM?**

A function template solves the problem by allowing you to write just one function that serves as a skeleton, or, template, for a family of functions whose tasks are all similar.

This function template does not specify the actual types of the arguments that the function accepts; instead, it uses a generic, or parameterized type, as a " place holder", until you determine the specific types. The process of invocation of these functions with actual parameter types is called the ***template instantiation***.

✓ **HOW TO WRITE A FUNCTION TEMPLATE?**

A function template should be written at the start of the program in the global area, or you may place it into a header file. All function templates start with a template declaration.

The syntax is:

Ø The C++ keyword template

Ø A left angle bracket (<)

Ø A comma separates a list of generic types, each one. A generic type consists of two parts:

1. The keyword class (this usage of class has nothing to do with the keyword class used to create user-defined type.)

2. A variable that represents some generic type, and will be used whenever this type needs to be written in the function definition. Typically the name T is used, but any valid C++ name will do.

A right angle bracket (>).

E.g.

```
template <class T>
T max(char x, char y)
{
return ( x > y) ? x : y ;
}
void main()
```

```
{
cout<<max(1,2)<<endl;
cout<<max(5.62,3.48)<<endl;
cout<<max('A','a')<<endl;
cout<<max(4,3)<<endl;
}
```

The **output** is :

```
2
5.62
a
6
```

Each of first three max () function class causes a template function to be instantiated, first with an int, then with a double and then with a char. The last call using two integers does not cause another instantiation to occur because this call can use the instantiated function that was generated as a result of the first class that also uses two integers.

CLASS TEMPLATES

In addition to function templates, C++ also supports the concept of class templates. By definition, a class template is a class definition that describes a family of related classes. The philosophy is essentially the same as that of function templates, i.e., the ability to create a class (or structure) that contains one or more types that are generic, or parameterized.

A class template is defined in a manner similar to that of a function template. You start by writing a template declaration followed by the class definition:

E.g.

```
Template <class T>
class test
{
private : T item;

// data and functions
};
```

The generation of a class from class definition is called template instantiation. We can declare variables of this class as follows:

```
void main()
{
test<int> intobj;
test<double> doubleobj;
}
```

In the first instantiation the entire template types i.e. variables of type T will be converted as integers. In the second case they are converted as double variables. Of course, you may have more than one parameterized type between the angle brackets.

Template <class T1, class T2, class T3>
class classname;

STREAM CLASS HIERARCHY

DEMONSTRATED THROUGH QUESTIONS

Q1. Describe the stream class hierarchy in C++. [JUN02;Q4(c)]

 # Describe the I/O stream hierarchy in C++? Write a program that write an object to a disk file.

 # What are the various stream classes in C++? Describe with the help of examples how these classes may be used in inputting objects from an input file and outputting objects to an output file. [JUN01;Q3]

The I/O system of C++ contains a set of classes that define the file handling methods. These include ifstream, ofstream and fstream. These classes are derived from fstreambase and from the corresponding iostream.h class as shown in Figure. These classes, designed to manage the disk files, are declared in fstream.h and therefore we must include this file in any program that uses files. Table shows the details of file operation classes. Note that these classes contain many more features. For more details, refer to the manual.

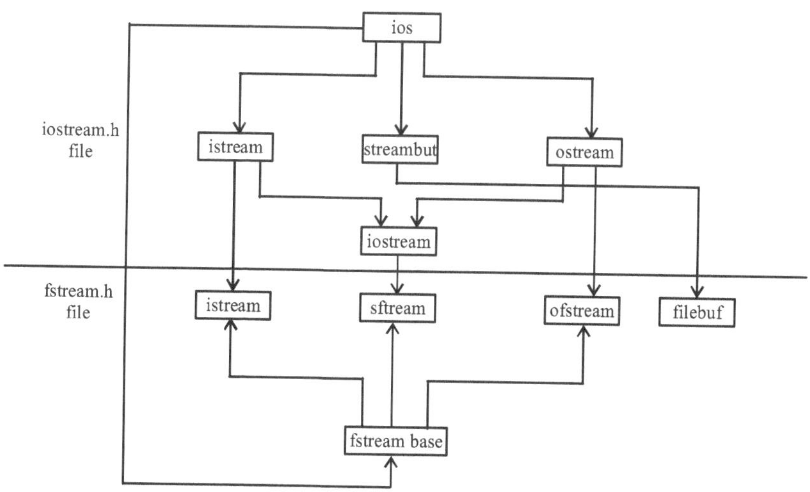

Class	Contents
filebuf	Its purpose is to set the file buffers to read and write. Contains **Openprot** constant in the open() of file stream. Also contains **close()** and **open()** as members.
fstreambase	Provides operations common to the file streams. Serves as a base for **fstream, ifstream** and **ofstream** classes. Contains **open()** and **close()** functions.
ifstream	Provides input operations. Contains **open()** with default input mode. Inherits the functions **get()**, **getline()**, **read()**, **seekg()** and tellg() functions from **istream.**
ofstream	Provides output operations. Contains **open()** with default output mode. Inherits **put()**, **seekp()**, **tellp()**, and **write()** functions from **ostream.**
fstream	Provides support for simultaneous input and output operations. Contains **open()** with default input mode. Inherits all the functions from **istream** and **ostream** classes through **iostream.**

example for inputting objects from an input file and outputting objects to an output file

```
#include<fstream.h>
#include<conio.h>
#include<string.h>
class me
{
int rollno;
char name[25];
public:
void getdata(int rno, char*n)
{
rollno=rno;
strcpy(name, n);
}
void display()
{
cout<<"Roll No="<<rollno<<"\n";
cout<<"Name="<<name<<"\n";
}
};
int main()
{
clrscr();
ofstream ofile("me.dat");
me obj;
obj.getdata(1111,"Rithik");
ofile.write((char*)&obj,sizeof obj);
ofile.close();
ifstream ifile;
ifile.open("me.dat", ios::in); //open file in input mode
```

```
ifile.read((char*)&obj,sizeof obj);
obj.display();
getch();
return 0;
}
```

Q2. How can files be used for input/output? Discuss with the help of an example.
[JUN03;Q6(b)]

Input/Output from Text Files

Reading a text file is very easy using an ifstream (input file stream).

1. Include the necessary headers.

2. #include <fstream>
using namespace std;

3. Declare an input file stream (ifstream) variable. For example,
ifstream myInput;

4. Open the file stream. For example,
myInput.open("C:\\temp\\datafile.txt");

Path names in MS Windows use backslashes (\). Because the backslash is also the string escape character, it must be doubled. If the full path is not given, most systems will look in the directory that contains the object program.

5. Check that the file was opened. For example, the open fails if the file doesn't exist, or if it can't be read because another program is writing to it. A failure can be detected with code like that below using the ! (logical not) operator:

6. if (!myInput) {
7. cerr << "Unable to open file datafile.txt";
8. exit(1); // call system to stop
}

9. Read from the stream in the same way as cin. For example,

10. while (myInput >> x) {
11. sum = sum + x;
}

12. Close the input stream. Closing is essential for output streams to make sure that all the information has been written to the disk, but is also good practice for input streams to release system resources and make the file available for other programs that might need to write it.
myInput.close();

Example

The following program reads integers from a file and prints their sum.

```
#include <iostream>
#include <fstream>
using namespace std;
int main() {
 ifstream myInput;
 int x;
int sum = 0;
```

```
myInput.open("test.txt");
if (!myInput) {
cerr << "Unable to open test.txt.";
exit(1);
}
while (myInput >> x) {
sum += x;
}
cout << "total = " << sum << endl;
myInput.close();
return 0; }
```

Q3. Design a template class that is used to create a circular linked list.
[JUN03;Q1(b)]

```
#include<iostream.h>
#include<conio.h>
#include<process.h>
template <class t>
class node
{
protected:
node* count;
node* p;
node* q;
node* first;
node* last;
public:
t data;                                //template type
node* ptr;
node()
{
count=NULL;
}
public:
void create(t a);
void display();
void insert(t,t);
void delete1(t &);
};
template <class t>
void node<t> :: create(t a)
{
int i;
p=new node;
cout<<"\ninput node information :";
```

```
cin>>p->data;
p->ptr=NULL;
first=p;
for(i=1;i<a;i++)
{
q=new node;
cout<<"\ninput node information :";
cin>>q->data;
p->ptr=q;
q->ptr=NULL;
p=q;
}
last=p;
p->ptr=first;
}
template <class t>
void node<t> :: display()
{
count=first;
p=first;
do
{
cout<<p->data<<" ";
p=p->ptr;
}while(p!=count);
}

template <class t>
void node<t>::insert(t a,t b)
{
if(last->data==a)
{
q=new node;
p=first;
do
{
if(p->data==a)
{
q->data=b;
q->ptr=p->ptr;
p->ptr=q;
}
p=p->ptr;
}while(p!=count);
p->ptr=first;
```

```
}
else
q=new node;
p=first;
do
{
if(p->data==a)
{
q->data=b;
q->ptr=p->ptr;
p->ptr=q;
}
p=p->ptr;
}while(p!=count);
}

template <class t>
void node<t>::delete1(t &item)
{
p=first;
if(p->data==item)
{
first=p->ptr;
delete p;
}
else
{
q=first;
p=p->ptr;
while(p!=NULL)
{
if(p->data==item)
{
q->ptr=p->ptr;
delete p;
break;
}
q=p;
}
}
}

void main()
{
clrscr();
```

```
int ch,i,n,po;
node<char> k;
do {
cin.clear();
cout<<"\n\t MAIN MENU"        ;
cout<<"\n   ------------"   ;
cout<<"\n  Single circular linked list";
cout<<"\n          1. create";
cout<<"\n          2. display";
cout<<"\n          3. insert";
cout<<"\n          4. delete";
cout<<"\n          5. exit";
cout<<"\n\n ENTER YOUR CHOICE...\t";
cin>>ch;
switch(ch)
{
case 1:
cout<<"\nhow many no. of nodes :";
cin>>n;
k.create(n);
k.display();
break;
case 2:
k.display();
getch();
break;
case 3:
cout<<"\ninsert after";
cin>>po;
cout<<"\nenter data to be inserted";
cin>>i;
k.insert(po,i);
break;
case 4:
cout<<"\nnode to be deleted:";
cin>>po;
k.delete1(po);
k.display();
break;
case 5:     exit(0);
}
}while(ch!=5);
}
```

Q4. Design a template class for a binary search tree having only the search and insert function. Make suitable assumptions, if any. [DEC02;Q1(b)]

```
#include<iostream.h>
#include<stdio.h>
#include<conio.h>
#include<process.h>
template <class t>
class tree
{
public:
t info;
t val;
tree *left;
tree *right;
tree* create(tree*);
tree* inserttree(tree*,tree*);
bool search( tree *node,t val);
void traverse(tree<t> *node);
};

void main()
{
int ch;
bool sh;
tree<int> *root;
tree<int> obj;

//    clrscr();
do
{
cout<<"\n    M E N U   ";
cout<<"\n 1 Create a Tree";
cout<<"\n 2 Search ";
cout<<"\n 3 Traverse ";
cout<<"\n 4 Exit";
cout<<"\n Enter your Choice: ";
cin>>ch;
switch(ch)
{
case 1:
root=obj.create(root);
break;
```

```
case 2:
cout<<"Enter the search value";
cin>>obj.val;
sh=obj.search(root,obj.val);
if(sh==true)
{
cout<<"value found ";
}
else
{
cout<<"value not found";
}
getch();
break;
case 3:
obj.traverse(root);
getch();
break;
case 4:
cout<<"\nExit";
getch();
break;
default:
cout<<"\n Wrong choice";
getch();
}
}
while(ch!=4);
}

template <class t>
void tree<t>::traverse(tree<t> *node)
{
if(node)
{
traverse(node->left);
printf(" %d -> ",node->info);
traverse(node->right);
}
}

template <class t>
bool tree<t>::search(tree<t> *node, t val)
```

```
{
if(node)
{
if(node->info==val)
{
return true;
}
else if(val<node->info)
{
return search(node->left,val);
}
else
{
return search(node->right,val);
}
}
return false;
}


template <class t>
tree<t>* tree<t>::create(tree<t> *root)
{
t num;
tree *p;
root=NULL;
cout<<"\n Enter tree info: ";
cin>>num;
do
{
p=new tree;
p->info=num;
p->left=NULL;
p->right=NULL;
root=inserttree(root,p);
cout<<"\n Enter tree info(0 to stop: )";
cin>>num;
}while(num!=0);
return root;
}
template <class t>
tree<t>* tree<t>::inserttree(tree<t> *r,tree<t> *p)
{
```

```
if(r==NULL)
r=p;
else
{
if(p->info>=r->info)
r->right=inserttree(r->right,p);
else
r->left=inserttree(r->left,p);
}
return r;
}
```

Q5. Design a class for a circular queue using pointer.

```
#include<iostream.h>
#include<stdio.h>
#include<ctype.h>
#include<alloc.h>
#define FALSE 0
#define NULL 0
struct listelement
{
int    dataitem;
struct listelement *link;
};
class queue :public listelement
{
public:
listelement * lp,* tempp;

void Menu (int *choice);
listelement * AddQ (listelement * listpointer, int data);
listelement * DeleteQ (listelement * listpointer);
void PrintQueue (listelement * listpointer);
void ClearQueue (listelement * listpointer);
};
void main ()
{
listelement *listpointer;
queue x;
int    data,choice;
listpointer = NULL;
do {
x.Menu (&choice);
```

```
switch (choice) {
case 1:
cout<< ("Enter data item value to add ");
cin>>data;
listpointer=x.AddQ (listpointer, data);
break;
case 2:
if(listpointer==NULL)
cout<<"Queue empty!\n";
else
listpointer=x.DeleteQ (listpointer);
break;
case 3:
x.PrintQueue (listpointer);
break;
default:
cout<<"Invalid menu choice - try again\n";
break;
}
} while (choice !=4);
x.ClearQueue (listpointer);
}
/* main */
void queue::Menu (int *choice)
{

char   local;

cout<<"\nEnter\t1 to add item,\n\t2 to remove item\n\
\t3 to print queue\n\t4 to quit\n";
do {
local = getchar ();
if((isdigit (local)==FALSE) && (local != '\n'))
{
cout<< "\nyou must enter an integer.\n";
cout<< "Enter 1 to add, 2 to remove, 3 to print, 4 to quit\n";
}
} while (isdigit ((unsigned char) local)==FALSE);
*choice = (int) local - '0';
}

listelement * queue:: AddQ (listelement * listpointer, int data)
{
```

```
lp = listpointer;

if(listpointer != NULL)
{
while (listpointer -> link != NULL)
listpointer = listpointer -> link;
listpointer -> link = new listelement;
listpointer = listpointer -> link;
listpointer -> link = NULL;
listpointer -> dataitem = data;
return lp;
}
else {
listpointer = new listelement;
listpointer -> link = NULL;
listpointer -> dataitem = data;
return listpointer;
}
}
listelement * queue ::DeleteQ (listelement * listpointer)
{
cout<<"Element removed is"<<listpointer -> dataitem;
tempp = listpointer -> link;
free (listpointer);
return tempp;
}
void queue ::PrintQueue (listelement * listpointer)
{
if(listpointer == NULL)
cout<<"queue is empty!\n";
else
while (listpointer != NULL) {
cout<<listpointer -> dataitem<<" ";
listpointer = listpointer -> link;
}
cout<<"\n";
}
void queue::ClearQueue (listelement * listpointer)
{
while (listpointer != NULL) {
listpointer = DeleteQ (listpointer);
}
}
```

Q6. Design a template class for a circular queue. Make suitable assumptions, if any. [JUN02;Q1(b)]

```
//circular queue implementation
#include<iostream.h>
#define MAX 10
#include<conio.h>
template<class T>
class queue
{
private:
T arr[MAX];
T front,rear;
public:
queue()
{
front=-1;
rear=-1;
}
void addq(T item)
{
if((rear==MAX-1&&front==0)||(rear+1==front))
{
cout<<endl<<"Queue is full";
return;
}
if(rear==MAX-1)
rear=0;
else
rear=rear+1;
arr[rear]=item;
if(front==-1)
front=0;
}
T delq()
{
T data;

if(front==-1)
{
cout<<endl<<"Queue is Empty";
return NULL;
}
else
{
```

```
data=arr[front];

if(front==rear)
{
front=-1;
rear=-1;
}
else
{
if(front==MAX-1)
front=0;
else
front=front+1;
}

return data;
}
}
};
void main()
{
queue <int>a;
clrscr();
a.addq(11);
a.addq(12);
a.addq(13);
a.addq(14);
a.addq(15);
a.addq(16);
a.addq(17);
a.addq(18);
a.addq(19);
a.addq(20);
a.addq(21);
T i=a.delq();
cout<<endl<<"item deleted="<<i;
i=a.delq();
cout<<endl<<"item deleted="<<i;
i=a.delq();
cout<<endl<<"item deleted="<<i;
getch();
}
```

Q7. Write template class for stack. [DEC01;Q1(b)]

```
#include<iostream.h>
#include<stdio.h>
#include<conio.h>
#include<process.h>
template <class t>
class st
{
public :
t stack[20];
int top;
t val;
int choice;
st()
{top=-1;
}
int pop(t stack[ ],int &top);
void push(t stack[ ],int &top,t val,int n);
void display(t stack[ ],int top);
};
//Insert in stack
template <class t>
void st<t>::push(t stack[ ],int &top,t val,int n)
{
if(top < n)
{
top++;
stack[top]=val;
}
else
cout<<"Stack is full";
}
//deletion in stack
template <class t>
int st<t>::pop(t stack[ ],int &top)
{
int delvalue;
if(top>=0)
{
delvalue=stack[top];
top--;
return delvalue;
}
else
{
```

```
cout<<"\n Stack is empty";
return(-9999);
}
}
//Display in stack
template <class t>
void st<t>::display(t stack[ ],int top)
{
int i;
if(top>=0)
{
cout<<"\n";
for(i=top;i>=0;i--)
{
cout<<stack[i];
}
getch();
fflush(stdin);
}
}
void main()
{
st<char> obj;
do
{
cout<<"\n         Menu     ";
cout<<"\n 1 ==> Push   2 ==> Pop";
cout<<"\n 3 ==> Display  4 ==>Quit ";
cout<<"Enter your choice";
cin>>obj.choice;
switch(obj.choice)
{
case 1: cout<<"Enter the value to pushed";
cin>>obj.val;
obj.push(obj.stack,obj.top,obj.val,30);
break;
case 2: obj.val=obj.pop(obj.stack,obj.top);
if(obj.val!=-9999)
cout<<"\n the popped last value of stack  is "<<obj.val;
break;
case 3: obj.display(obj.stack,obj.top);
break;
case 4: exit(0);
default:
cout<<"wrongh value ";
        }
    }while(obj.choice!=4);
}
}
```

CHAPTER-8

EXCEPTION HANDLING

- **Overview**
- **Use of Exception Handling**
- **Programming Errors**
- **Process of Error Handling**
- **Control on Errors**

EXCEPTION HANDLING

The extensibility of C++ can increase substantially the number and kind of errors that can occur. The feature presented here enable programmers to write clearer, more robust, more fault tolerant programs.

There are many popular means of dealings with errors. Most commonly, error handling. Code is interspersed throughout a system code. Errors are dealt with at the place in the code where the errors can occur. The advantage of this approach is that a programmer reading code can see the error processing in the immediate vicinity of the code and determine if the proper errors checking has been implemented. The problem with this scheme is that code became polluted with the error processing. It becomes more difficult for a programmer concerned with the application itself to read the code and determine if the code is functioning correctly. This make its more difficult to understand and to maintain the code.

Some common example of exception are failure of new to obtain a requested amount of memory, an out range, arithmetic overflow, division by zero.

C++ exception handling features enables the programmer to remove the error handling code from the main line of a program execution. This improve the program reading and modifiability.

Exception handling is not designed to deal with asynchronous, situations such as disk I/O.

USE OF EXCEPTION HANDLING

Exception handling is used in situations is which the system can recover from the error causing the exception. The recovery procedure is called an exception handler. Exception handling is typically used when the error will be dealt by different part of the program from which detected the error.

Exception handling is especially appropriate for situation in which the program will not be able to recover, but needs to provide orderly clean up, then shutdown "gracefully".

1) Use exceptions for errors that must be processed in a different scope from which they occur. Use other means of error handling for errors that will be processed in the scope in which they occur.
2) Avoid using exception handling for purposes other than error handling because this can reduce program clarity.

Performance unit
1) Although it is possible to use exception handling for purposes other than error handling, this can reduce program performance.
2) Exception handling is generally implemented in compilers in such a manner that when an exception does not occurs, little or no overhead is imposed by the presence of exception handling code. When exception happen, they do in occur execution time overhead. Certainly the presence of exception handling code made the program consume more memory.
3) Another reason exception can be dangerous as an alternativc to normal flow of control is that the stack is unwound and resources allocated prior to the occurrence of the exception may not be freed. This problem can be avoided by careful programming.

Example of new throwing bad_alloc when memory is not allocated.
1)
```
# include <iostream.h>
using std :: cont ;
using.std :: cin;
# include < new>
using std : : bad_alloc;

int main ()
{
double * ptr [50];
try
{
for (int I=0; 1< 50; I++)
{
ptr (I)=new double [ 500000];
cont << "Allocte 500000 double in ptr"<< I;
}
}
catch ( bad_alloc.exception )
{
cont << "Exception Occurred"<<exception.what () << end 1;
}
return 0 ;
}
```

PROGRAMMING ERRORS

1) Aborting a program could leave a resource in a state in which other program would not be able to acquire the resource, hence the program would have a so-called "resource-leak".

2) Exception should be thrown only within try block. An exception thrown outside a try block cause a call to terminate.

3) It is possible to throw a conditional expression. But be careful because promotion rules may cause the value returned by the conditional expression to be of a different type than you may expect for example when throwing an int or double form the same conditional expression, the conditional expression will convert the int into Double. Therefore the result will always be caught by a catch with a double argument rather than sometimes catching double and sometime catching int.

4) Specifying a Comma separated list of catch argument is a syntax error.

5) Placing catch () before other catch blocks would prevent those blocks from ever being executed, catch () must be placed last in the list of handlers following a try block.

6) Assuming that after an exception is processed control return to the first statement after the throw is a logic error.

7) Placing an empty throw statement outside a Catch handler; executing such a throw causes a call to terminate.

8) User defined exception classes need not be derived from class exception. Thus writing catch (exception) is not guaranteed to catch all exception a program may encounter.

PROCESS OF ERROR HANDLING

Q1. What is an exception in C++? How is it handled? Describe with the help of an example.

#: How can the errors be handled in C++ program? Describe by giving an example.

[DEC01;Q4(b)]

The exception mechanism of C++ uses three new *keywords: throw, catch,* and try. Also, we need to create a new kind of entity called an *exception class.*

Suppose we have an application that works with objects of a certain class. If during the course of execution of a member function of this class an error occurs, then this member function informs the application that an error has occurred. This process of informing is called *throwing* an exception. In the application we have to create a separate section of code to tackle the error. This section of code is called an *exception handler* or a *catch block.* Any code in the application that uses objects of the class is enclosed in *a try block.* Errors generated in the try block are caught in the catch block. Code that doesn't interact with the class need not be in a *try* block. The following code shows the organisation of these blocks. It is not a working program, but it clearly shows how and where the various elements of the exception mechanism are placed.

```
class sample
{
public:
//exception class
class errorclass
{
};
void fun()
{
if(some error occurs)
throw errorclass(); //throws exception
}
};
//application
void main()
{
//try block
try
{
sample s;
s.fun();
}
catch(sample::errorclass) //exception handler or catch block
{
//do something about the error
}
}
```

Here sample is any class in which errors might occur. An exception class called *errorclass,* is specified in the *public* part of *sample*. In *main()* we have enclosed part of the program that uses *sample* in a try block. If an error occurs in *sample::fun()* we throw an exception, using the keyword *throw* followed by the constructor for the *errorclass:*

throw errorclass();

When an exception is thrown control goes to the *catch* block that immediately follows the *try* block.

CS-72

Solved Papers

GUESS PAPER-I

Q1(a). What is polymorphism? How is polymorphism exhibited by virtual functions. Illustrate by an example. [5]

(b) Design a class template to implement a doubly linked list for insertion and deletion only. [5]

(c) Design & implement a class hierarchy for the following. [10]

- class should represent coordinates of a plane in x and y.
- it should have overloaded operator for addition & subtraction of two points.
- An attempt to divide one point by other should generate an error.
- class should have suitable constructors, destructors, copy constructors & assignment operator.

Write appropriate main( ). Make suitable assumptions, if any.

(d) What are the access control violations in the following program segment [10]

```
class basefirst
{
        int val;
        protected;
        int n;
        public;
        int m;
        void print();
};
class derived first : public basefirst
{
        protected :
        int l;
        public:
        void getdata() {cout <<val;}
};
class derived: private derived first
{
        public :
        void put() { cout << l << val;}
};
void main()
{
        derived third t3;
        t3.getdata();
        t3.put();
        derived first f1;
```

```
    f1.getdata();
}
```

Q2(a). What is operator overloading? Illustrate by overloading unary operator ++. [6]

(b). Explain the concept of pointer to functions in C++. Give an example of it. [4]

Q3(a). How can you overload output operator in C++? Describe with an example. [5]

(b) Give differences between a stack & a queue through a program code.

Q4(a). What do you understand by abstract class & its relation to virtual functions? [5]

(b) Explain copy constructor & overloaded assignment operator. Use with example [5]

Q5. Design a class in C++ to implement record input of an employee in a file. Record has name, code, address of employee.
There should provision for traversal, insertion at last, deletion of a record. [10]

Q6. Describe the following with help of one example. [10]

(a) C++ free store
(b) Pointer & reference
(c) ios class
(d) Containership

GUESS PAPER-II

Q1(a). What is object oriented paradigm? Relate it to polymorphism & overloading? [5]

(b) Explain 'const' keyword with respect to parameters in functions? Give an example of code. [5]

(c) Design a circular queue through linked list / through array. Implement functions of addition and deletion. [10]

(d) What are access control violations in following program :

```
class init
{
        private;
        int k;
        public:
        void get() { cout<<k;}
};
class dinit : public init
{
        public :
        int j;
        void print() {cout<<k;}
        protected;
        int f;
};
class derived3; private dinit
{
        public;
        int b;
        void show ( );
};
void main()
{
        derived3 d3;
        d3.show();
        d3.print();
        dinit();
        i.show();
}
```

Q2(a). What is inheritance? Explain single & multiple inheritance by examples. [6]

(b). Explain references in C++ & differences from pointer. [4]

Q3(a). How you will overload binary operator * in C++. Explain using user Defined data type employee. [5]

(b). What are similarities / differences between class & structure when reviewed under OOP? [5]

Q4. Design a polymorphic class having following :

-It should represent polar co-ordinates r1 & r2.

-It should have overloaded operator for addition & subtraction of polar coordinates.

-There should no provision to divide polar co-ordinates. (error should appear).

-There should be constructors, destructors, copy constructors, assignment operator. Write appropriate main(). Make suitable assumption, if any. [10]

Q5(a). Explain function overloading and default arguments in C++ by examples. [5]

(b). Explain istream & ostream class function in class hierarchy of files. [5]

Q6. Explain with example.

a) Object slicing virtual functions.

b) Constructors in multiple inheritance.

c) Bridge Functions.

d) Global data.

CS-72 : C++ AND OBJECT ORIENTED PROGRAMMING

JUNE 2001

Note : *There are* **six** *questions in this paper. Question* **1** *is* **compulsory** *and carries 30 marks. Attempt any three from the rest.*

1(a). What are the advantages of object oriented programming? How is it different from procedural programming? What are the disadvantages of object oriented systems? **[5]**

Refer to Study Material, Chapter-1,Q1, Page no.- 1

(b) What is data abstraction? How is it implemented using C++? Describe with the help of an example. **[5]**

Refer to DEC2001, Q1(a), Page no.- 227

(c) What is meant by the term information violate information hiding? Describe with the help of an example. Does friend function violate information hiding? Justify your answer. **[5]**

The property of being a self-contained unit is called encapsulation. The idea that the encapsulated unit can be used without knowing how it works is called data hiding.

Encapsulation is the principle by which related contents of a system are kept together. It minimizes traffic between different parts of the work and it separates certain specific requirements from other parts of specification, which use those requirements. The important advantage of using encapsulation is that it helps minimize rework when developing a new system. The part of the work, which is prone to change, can be encapsulated together. Thus any changes can be made without affecting the overall system and hence changes can be easily incorporated. C++ supports the properties of encapsulation and data hiding through the creation of user-defined types, called classes.

Friend function has ability that can access the private data of the class. So, where the abstraction similarly if we use pointer. Pointer can access the address of any part of data. Either, so again where is the security in it. So both pointer and function access rules violated in C++. For example,

```
class x
{
int data;

void add( );
public:
friend void add( x obj; y obj2);
}
```

```
void add(x obj; obj2)
{
int sum;
sum = obj.data + obj.2data;
}
class y
int 2data;
public:
friend void add( x obj; y obj2);
}

main()
{
x obj2;
y obj3;
obj2.data = 10;
obj3.2data = 20;
data (obj2, obj3)
}
```

(d) What is single and multiple inheritance? Explain with the help of an example. What are the problems relating to multiple inheritance? **[5]**

In single inheritance a single class is derived from a single class (see figure below).

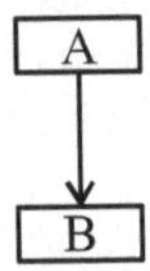

a) Single inheritance

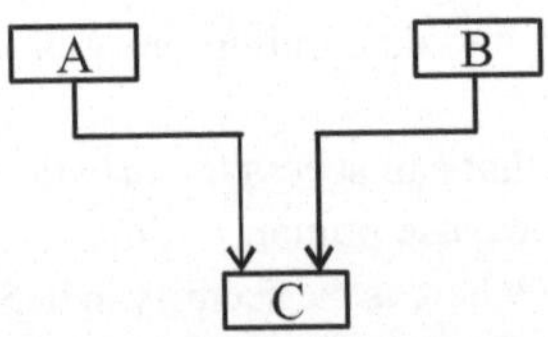

b) Multiple inheritance

Multiple Inheritance : Multiple inheritance, as the name suggests, is deriving a class from more than one class. The derived class inherits all the properties of all its base classes. Consider the following example:

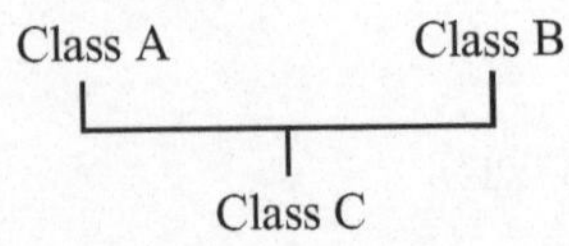

Multiple Inheritance

```
class Aclass
{
    :
    :
};
class Bclass
{
    :
    :
};

class Cclass : public Aclass , public Bclass
{

private :
        :
        :
public :
Cclass(...) : Aclass (...), Bclass(...)
{
};
};
```

The class Cclass in the above example is derived from two classes - Aclass and Bclass - therefore the first line of its class definition contains the name of two classes, both publicly.

Problems with multiple inheritance : If a class has been derived from two base classes having functions with same name say f() while derived class has no function with this name. Then there is ambiguity if derived class object tries to call the function f(). So, we should explicitly write :

```
derived d;
d.f();          //error
d.base1::f();
d.base2::f();
```

base1 and base2 are base classes.

(e) What is Dynamic binding? How is it useful in implementing polymorphism in object orient systems? Explain with the help of an example. **[5]**

Refer to JUNE2003, Q6(c), Page no.- 192

(f) Write a template for a list class name it as linked-list-single. **[5]**

Refer to JUNE2003, Q6(b), Page no.- 178

2. Write a program in C++ for merging two strings into one. You must design the program using pointers. Strings should be represented using pointers. [10]

Refer to DEC2001, Q1(c), Page no.- 229

3. What are the various stream classes in C++? Describe with the help of examples how these classes may be used in inputting objects from an input file; and outputting objects to an output file. [10]

Refer to DEC2001, Q4(a), Page no.- 234

4. Design a class hierarchy in C++ for employees of a company. Employees can be of two types, full time and part-time, all employees are employed for a particular department. One of the employees in the department is designated as manager. In your design you may include the data members, constructor, destructor and one polymorphic function for printing the details. [10]

```
#include<iostream.h>
#include<conio.h>
#include<string.h>
class employee
{
protected:
int no;
char name[15];
char deptname[25];
char desig[25];
public:
void getdata()
{
cout<<"Enter No:";
cin>>no;
cout<<"\nEnter Name:";
cin>>name;
cout<<"\nEnter Department name:";
cin>>deptname;
}
void putdata()
{
cout<<"No="<<no;
cout<<"\nName="<<name<<"\n";
cout<<"Dept Name="<<deptname<<"\n";
}
};
class Fulltimeemp:public employee
{
protected:
```

```
float salary;
public:
void getdata()
{
employee::getdata();
cout<<"\nEnter salary:";
cin>>salary;
}
void putdata(void)
{
employee::putdata();
cout<<"Salary="<<salary<<"\n";
}
};
class parttime:public employee
{
protected:
float salary;
public:
void getdata()
{
employee::getdata();
cout<<"\nEnter fees:";
cin>>salary;
}
void putdata(void)
{
employee::getdata();
cout<<"Salary="<<salary<<"\n";
}
};
int main()
{
int ch,i=0,j=0,n,k;
do
{
clrscr();
cout<<"1.FullTime Employee\n";
cout<<"2.PartTime Employee\n";
cout<<"3.Exit\n";
cout<<"Enter choice(1/2/3):";
cin>>ch;
switch(ch)
{
case1: Fulltimeemp ob1[10];
```

```
ob1[i++].getdata();
break;
case2: parttime ob2[10];
ob2[j++].getdata();
break;
case3: if(i!=0||j!=0)
{
n=i;
int k=0;
for(;k<n;K++)
ob1[k].putdata();
n=j;
k=0;
for(;k<n;k++)
ob2[k].putdata();
getch();
}
}
}while(ch!=3);
return 0;
}
```

5. Describe the following with one example each: **[10]**

(a) Error handling during file operation

Refer toJUNE2002, Q3(b), Page no.- 214

(b) Binary operator overloading

In this program, we are showing the binary operator +overloading.

```
#include <iostream.h>
class point
{
int x;
int y;
public:
point() {x=0; y=0 }
point(int l, int g)
{
x=l;
y=g;
}
void show()
{
cout<< x << " ";
cout<< y << "\n";
```

```
}
point operator+(point op2);
};
point::operator+(point op2)
{
int x1=x+op2.y;
int y1=y+op2.y;
return point(x1,y1);
}
void main()
{
point ob1(10,20), ob2(5,30);
ob1=ob1+ob2;
ob1.show();
}
```

As you can see, operator+() has only one parameter even though it overloads the binary + operator. The reason that operator+() takes only one parameter is that the operand on the left side of the + is passed implicitly to the function through the this pointer. The operand on the right is passed in the parameter op2.
The fact that the left operand is passed using this also implies one important point : When binary operators are overload, it is the object on the left that generates the call to the operator function.

(c) Bridge function
Refer to JUNE2003, Q6(a), Page no.- 189

(d) Function overloading
Function overloading is a form of polymorphism. Function overloading facilitates defining one function having many forms. In other words it facilitates defining several functions with the same name, thus overloading the function names. Like in operator overloading, even here, the compiler uses context to determine which definition of an overloaded function is to be invoked.
Function overloading is used to define a set of functions that essentially, do the same thing, but use different argument lists. The argument list of the function is also called as the function's signature. You can overload the function only if their signatures are different.

The differences can be
1. In number of arguments,
2. Data types of the arguments,
3. Order of arguments, if the number and data types of the arguments are same.
E.g.
int add(int, int);

```
int add( int, int, int );
float add( float, float );
float add( int, float, int );
float add(int,int,float);
```

The compiler cannot distinguish if the signature is same and only return type is different. Hence, it is a must, that their signature is different. The following functions therefore raise a compilation error.

E.g.

```
float add( int, float, int );
int add( int, float, int );
```

Consider the following example, which raises a given number to a given power and returns the result.

```
long long_raise_to(int num, int power)
{
  long lp = 1;

     for( int i = 1; i <= power ; i++ )
     {
          lp = lp * num ;
     }
     return lp;
}
double double_raise_to( double num, int power)
{
  double dp = 1;

  for( int i = 1; i <= power ; i++ )
     {
        dp = dp * num ;
     }
     return dp;
}

void main(void)
{
   cout<<"2 raise to 8 is <<long_raise_to(2,8);
   cout<<"2.5 raise to 4 is <<double_raise_to(2.5,4);
}
```

6. Design and implement (using C++) a class complex having the following functionality: [10]

- **It allows representation of complex numbers**
- **It allows addition of two complex numbers**
- **It has overloading constructors and a copy constructor**
- **It allows assignment of one complex number to other.**

Refer to Study Material, Chapter-6,Q3, Page no.- 91

CS-72 : C++ AND OBJECT ORIENTED PROGRAMMING

DEC 2001

Note : *There are* **six** *questions in this paper. Question number* **1** *is* **compulsory** *and carries 30 marks. Attempt any* **three** *from the rest.*

1(a) What is the meaning of data abstraction? What is encapsulation? How does C++ achieve these two concepts? Describe with the help of an example. [5]

Refer to DEC2002, Q1(a), Page no.- 194

(b) Write template class for stack. [5]

```
#include<iostream.h>
#include<stdio.h>
#include<conio.h>
#include<process.h>
template <class t>
class st
{
public :
t stack[20];
int top;
t val;
int choice;
st()
{top=-1;
}
int pop(t stack[],int &top);
void push(t stack[],int &top,t val,int n);
void display(t stack[],int top);
};
//Insert in stack
template <class t>
void st<t>::push(t stack[],int &top,t val,int n)
{
if(top < n)
{
top++;
stack[top]=val;
}
else
cout<<"Stack is full";
```

```
}
//deletion in stack
template <class t>
int st<t>::pop(t stack[ ],int &top)
{
int delvalue;
if(top>=0)
{
delvalue=stack[top];
top--;
return delvalue;
}
else
{
cout<<"\n Stack is empty";
return(-9999);
}
}
//Display in stack
template <class t>
void st<t>::display(t stack[ ],int top)
{
int i;
if(top>=0)
{
cout<<"\n";
for(i=top;i>=0;i--)
{
cout<<stack[i];
}
getch();
fflush(stdin);
}
}
void main()
{
clrscr();
st<char> obj;
do
{
cout<<"\n        Menu     ";
cout<<"\n 1 ==> Push   2 ==> Pop";
cout<<"\n 3 ==> Display 4 ==>Quit ";
```

```
cout<<"Enter your choice";
cin>>obj.choice;
switch(obj.choice)
{
case 1: cout<<"Enter the value to pushed";
cin>>obj.val;
obj.push(obj.stack,obj.top,obj.val,30);
break;
case 2: obj.val=obj.pop(obj.stack,obj.top);
if(obj.val!=-9999)
cout<<"\n the popped last value of stack  is "<<obj.val;
break;
case 3: obj.display(obj.stack,obj.top);
break;
case 4: exit(0);
default:
cout<<"wrongh value ";
}
}while(obj.choice!=4);
}
```

(c) Write a C++ program having the following functionality: **[15]**

- **The program have a class string in it.**
- **The string class have the data member as pointer to character.**
- **The class has overloaded constructor and copy constructor.**
- **The class have overloaded + operator which concatenates two strings.**
- **The class have a destructor.**
- **The class have functions for string comparison.**

Also write the appropriate main function that demonstrate the complete functionality of the class string.

Refer to Study Material, Chapter-3,Q8, Page no.- 41

(d) What are the access control violations in the following program segment: **[5]**

```
class X {
int one ;
protected :
int two ;
public :
int three;
void X1() {
one=1;
two=2;
three=3;
```

```
};
class Y : publicX {
int four;
public:
void Y2 () {
one=2;
two=3;
three=4;
four=5;
}
};
void main () {
X a;
Y b;
a.X1 () ;
a.one=5;
b.one=10;
b.Y2 ();
};
```

Class y	
(1)	Private member
	int four
(2)	protected member
	int two
(3)	public member
	int three
	void X1 ( )
	void Y2 ( )

Reason -> (i) a.one=5 is not accessible become t is nota public member variable (ii) One is not a member of class y because private data never inherit.

2. Design a polymorphic class hierarchy for four-side objects. The four-side objects which may be included in this class may be square, rectangle or rombus. The class should have explicit constructors. The class should have polymorphic functions for area calculations and printing. Write the appropriate main( ) function that have 10 such objects and find the area of these objects /print those objects using polymorphic function. **[10]**

```
#include<iostream.h>
#include<conio.h>
#include<stdio.h>
```

```
class four_sided_objects
{
protected:
int length;
int width;
int height;
int area;

public:
virtual void getdata()=0;
virtual void calcarea()=0;
virtual void printarea()=0;
};


class square:public four_sided_objects
{
public:
square()
{
length=10;
}
~square(){}
void getdata()
{
cout<<"Enter side of square in pixel";
cin>>length;
}
void calcarea()
{
area=length*length;
}
void printarea()
{
cout<<"Area of square is"<<area;
}
};

class rectangle:public four_sided_objects
{
public:
rectangle()
{
```

```
length=10;
width=5;
}
~rectangle(){}
void getdata()
{
cout<<"Enter length and breadth of rectangle in pixel";
cin>>length>>width;
}
void calcarea()
{
area=length*width;
}
void printarea()
{
cout<<"Area of rectangle is"<<area;
}
};

class rhombus:public four_sided_objects
{
public:
rhombus()
{
length=10;
height=5;
}
~rhombus(){}
void getdata()
{
cout<<"Enter longer side & distance between longer sides in pixel";
cin>>length>>height;
}
void calcarea()
{
area=length*height;
}
void printarea()
{
cout<<"Area of rhombus is"<<area;
}
};
void main()
```

```
{
clrscr();
four_sided_objects *fs[3];
square s1;
rectangle r1;
rhombus h1;
fs[0]=&s1;
fs[1]=&r1;
fs[2]=&h1;

cout<<"Enter the data:\n";

for(int i=0;i<10;i++)
for(int j=0;j<3;j++)
if(j==0)
{
cout<<"\n\nEnter data for square:"<<i+1<<"\n";
fs[j]->getdata();
cout<<"\n";
fs[j]->calcarea();
fs[j]->printarea();
}
else
if(j==1)
{
cout<<"\n\nEnter data for rectangle:"<<i+1<<"\n";
fs[j]->getdata();
cout<<"\n";
fs[j]->calcarea();
fs[j]->printarea();
}

else

{
cout<<"\n\nEnter data for rhombus:"<<i+1<<"\n";
fs[j]->getdata();
cout<<"\n";
fs[j]->calcarea();
fs[j]->printarea();
}
getch();
}
```

3(a). Describe the following terms with one example each: **[10]**

(a) Reference types in C++

Refer to JUNE2003, Q1(a), Page no.- 177

(b) The use of "this" pointer in C++

Refer to JUNE2003, Q4(a), Page no.- 188

(c) Multiple inheritance

Refer to JUNE2002, Q3(a), Page no.- 214

(d) Friend functions

Refer to JUNE2003, Q6(a), Page no.- 189

4(a). Describe the I/O stream hierarchy in C++? Write a program that write an object to a disk file. **[5]**

The I/O system of C++ contains a set of classes that define the file handling methods. These include **ifstream, ofstream** and **fstream.** These classes are derived from **fstreambase** and from the corresponding *iostream.h* class as shown in Fig. 11.3. These classes, designed to manage the disk files, are declared in *fstream.h* and therefore we must include this file in any program that uses files. Table shows the details of file operation classes. Note that these classes contain many more features. For more details, refer to the manual.

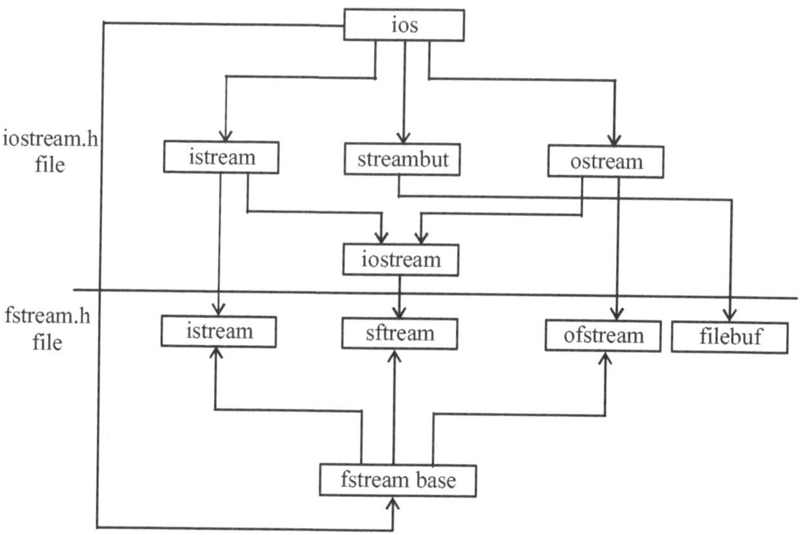

Class	Contents
filebuf	Its purpose is to set the file buffers to read and write. Contains **Openprot** constant in the open() of file stream. Also contains **close()** and **open()** as members.
fstreambase	Provides operations common to the file streams. Serves as a base for **fstream, ifstream** and **ofstream** classes. Contains **open()** and **close()** functions.
ifstream	Provides input operations. Contains **open()** with default input mode. Inherits the functions **get()**, **getline()**, **read()**, **seekg()** and tellg() functions from **istream.**
ofstream	Provides output operations. Contains **open()** with default output mode. Inherits **put()**, **seekp()**, **tellp()**, and **write()** functions from **ostream.**
fstream	Provides support for simultaneous input and output operations. Contains **open()** with default input mode. Inherits all the functions from **istream** and **ostream** classes through **iostream.**

```
#include <fstream.h>
void main ( )
{
struct employee
{
char name[20] ;
int age ;
float basic ;
float gross ;
} ;
employee e ;
char ch = 'y' ;
\\ create file for output
ofstream outfile ;
outstream outfile ;
outfile.open ( " EMPLOYEE.DAT", ios::out | ios::binary ) ;
while ( ch == 'y' )
{
cout << end| << "enter a record";
cin >> e.name >> e.age >> e.basic >> e.gross ;
outfile.write ((char *) &e, sizeof (e) ) ;
cin >> ch ;
}
outfile.close( )
\\ create file for input
ifstream in file ;
infile.open (EMPLOYEE.DAT", ios ::out | ios::binary ) ;
while (infile.read ((char *) &e, sizeof (e) ) )
{
```

```
cout << endl <<e.name << '\t' << e.age << '\t'
<<e.basic << '\t' <<e.gross ;
}
```

(b) How can the errors be handled in C++ program? Describe by giving an example. [5]

Refer to DEC2002, Q3(a), Page no.- 201

5(a). Design and implement a table class in C++ having the following requirements:

- **The table may have only floating point values. [10]**
- **The sum of a row or a column can be calculated with the help of overloaded sum function**
- **There is a copy constructor and other constructor for the table**
- **There are functions to find largest and the smallest values from the table and its positions in the table.**
- **It allows addition and subtraction of two tables having similar size.**

Refer to Study Material, Chapter-6,Q3, Page no.- 91

6(a). What is the meaning of having "const and classname" as a parameter in a function? Describe. [3]

If we want that an argument passed to an ordinary function by reference should not get modified then the argument should be made const in the function declaration (and definition). This holds good for member functions as well.

```
#include <iostream.h>
class sample
{
private :
int data ;
public :
sample ()
{
data = 0
}
void changedata()
{
data = 10 ;
}
void showdata () const
{
cout << end | << "data = " << data ;
}
void add (sample cont &s, sample const &t )
{
data = s. data + t.data ;
```

```
}
void getdata( )
{
cin >> data ;
}
};
void main ( )
{
sample s1
s1. Changedata( )
sample s3;
s3.add (s1, s2) ;
s3.showdata( ) ;
}
```

In this program the arguments to the function add ( ) are passed by reference, and we want to make sure that add ( ) won't modify these arguments. To ensure this we have declared the arguments as const.

(b) How can the operators << be overloaded in C++? **[4]**

Refer to JUNE2002, Q6(c), Page no.- 225

(c) What is an abstract class? What is late binding? **[3]**

A class that serves only as a base class from which classes are derived. No objects of an abstract base class are created. A base class that contains pure virtual functions is an abstract base class.

Late Binding : At the design level, when a software engineer is deciding what type of action is appropriate for a given object, he or she should not be concerned about how the object interprets the action (message) and implements the methods but only what the effect of the action is on the object. Object-oriented languages like C++ and Smalltalk allow a programmer to send identical messages to dissimilar but related objects and achieve identical actions while letting the software system decide how to achieve the required action for the given object. A key issue associated with polymorphism is the timing of the software system's implementations decision. If the system decides how to implement an action at compile time, this is called early binding. If the decision is made dynamically at run-time, it is called **late binding**.

CS-72 : C++ AND OBJECT ORIENTED PROGRAMMING

JUNE 2002

Note : *There are* **six** *questions in this paper. Question* ***1*** *is* **compulsory** *and carries 30 marks. Attempt any three from the rest.*

1(a). What is Object Oriented Programming? How is it different from procedural programming? Does object oriented programming paradigm not use procedural programming at all? Justify your answer. **[5]**

Refer to Study Material, Chapter-1,Q1, Page no.- 1

(b) Design a template class for a circular queue. Make suitable assumptions, if any. **[5]**

```
//circular queue implementation
#include<iostream.h>
#define MAX 10
#include<conio.h>
template<class T>
class queue
{
private:
T arr[MAX];
T front,rear;
public:
queue()
{
front=-1;
rear=-1;
}
void addq(T item)
{
if((rear==MAX-1&&front==0)||(rear+1==front))
{
cout<<endl<<"Queue is full";
return;
}
if(rear==MAX-1)
rear=0;
else
rear=rear+1;
arr[rear]=item;
if(front==-1)
front=0;
```

```
}
T delq()
{
T data;

if(front==-1)
{
cout<<endl<<"Queue is Empty";
return NULL;
}
else
{
data=arr[front];

if(front==rear)
{
front=-1;
rear=-1;
}
else
{
if(front==MAX-1)
front=0;
else
front=front+1;
}

return data;
}
}
};
void main()
{
queue <int>a;
clrscr();
a.addq(11);
a.addq(12);
a.addq(13);
a.addq(14);
a.addq(15);
a.addq(16);
a.addq(17);
a.addq(18);
a.addq(19);
a.addq(20);
```

```
a.addq(21);
T i=a.delq();
cout<<endl<<"item deleted="<<i;
i=a.delq();
cout<<endl<<"item deleted="<<i;
i=a.delq();
cout<<endl<<"item deleted="<<i;
getch();
}
```

(c) What are the access control violations in the following program segment: **[5]**

```
Class A {
int x;
protected:
int y;
public:
A() {x = 5, y = 10}
print(); //prints A.
};

Class B : public A {
int z;
public:
B() {
z = 5;
x = 1;
y = 2;
}    };

main() {
A a;
B b;
a.z = 5;
b.print();
b.x = 10;
};
```

Class B	
	Private member
	int z
	int y
	Public
	A( )
	Print ( )
	B ( )

Reason -> (i) a.z=5

It is not possible to access a class in reverse order mean how can you implement or access a class that is not yet create. Z is a member of class B not A.

(ii) b.x=10:

is a not a part of class B because private data can never be inherited.

(d) Design and implement a class vector having the following requirements: [15]

· It represents a single dimensional array of arbitrary length using dynamic array. (Use pointers)

· The class has constructors and destructors. However, the constructor which does not have any parameter creates a vector of size 10.

· The class has explicit destructor.

· Addition of two vectors is done in case they have same number of elements else an error message is generated.

· There is a provision of copy constructor and assignment among two vectors.

· There is a print function for vector.

Write the appropriate main( ) function that checks the functionality of the class.

Same method as Jun 2003 Q5. 188

2 Design a polymorphic class hierarchy for the students of a university. Each student is attached to a department. However, there are two types of students: day scholars and hostelers. Day scholars get a 30% concession in fee as they are not availing hostel fee. Design the suitable constructors/destructors and polymorphic function for fee calculation. Implement the classes. Write appropriate main( ) function which calculates the fee of the students of a batch of 100 belonging to two departments. Make and state suitable assumptions. [10]

Refer to Study Material, Chapter-6,Q14, Page no.- 109

3. Describe the following with the help of one example each: [10]

(a) Multiple Inheritance in C++

Multiple Inheritance : Multiple inheritance, as the name suggests, is deriving a class from more than one class. The derived class inherits all the properties of all its base classes. Consider the following example:

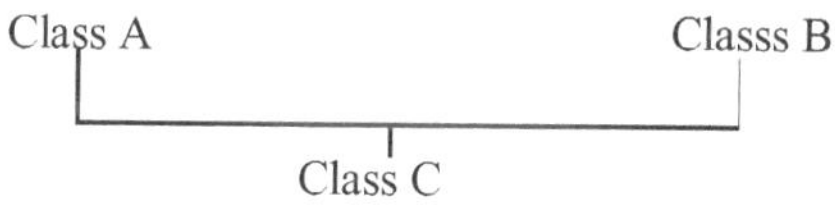

Multiple Inheritance

```
class  Aclass
{
:
:
};

class  Bclass
{
:
:
};

class Cclass : public Aclass , public Bclass
{

private :
:
:
public  :

Cclass(...) : Aclass (...), Bclass(...)
{
};
};
```

The class Cclass in the above example is derived from two classes - Aclass and Bclass.

(b) Input/Output from a file with error detection in C++

Reading a text file is very easy using an ifstream (input file stream).

1. Include the necessary headers.

2. #include <fstream>
   using namespace std;

3. Declare an input file stream (ifstream) variable. For example,
   ifstream myInput;

4. Open the file stream. For example,
   myInput.open("C:\\temp\\datafile.txt");

Path names in MS Windows use backslashes (\). Because the backslash is also the string escape character, it must be doubled. If the full path is not given, most systems will look in the directory that contains the object program.

5. Check that the file was opened. For example, the open fails if the file doesn't exist, or if it can't be read because another program is writing it. A failure can be detected with code like that below using the ! (logical not) operator:

6. if (!myInput) {
7. cerr << "Unable to open file datafile.txt";
8. exit(1); // call system to stop
}

9. Read from the stream in the same way as cin. For example,

10. while (myInput >> x) {
11. sum = sum + x;
}

12. Close the input stream. Closing is essential for output streams to be sure all information has been written to the disk, but is also good practice for input streams to release system resources and make the file available for other programs that might need to write it.

myInput.close();

(c) Const member functions and their applications in C++

Constant member functions are used in classes to protect changes to class's data For example, in the case definition:

```
Class ConstClass
{
private:
declarations
public:
int ConstFunc (args) const;
};
```

The const after the declaration of ConstFunc ( ) states that ConstFunc ( ) is not allowed to change any fields of the object that calls it. For example, with the code fragment:

```
ConstClass Object;
Object.ConstFunc ( );
```

The call to ConstFunc ( ) must not alter any of the values of any of the data fields of Object. This is another safety feature in C+ designed to help you catch programming errors early. If you declare a function as const in this fashion and then inadvertently insert some statements into the definition of that function that alter some of the fields of the object calling the function, the compiler will flag an error. It is therefore a good idea to think carefully about whether or not a function *should* be allowed to alter data fields and, if not, declare it as const.

(d) Functions with varying number of arguments in C++

A c++ function prototype can declare that one or more of the function's parameters have default values. What a call to the function omits the corresponding arguments,

the compiler inserts the default values where it expects to see the arguments.
We can declare default values for arguments in a C++ function prototype in the following way:

```
Void myfunc(int=5,double=1.23);
```

The expression declare default values for the arguments. The C++ compiler substitutes the default values if you omit the arguments when you call the function.
We can call the function by using any of the following ways:

```
myfunc(12,3.45); // overrides both defaults
myfunc(3);       // effectively func(3, 1.23);
myfunc();        // effectively func(5,1.23);
```

To omit first parameter in these examples, you must omit the second one; however, you can omit a parameter unless you omit the parameters to its right.
Here is the example:

```
#include<iostream.h>
void show(int=1,float=2.3,long=4);
main()
{
show(); //all three parameters default
show(5);//provide 1st parameter
show(6,7.8);      //provide all three parameters
}
void show(int first, float second, long third)
{
cout<<"\nfirst= "<<first;
cout<<"second="<<second;
cout<<"third="<<third;
}
```

4(a). What is an exception in C++? How is it handled? Describe with the help of an example. **[5]**

Refer to DEC2003, Q3(a), Page no.- 167

(b) What is dynamic binding? How is it different to static binding? **[2]**

At the design level, when a software engineer is deciding what type of action is appropriate for a given object, he or she should not be concerned about how the object interprets the action (message) and implements the methods but only what the effect of the action is on the object. Object-oriented languages like C++ and Smalltalk allow a programmer to send identical messages to dissimilar but related objects and achieve identical actions while letting the software system decide how to achieve the required action for the given object. A key issue associated with polymorphism is the timing of the software system's implementations decision. If the system decides how to implement an action at compile time, this is called early binding. If the decision is made dynamically at run-time, it is called **late biding**. Generally late biding offers the advantages of flexibility and a high level of problem abstraction.

Example

```
#include<iostream.h>
class x                                //base class
{
public:
virtual void show()                    //virtual function
{
cout<<"x";
}
};

class y: public x                      //derived class
{
public:
void show()
{
cout<<"y";
}
};

class z:public y                       //super class
{
public:
void show()
{
cout<<"z";
}
};
```

Static/Early Binding refers to events that occur at compile time. In essence, early binding occurs when all information needed to call a function is known at compile time. (you can say, early binding means that an object and function call are bound during compilation.) Examples of early binding include normal function calls (including standard library functions), overloaded function calls, and overloaded operators. The main advantage early binding is efficiency. Becaue all information necessary to call a function is determined at compile time, these types of function calls are very fast.

(c) Describe the stream class hierarchy in C++. **[3]**

The I/O system of C++ contains a set of classes that define the file handling methods. These include **ifstream, ofstream** and **fstream.** These classes are derived from **fstreambase** and from the corresponding *iostream.h* class as shown in Fig. 11.3. These classes, designed to manage the disk files, are declared in *fstream.h* and therefore we must include this file in any program that uses files. Table shows the details of file operation classes. Note that these classes contain many more features.

For more details, refer to the manual.

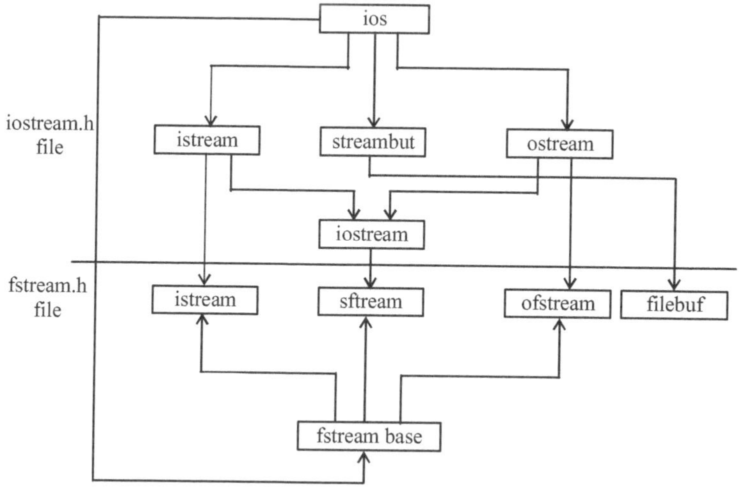

Class	Contents
filebuf	Its purpose is to set the file buffers to read and write. Contains **Openprot** constant in the open() of file stream. Also contains **close()** and **open()** as members.
fstreambase	Provides operations common to the file streams. Serves as a base for **fstream, ifstream** and **ofstream** classes. Contains **open()** and **close()** functions.
ifstream	Provides input operations. Contains **open()** with default input mode. Inherits the functions **get()**, **getline()**, **read()**, **seekg()** and tellg() functions from **istream.**
ofstream	Provides output operations. Contains **open()** with default output mode. Inherits **put()**, **seekp()**, **tellp()**, and **write()** functions from **ostream.**
fstream	Provides support for simultaneous input and output operations. Contains **open()** with default input mode. Inherits all the functions from **istream** and **ostream** classes through **iostream.**

5. Design and implement a class linked list having constructors/destructors and operations of adding an item for searching a value and inserting a value after a searched item. (Please assume singly linked list). Make suitable assumptions, if any. **[10]**

```
#include<iostream.h>
#include<conio.h>
class Linklist
{
public:
```

```
int info;
Linklist *next;
Linklist *first;
Linklist()
{
first=0;
next='\0';
}
~Linklist()
{
delete next;
delete first;
}
void addnode(void);
void insnode(void);
void display(void);

};
void Linklist::addnode()
{
Linklist *curr;
static Linklist *last=0;
curr=new Linklist();
cout<<"Enter number:";
cin>>curr->info;
curr->next='\0';
if (last)
last->next=curr;
else
first=curr;
last=curr;
}
void Linklist::display()
{
Linklist *l;
l=first;
do
{
cout<<l->info<<"\n";
l=l->next;
} while(l!='\0');
}
void Linklist::insnode()
{
Linklist *curr,*last,*l,*n;
```

```
int no,val,flag=0;
l=first;
cout<<"Enter value which you want to search :";
cin>>no;
cout<<"Enter value which you want to insert :";
cin>>val;
while(l!='\0')
{
if(l->info==no)
{
curr=l;
flag=1;
break;
}
else
{
l=l->next;
}
}
if(flag==0)
{
cout<<"not found";
getch();
return ;
}
else
{
n=new Linklist();
n->info=val;
n->next='\0';
last=l->next;
curr->next=n;
n->next=last;
}
}
void main()
{
clrscr();
Linklist ob;
int ch,f;
```

```
do{
clrscr();
cout<<"1.Add Node\n";
cout<<"2.Insert Node\n";
cout<<"3.Display and Exit\n";
cout<<"Enter choice:";
cin>>ch;
switch(ch)
{
case 1:ob.addnode();
break;
case 2:ob.insnode();
break;
case 3:ob.display();
getch();
break;
}
}while(ch!=3);
}
```

6(a). What is the purpose of using friend functions? Describe with an example. Can a class be made friend of other class? Justify your answer. [3]

The concept of data encapsulation sometimes takes information hiding too far. There are situations where a rigid and controlled access leads to inconvenience and hardships.

For instance, consider a case where a function is required to operate on object of two different classes. This function cannot be made a member of both the classes. What can be done is that a function can be defined outside both the classes and made to operate on both. That is, a function not belonging to either, but able to access both. Such a function is called as a friend function. In other words, a friend function is a nonmember function, which has access to a class's private members.

Using a Friend

Using a friend function is quite simple. The following example defines a friend function to access members of two classes.

```
class Bclass;                              // Forward Declaration
class Aclass
{
public :
Aclass(int v)
{
Avar = v;
}

friend int addup(Aclass &ac, Bclass &bc);
```

```
private :
int Avar;
};

class Bclass
{
public :
Bclass(int v)
{
Bvar = v;
}

friend int addup(Aclass &ac, Bclass &bc);
private :
int Bvar;
};

int addup(Aclass &ac, Bclass &bc)
{
return( ac.Avar + bc.Bvar);
}
void main()
{
Aclass aobj;
Bclass bobj;

int total;
total = addup(aobj,bobj);
}
```

The program defines two classes - Aclass and Bclass. It also has constructors for these classes. A friend function, addup(), is declared in the definition of both the classes. Sometimes friend functions can be avoided using inheritance and they are preferred. Excessive use of friend over many classes suggests a poorly designed program structure. But sometimes they are unavoidable.

Granting friendship to another class

To grant friendship to another class, write the keyword followed by the class name. The keyword class is optional. Note that this declaration also implies a forward declaration of the class to which the friendship is being granted. The implication of this declaration is that all off the member functions of the friend class are friend functions of the class that bestows the friendship.

```
class Aclass
{
public :
:
```

```
:
:
friend class Bclass;                    // Friend declaration.
private :
int Avar;
};
class Bclass
{
public :
:
:
void fn1(Aclass ac)
{
Bvar = ac. Avar;                        //Avar can be accessed.
}
private :
int Bvar;
};
void main()
{
Aclass aobj;
Bclass bobj;
Bobj,fn1(aobj);
}
```

The program declares class Bclass to be a friend of Aclass. It means that all member functions of Bclass have been granted direct access to all member functions of Aclass.

(b) Why do you need references in C++? How can a reference be used in parameter passing? Describe with the help of an example. [3]

C++ contains a feature that is related to pointer called reference. A reference is essentially an implicit pointer. There are three ways that a reference can be used :

(i) As a function parameter.

(ii) As a function return value, or

(iii) As a stand-alone reference.

The most important use of a reference is to allow us to create functions that automatically use call-by-reference parameter passing.

The syntax for this is:

int RefFunction (int &Arg1, float &Arg2);

Note that each argument is prefixed by an ampersand. Such a function is called in exactly the same way as one where the arguments are passed by value:

ReturnedInt = RefFunction (Int, Float2);

The difference between IntFunction and RefFunction is that the *addresses* of the arguments are passed in RefFunction, and not the actual values. As such, no extra memory is reserved within the function, since no copy of the arguments need to be made. This variable Arg1 within the function and the variable Int1 passed to it are identical: they share the same address in memory. In this case, any change made to Arg1 within the function will also affect Int1 I the calling routine.

Advantage Of Passing By Reference

This sounds like a good reason to always pass by reference, but if you are awake you should spot a danger here. Remember that one difference between that two methods of passing a variable is that in one case, any changes made on the variable within the function have no effect on the calling routine, while in the other case, the changes *do* affect the variable in the calling routine. If you pass a variable by reference and inadvertently make changes to it within the function that you don't fortunately, C++ has a mechanism that allows you to protect against such an error, even if you pass the variable by reference.

(c) How can you overload the output operator in C++? Describe with the help of an example. [4]

We can overload output operator << by using istream & ostream classes along with friend functions for a better interface (same as used with cout).

Example is given below :

```
#include<iostream.h>
class de
{
public:
int a,b,c;
friend istream & operator >>(istream & os ,de &obj);
friend ostream & operator <<(ostream & os , de &obj);
};

//overloading output operator
ostream& operator <<(ostream & os,de &obj)
{
os<<obj.a<<obj.b<<obj.c;
return os;
}
void main()
{
de e;
cin>>e.a>>e.b>>e.c;
cout<<e;
getch();
}
```

Feedback is the breakfast of Champions.

Ken Blanchard

You can Help other students.
"Inform any error or mistake in this book."

We and Universe
will reward you for Your Kind act.

Email at : feedback@gullybaba.com
or
WhatsApp on 9350849407

CS-72 : C++ AND OBJECT ORIENTED PROGRAMMING

DEC 2002

Note : *There are* **six** *questions in the Paper. Q. No.* ***1*** *is* **compulsory** *and carries 30 marks. Attempt any three from the rest.*

1(a). What is data abstraction? How is it related to/different encapsulation and polymorphism? Discuss with the help of an example. [5]

Abstraction : Abstraction refers to the act of representing essential features without including the background details or explanations. Classes use the concept of abstraction and are defined as a list of abstract attributes such as size, weight and cost, and functions to operate on these attributes. They encapsulate all the essential properties of the objects that are to be created. Since the classes use the concept of data abstraction, they are known as Abstract Data Types (ADT).

e.g.
```
int a;
float b;
```
are used for storage of numbers by user without caring for internal storage details.

The property of being a self-contained unit is called encapsulation. The idea that the encapsulated unit can be used without knowing how it works is called data hiding.

Encapsulation is the principle by which related contents of a system are kept together. It minimizes traffic between different parts of the work and it separates certain specific requirements from other parts of specification, which use those requirements.

e.g.
```
class A {
int a;
public:
void getdata();
};
void main()
{
A a1;
}
```
Here, a1(object) is an encapsulated unit, containing attributes and functionality together.

The important advantage of using encapsulation is that it helps minimize rework when developing a new system. The part of the work, which is prone to change, can be encapsulated together. Thus any changes can be made without affecting the overall system and hence changes can be easily incorporated.

C++ supports the properties of encapsulation and data hiding through the creation of user-defined types, called classes.

(b) Design a template class for a binary search tree having only the search and insert function. Make suitable assumptions, if any. [5]

```
#include<iostream.h>
#include<stdio.h>
#include<conio.h>
#include<process.h>
enum bool{true,false};
template <class t>
class tree
{
public:
t info;
t val;
tree *left;
tree *right;
tree* create(tree*);
tree* inserttree(tree*,tree*);
bool search( tree *node,t val);
void traverse(tree<t> *node);
};

void main()
{   clrscr();
int ch;
bool sh;
tree<int> *root;
tree<int> obj;

do
{
cout<<"\n   M E N U  ";
cout<<"\n 1 create a tree";
cout<<"\n 2 Search";
cout<<"\n 3 Traverse ";
cout<<"\n 4 Exit";
cout<<"\n Enter your choice: ";
cin>>ch;
switch(ch)
{
case 1:
root=obj.create(root);
break;
case 2:
```

```
cout<<"Enter the search value";
cin>>obj.val;
sh=obj.search(root,obj.val);
if(sh==true)
{
cout<<"value found ";
}
else
{
cout<<"value not found";
}
getch();
break;
case 3:
obj.traverse(root);
getch();
break;
case 4:
break;
default:
cout<<"\n Wrong choice";
getch();
}
}
while(ch!=4);
}

template <class t>
void tree<t>::traverse(tree<t> *node)
{
if(node)
{
traverse(node->left);
printf(" %d -> ",node->info);
traverse(node->right);
}
}

template <class t>
bool tree<t>::search(tree<t> *node, t val)
{
if(node)
{
```

```
if(node->info==val)
{
return true;
}
else if(val<node->info)
{
return search(node->left,val);
}
else
{
return search(node->right,val);
}
}
return false;
}


template <class t>
tree<t>* tree<t>::create(tree<t> *root)
{
t num;
tree *p;
root=NULL;
cout<<"\n Enter tree info: ";
cin>>num;
do
{
p=new tree;
p->info=num;
p->left=NULL;
p->right=NULL;
root=inserttree(root,p);
cout<<"\n Enter tree info(0 to stop: )";
cin>>num;
}while(num!=0);
return root;
}
template <class t>
tree<t>* tree<t>::inserttree(tree<t> *r,tree<t> *p)
{
if(r==NULL)
r=p;
else
```

```
{
if(p->info>=r->info)
r->right=inserttree(r->right,p);
else
r->left=inserttree(r->left,p);
}
return r;
}
```

(c) What are the access control violation in the following program segment: [5]

```
class All_public {
public :
int all_pub ;
All_public ( ) { }
void print ( );
};

class Inherited : Private All_public {
private:
int some_private_data;
public:
int read( );
void print( );
}

void main ()
{
All_public first;
Inherited second ;
second.all_pub = 10;
second.all_public::print( );
first.all_pub = 50;
second. some_ private _ data = 200;
}.
```

The following access violations are there:

1) All_public::all_pub is not accessible because in this example our subclass Inherited is privately inherited not publicly.

2) All_public::print() is not accessible in void main because of private inheritance.

3) Inherited::Second.some_private_data=200; is not accessible because it is defined private in subclass Inherited.

(d) Design and implement a class matrix having the following requirements: [15]

· It represents matrix in two dimensional arrays. The maximum size of array can be 100 × 100.

· There is a constructor that allocates the array of maximum size to the matrix object.

· You can store any matrix of size m × n (m £ 100 and n £ 100) in this class. There is an additional initialisation function to do so.

· It prints the stored matrix in row/column format.

· It adds and subtracts two matrices of same size.

· It multiplies two given matrices after checking the necessary time constraints.

· The class has provision for copy constructor and overloaded assignment operation.

Write the appropriate main( ) function. Make suitable assumptions, if any.

Refer to Study Material, Chapter-3,Q4, Page no.- 29

2. Design and implement a class linked-queue which is implemented using pointers. The class includes AddQ, DeleteQ and Empty operations (standard operations of Data Structure Queue). Make suitable assumptions, if any. [10]

```
#include<iostream.h>
#include<stdio.h>
#include<ctype.h>
#include<alloc.h>
#define FALSE 0
#define NULL 0
struct listelement
{
int    dataitem;
struct listelement *link;
};
class queue :public listelement
{
public:
listelement * lp,* tempp;

void Menu (int *choice);
listelement * AddQ (listelement * listpointer, int data);
listelement * DeleteQ (listelement * listpointer);
void PrintQueue (listelement * listpointer);
void ClearQueue (listelement * listpointer);
};
void main ()
{
listelement *listpointer;
queue x;
int    data,choice;
listpointer=NULL;
do {
x.Menu (&choice);
```

```
switch (choice) {
case 1:
cout<< ("Enter data item value to add ");
cin>>data;
listpointer = x.AddQ (listpointer, data);
break;
case 2:
if (listpointer == NULL)
cout<<"Queue empty!\n";
else
listpointer = x.DeleteQ (listpointer);
break;
case 3:
x.PrintQueue (listpointer);
break;
default:
cout<<"Invalid menu choice - try again\n";
break;
}
} while (choice != 4);
x.ClearQueue (listpointer);
}
/* main */
void queue::Menu (int *choice)
{

char   local;
cout<<"\nEnter\t1 to add item,\n\t2 to remove item\n\
\t3 to print queue\n\t4 to quit\n";
do {
local = getchar ();
if ((isdigit (local) == FALSE) && (local != '\n'))
{
cout<< "\nyou must enter an integer.\n";
cout<< "Enter 1 to add, 2 to remove, 3 to print, 4 to quit\n";
}
} while (isdigit ((unsigned char) local) == FALSE);
*choice = (int) local - '0';
}

listelement * queue:: AddQ (listelement * listpointer, int data)
{
lp = listpointer;
if (listpointer != NULL)
{
```

```
while (listpointer -> link != NULL)
listpointer = listpointer -> link;
listpointer -> link = new listelement;
listpointer = listpointer -> link;
listpointer -> link = NULL;
listpointer -> dataitem = data;
return lp;
}
else {
listpointer = new listelement;
listpointer -> link = NULL;
listpointer -> dataitem = data;
return listpointer;
}
}
listelement * queue ::DeleteQ (listelement * listpointer)
{
cout<<"Element removed is"<<listpointer -> dataitem;
tempp = listpointer -> link;
free (listpointer);
return tempp;
}
void queue ::PrintQueue (listelement * listpointer)
{
if(listpointer == NULL)
cout<<"queue is empty!\n";
else
while (listpointer != NULL) {
cout<<listpointer -> dataitem<<" ";
listpointer = listpointer -> link;
}
cout<<"\n";
}
void queue::ClearQueue (listelement * listpointer)
{
while (listpointer != NULL) {
listpointer = DeleteQ (listpointer);
}
}
```

3(a). How can you handle error in C++ ? Describe with the help of an example. What is the need of having error handling capabilities in C++ ? [5]

Exception Handling in C++

The exception mechanism of C++ uses three new *keywords: throw, catch,* and try. Also, we need to create a new kind of entity called an *exception class.*

Need : Suppose we have an application that works with objects of a certain class. If during the course of execution of a member function of this class an error occurs, then this member function informs the application that an error has occurred. This process of informing is called *throwing* an exception. In the application we have to create a separate section of code to tackle the error. This section of code is called an *exception handler* or a *catch block.* Any code in the application that uses objects of the class is enclosed in *a try block.* Errors generated in the try block are caught in the catch block. Code that doesn't interact with the class need not be in a *try* block. The following code shows the organisation of these blocks. It is not a working program, but it clearly shows how and where the various elements of the exception mechanism are placed.

```
class sample
{
public:
//exception class
class errorclass
{
};
void fun()
{
if(some error occurs)
throw errorclass(); //throws exception
}
};
//application
void main()
{
//try block
try
{
sample s;
s.fun();
}
catch(sample::errorclass) //exception handler or catch block
{
//do something about the error
}
}
```

Here sample is any class in which errors might occur. An exception class called *errorclass,* is specified in the *public* part of *sample.* In *main()* we have enclosed part of the program that uses *sample* in a try block. If an error occurs in *sample::fun()* we throw an exception, using the keyword *throw* followed by the constructor for the *errorclass:*

throw errorclass();

When an exception is thrown control goes to the *catch* block that immediately follows the *try* block.

(b) What is a reference variable? What is the usage of references in parameter passing? Why are references needed when call by value exists? What is the purpose of "const" keyword with respect to references? [10]

Refer to Study Material, Chapter-4,Q4, Page no.- 62

4. Describe the following with the help of one example each: [10]

(a) Reusability of objects/classes

Refer to JUNE2003, Q4(b), Page no.- 188

(b) Input/Output streams in C++

Streams :-

C++ streams are implemented as classes. The cout and cin objects are global instances of those classes, Which derive from a base class named ios and which are declared by the system.

The ostream Class

Stream output is managed by a class named ostream, which is derived from ios. The following statement :-

Cout <<"Hello, Dolly";

The cout object is an external object of the ostream class. The cout object is declared in the library, and an extern declaration of it appears in iostream.h so that is available to be used by any program that includes iosteream.h

The istream class

The istream class manages stream input in the same way that the ostream class manages output. The istream class is externally declared in iostream.h. The cin object reads data values from the standard input device.

The iostream class

The iostream class is derived from the istream and ostream classes. A program uses it for the declaration of object that do both input and output. You do not often need to deal with the iosteream class in basic input/output operations. The fstream class, which manages file input/output, derives from the iosream class.

The ofstream class

The ofstream class object are files that a program can write to. In the most elementary use of ofstream, the program declares an object an object of type ofstream, gives it a name, and writes to it. When the object goes out of scope, the file closes.

Example:-

```
#include <fstream.h>
main()
{
ofstream tfile( "test,dat");
tfile << "This is test data ";
}
```

The ifstream class

The ifstream class object are input files. A program can declare an input file stream object and read it. The following example reads a text file a one character at a time, sending each character to cout and stopping at end-of-file.

Example:-

```
#include <fstream.h>
main( )
{
ifstream tfile( "test,dat");
while (!tfile.eof( ) )
{
char ch;
tfile.getch(ch);
cout <<ch;
}
}
```

The fstream class

The fstream class supports file stream objects that a program opens for both input and output.

(c) Macros and Inline functions

Refer to DEC2003, Q6(i), Page no.- 171

(d) Inheritance and its need : Let us now consider a situation, where two classes are generally similar in nature with just couple of differences. Would you have to rewrite the entire class ?

Inheritance is the OOPS feature which allows derivation of the new objects from the existing ones. It allows the creation of new class, called the derived class, from the existing classes called as base class.

The concept of inheritance allows the features of base class to be accessed by the derived classes, which in turn have their new features in addition to the old base class features. The original base class is also called the parent or super class and the derived class is also called as subclass.

For Example Cars, mopeds, trucks have certain features in common i.e. they all have wheels, engines, headlights etc. They can be grouped under one base class called automobiles. Apart from these common features they have certain distinct features which are not common like mopeds have two wheels and cars have four wheels, also cars uses petrol and trucks run on diesel. The derived class has its own features to in addition to the class from which they are derived.

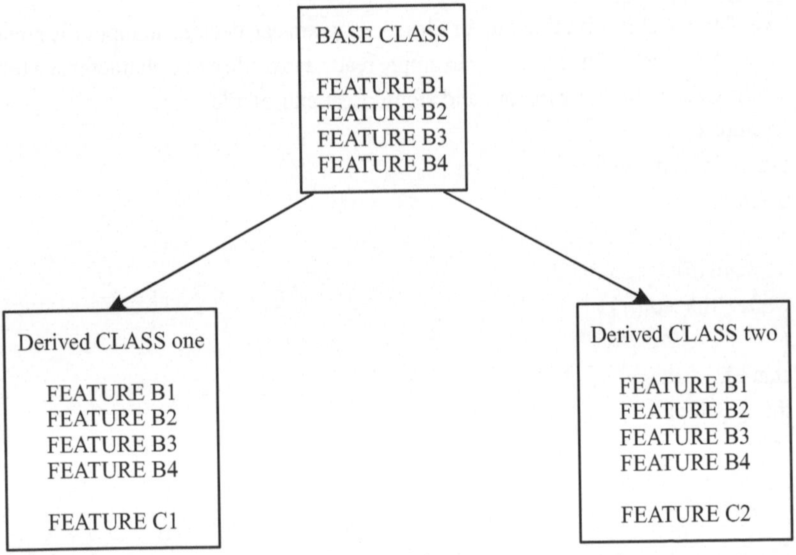

Figure : Inheritance

In the above figure, Classes one and two are derived from base class. Note that both derived classes have their own features C1 and C2 in addition to derived features B1,B2, B3, B4 from base class.

Let us extend our example of employee class in the context of Inheritance. After creating the class Employee, you might make a subclass called Manager, which defines some manager-specific operations on data of the subclass 'manager'. The feature, which can be included, may be to keep track of employee being managed by the manager.

Inheritance also promotes reuse. You do not have to start from scratch when you write a new program. You can simply reuse an existing repertoire of classes that have behaviour similar to what you need in the new program.

5(a). How can you overload the input operator in C++? Describe with the help of example. [4]

```
//overloading input operator
#include<iostream.h>
class input
{
public:
int a,b,c;
friend istream & operator >>(istream & os ,input &obj);
};
istream& operator >>(istream & os,input &obj)
{
```

```
os>>obj.a>>obj.b>>obj.c;
return os;
}

void main()
{
input object;
cin>>object;
cout<<object.a<<object.b<<object.c ;
cin.get();
}
```

(b) The access rules violated by friend functions and pointers." Comment on the above statement. Give reasons in support or against the above statement. [3]

Friend function has ability that can access the private data of the class. So, where the abstraction similarly if we use pointer. Pointer can access the address of any part of data. Either, so again where is the security in it. So both pointer and function access rules violated in C++. For example,

```
class x
{
int data;

void add( );
public:
friend void add( x obj; y obj2);
}

void add(x obj; obj2)
{
int sum;
sum = obj.data + obj2.data;
}

class y
{
int data
int 2data;
public:
friend void add( x obj; y obj2);
}
main( )
{
x obj2;
y obj3;
```

```
obj2.data = 10;
obj3data = 20;
add(obj2,obj3);
}
```

Advantage : Generalization extended (in Support)
Disadvantages : Data hiding violation (in against)

(c) What is late binding? Is it different from dynamic binding? Justify your answer with the help of an example. [3]

Refer to JUNE2003, Q6(c), Page no.- 192

6. Design a polymorphic class hierarchy for the Windows based software. Assume that a window consist of Menu, Tools, Buttons and Interaction area. Your class should include necessary data members, constructor/destructor and at least one polymorphic function. Make and state suitable assumptions, if any. [10]

```
#include<iostream.h>
#include<conio.h>
#include<stdio.h>
class windows
{
protected:
int length;
int width;
public:
void getwindowdimensions()
{
cout<<"Enter window length in pixels";
cin>>length;
cout<<"Enter window breadth in pixels";
cin>>width;
}
virtual void getdata()=0;
};


class Menu:public windows
{
char name[20][20];
int no_menu;
public:
Menu()
{
no_menu=0;
```

```
}
~Menu(){}
void getdata()
{
cout<<"Enter length & width of menu in pixels";
cin>>length>>width;
cout<<"Enter no: of menus";
cin>>no_menu;
cout<<"Enter menu names\n";
for(int i=0;i<no_menu;i++)
{
cout<<"\nMenu:"<<i+1<<":";
gets(name[i]);
}
}
};

class Tools:public windows
{
char name[20][20];
int no_tools;
public:
Tools()
{
no_tools=0;
}
~Tools(){}
void getdata()
{
cout<<"Enter no: of tools";
cin>>no_tools;
cout<<"Enter tool names\n";
for(int i=0;i<no_tools;i++)
{
cout<<"\nTool:"<<i+1<<":";
gets(name[i]);
}
}
};


class Buttons:public windows
{
char text[20][20];
int no_buttons;
```

```
public:
Buttons()
{
no_buttons=0;
}
~Buttons(){}
void getdata()
{
cout<<"Enter length & width of button in pixels";
cin>>length>>width;
cout<<"Enter no: of buttons";
cin>>no_buttons;
cout<<"Enter button names\n";
for(int i=0;i<no_buttons;i++)
{
cout<<"\nButton:"<<i+1<<":";
gets(text[i]);
}
}
};

class Interaction_Area:public windows
{
char message[50];
public:
Interaction_Area()
{
length=639;
width=479;
}
~Interaction_Area(){}
void getdata()
{
cout<<"Enter length & width of interaction area in pixels";
cin>>length>>width;
cout<<"Enter the message to appear by default";
gets(message);
}
};

void main()
{
clrscr();
windows *w[4];
Menu m1;
```

```
w[0]=&m1;
w[0]->getwindowdimensions();

Tools t1;
w[1]=&t1;

Buttons b1;
w[2]=&b1;

Interaction_Area a1;
w[3]=&a1;

cout<<"Enter data for windows & other elements\n";

for(int i=1;i<4;i++)
{
w[i]->getdata();
cout<<"\n\n";
}

getch();
}
```

CS-72 : C++ AND OBJECT ORIENTED PROGRAMMING

JUNE 2003

Note : *There are six questions in this paper. Question **1** is **compulsory** and carries 30 marks. Attempt any **three** from the rest.*

1(a). What is the purpose of "references" in C ++? How are they similar/different to pointers? [5]

C++ provides a second way of passing a variable to a function called *passing by reference*. The syntax for this is:

Int RefFunction (int &Arg1, float &Arg2);

Note that each argument is prefixed by an ampersand. Such a function is called in exactly the same way as one where the arguments are passed by value:

ReturnedInt = RefFunction (Int, Float2);

The difference between IntFunction and RefFunction is that the *addresses* of the arguments are passed in RefFunction, and not the actual values. As such, no extra memory is reserved within the function, since no copy of the arguments need to be made. This variable Arg1 within the function and the variable Int1 passed to it are identical: they share the same address in memory. In this case, any change made to Arg1 within the function will also affect Int1 I the calling routine.

Advantage of Passing By Reference

This sounds like a good reason to always pass by reference, but if you are awake you should spot a danger here. Remember that one difference between that two methods of passing a variable is that in one case, any changes made on the variable within the function have no effect on the calling routine, while in the other case, the changes *do* affect the variable in the calling routine. If you pass a variable by reference and inadvertently make changes to it within the function that you don't fortunately, C++ has a mechanism that allows you to protect against such an error, even if you pass the variable by reference.

Passing By Pointers

It is important to note that there is no way of telling from the function call whether your variables are being passed to the function by value or by reference: you can only tell this if you examine the function declaration or definition itself. For this reason, some purists do not like the reference passing facility in C++ (which is not present in C), preferring to actually make explicit the fact that they are passing a pointer to a variable by using the syntax:

int PointerFunction (Int *Arg1, float *Arg2) {....}

for defining the function, and the syntax:

ReturnedInt = PointerFunction (&Int1, &Float2);

(b) Design a template class that is used to create a circular linked list. **[5]**

```
#include<iostream.h>
#include<conio.h>
#include<process.h>
template <class t>
class node
{
protected:
node* count;
node* p;
node* q;
node* first;
node* last;
public:
t data;                                   //template type
node* ptr;
node()
{
count=NULL;
}
public:
void create(t a);
void display();
void insert(t,t);
void delete1(t &);
;
template <class t>
void node<t> :: create(t a)
{
int i;
p=new node;
cout<<"\nInput node information :";
cin>>p->data;
p->ptr=NULL;
first=p;
for(i=1;i<a;i++)
{
q=new node;
cout<<"\ninput node information :";
cin>>q->data;
```

```
p->ptr=q;
q->ptr=NULL;
p=q;
}
last=p;
p->ptr=first;
}
template <class t>
void node<t> :: display()
{
count=first;
p=first;
do
{
cout<<p->data<<" ";
p=p->ptr;
}while(p!=count);
}

template <class t>
void node<t>::insert(t a,t b)
{
if(last->data==a)
{
q=new node;
p=first;
do
{
if(p->data==a)
{
q->data=b;
q->ptr=p->ptr;
p->ptr=q;
}
p=p->ptr;
}while(p!=count);
p->ptr=first;
}
else
q=new node;
p=first;
do
{
if(p->data==a)
{
```

```
q->data=b;
q->ptr=p->ptr;
p->ptr=q;
}
p=p->ptr;
}while(p!=count);
}

template <class t>
void node<t>::delete1(t &item)
{
p=first;
if(p->data==item)
{
first=p->ptr;
delete p;
}
else
{
q=first;
p=p->ptr;

while(p!=NULL)
{
if(p->data==item)
{
q->ptr=p->ptr;
delete p;
break;
}
q=p;
}
}
}

void main()
{
clrscr();
int ch,i,n,po;
node<char> k;
do {
cin.clear();
cout<<"\n\t MAIN MENU"        ;
cout<<"\n    ------------"   ;
cout<<"\n  Single circular linked list";
```

```
cout<<"\n          1. create";
cout<<"\n          2. display";
cout<<"\n          3. insert";
cout<<"\n          4. delete";
cout<<"\n     5. exit";
cout<<"\n\n ENTER YOUR CHOICE...\t";
cin>>ch;
switch(ch)
{
case 1:
cout<<"\nhow many no. of nodes :";
cin>>n;
k.create(n);
k.display();
break;
case 2:
k.display();
getch();
break;
case 3:
cout<<"\ninsert after";
cin>>po;
cout<<"\nenter data to be inserted";
cin>>i;
k.insert(po,i);
break;
case 4:
cout<<"\nnode to be deleted:";
cin>>po;
k.delete1(po);
k.display();
break;
case 5:     exit(0);
}
}while(ch!=5);
}
```

(c) What are the access control violations in the following program segment: **[5]**

```
class test_protected {
private:
int pri;
protected:
int pro:
public:
int pub;
```

```
test_protected () {};
void print (); };
class test_pro : private test_protected
private:
int sub_pri;
public:
int read ();
void print () {
cout << pri << pro << pub << sub_pri;
}
void main () {
test_protected t;
t.print ();
}
```

In the above program the derived class test_pro is subclasses vis private access modifier .So it will generate an error that
'test_protected'::pri is not accessible
that means pri is declared private variable in test_protected that's why it is not accessible in subclass's print function.

(d) Design and implement a class student_list having the following requirements: [15]

- **It stores details of two types of students "residential" and "non-residential".**
- **Different fee structures are stored for different types of students.**
- **Fee of the student is calculated on the basis of types and are vastly different.**
- **You need to define the class hierarchy of the student supporting above.**
- **The classes should include necessary constructors, destructors and fee calculation functions (make suitable assumptions.)**
- **The student name should be represented using pointers.**

Write the appropriate main () function. Make suitable assumptions, if any.

```
#include<iostream.h>
#include<conio.h>
class std_list
{
public :
char *name;
int length;
char res_type;
int total;
                                        //default constructor
std_list()
{
length=20;
name=new char[length+1];
```

```
total=0;
}
                                        //distructor
~std_list()
{
delete name;
}
void accept();                          //function for accepting the detail of student
void display();                         // function to displaying the student details
void fee();                             // function to accept fee;
};                                      //end of class
void std_list::fee()
{
if((res_type=='y')||(res_type=='Y'))
{
total=5000+5000+2000;
}
else
{
total=5000;
}
cout<<"total ==> "<<total;
}
void std_list::display()
{
cout<<"\n\n\n\nThe name of the student is \t";
cout<<name;
cout<<"\nThe residential type\t";
cout<<res_type;
cout<<"\nyour total fees \t";
cout<<total;
getch();
}

void std_list::accept()
{
cout<<"\nEnter your name =>\t";
cin>>name;
cout.flush();
cout<< "Choose The residential type "<<endl;
cout<<" 1 Residential   include Room rent + Food Cost + tutionfees   cost
==>12000"<<endl;
cout<<" 2 Non Residential include Tutionfees cost ==>5000 "<<endl;
cout<<"press 1 for Residential   \n";
cout<<"press 2 for non Residential\t";
```

```
cin>>res_type;

if((res_type=='y')||(res_type=='Y'))
{
cout<<"\n\n\nyou choose Residential option so your charges are as ";
cout<<"\nyour Room  Rent is  5000 \t";
cout<<"\nyour tuition Fees is 5000 \t";
cout<<"\nyour Food cost is   2000 \t";
}
else
{
cout<<"Your Tuition fee is 5000 \t";
}
}
void main()
{     clrscr();
std_list ob;
ob.accept();
ob.fee();
ob.display();
}
```

2(a). How can the process of error handling be controlled in C ++? Consider a program that multiplies two integers. What kind of error handling may be provided for such a program? [5]

Exception Handling in C++

The exception mechanism of C++ uses three new *keywords: throw, catch,* and try. Also, we need to create a new kind of entity called an *exception class.*

Suppose we have an application that works with objects of a certain class. If during the course of execution of a member function of this class an error occurs, then this member function informs the application that an error has occurred. This process of informing is called *throwing* an exception. In the application we have to create a separate section of code to tackle the error. This section of code is called an *exception handler* or a *catch block.* Any code in the application that uses objects of the class is enclosed in *a try block.* Errors generated in the try block are caught in the catch block. Code that doesn't interact with the class need not be in a *try* block. The following code shows the organisation of these blocks. It is not a working program, but it clearly shows how and where the various elements of the exception mechanism are placed.

```
class sample
{
public:
//exception class
```

```
class errorclass
{
};
void fun()
{
if(some error occurs)
throw errorclass(); //throws exception
}
};
//application
void main()
{
//try block
try
{
sample s;
s.fun();
}
catch(sample::errorclass) //exception handler or catch block
{
//do something about the error
}
}
```

Here sample is any class in which errors might occur. An exception class called *errorclass,* is specified in the *public* part of *sample.* In *main()* we have enclosed part of the program that uses *sample* in a try block. If an error occurs in *sample::fun()* we throw an exception, using the keyword *throw* followed by the constructor for the *errorclass:*

throw errorclass();

When an exception is thrown control goes to the *catch* block that immediately follows the *try* block.

```
//A simple exception handling example.
#include<iostream.h>
#include<conio.h>
#include<new>
void main()
{
int i,j;
cin>>i>>j;
try
{
int m=i*j;
}
catch(bad_calloc xa)
{
cout<<"Alloction Failure \n";
exit(0);
}
```

A program that multiplies two integers may need error handling for :

(i) Checking bounds of integers to see if numbers are not out of range at the time of initialization or after multiplication.

(ii) Multiplication symbol is correct.

(b) What are the usages of "const" keyword in functions and arguments? Describe with the help of example. [5]

We have met the const keyword already as a way of defining a constant value which can be used in place of a raw number within your program. The const keyword has several other uses in C++, particularly in relation to function definitions. Consider the function definition:

Int ConstArgs (const int &Arg1, const float &Arg2) {....}

The const keyword before each argument tells the compiler that although these arguments are being passed by reference, they are not allowed to be modified within the function body. They

become, in essence, 'read-only objects: their values may be accessed but not altered. Thus, the following function definition would give rise to a compile-time error:

```
int ConstArgs (const int &Arg1, const float &Arg2)
{
Arg1 *= 2;
}
```

Another use of the const keyword is *after* a function declaration in a class. For example, in the case definition:

```
Class ConstClass
{
private:
declarations
public:
int ConstFunc (args) const;
};
```

the const after the declaration of ConstFunc ( ) states that ConstFunc ( ) is not allowed to change any fields of the object that calls it. For example, with the code fragment:

```
    ConstClass Object;
    Object.ConstFunc ( );
```

the call to ConstFunc ( ) must not alter any of the values of any of the data fields of Object. This is another safety feature safety feature in C+ designed to help you catch programming errors early.

3. Design and implement a class point stack using pointers. (The data representation must not be an array). Implement constructor(s), destructor and other suitable functions. [10]

```
#include<iostream.h>
#include<conio.h>
#define max 100
class point_stack
{
int*arr;
int tos;
public:
point_stack()
{
tos=0;
cout<<"stack destroyed\n";
getch();}
void push(int i)
{
if(tos==max)
{
cout<<"Stack is full\n";
return;
}
*arr=i;
tos++;
arr++;
}
int pop()
{
if(tos==0)
{
cout<<"stack overflow\n";
return 1;
}
arr--;
return*arr;
}
};
void main()
{
clrscr();
point_stack a,b;
a.push(1);
b.push(2);
a.push(3);
b.push(4);
cout<<a.pop()<<"\n";
cout<<a.pop()<<"\n";
```

```
cout<<b.pop()<“\n”;
getch();
}
```

4. Describe the following with the help of an example each: [10]
(a) “this” pointer
(b) Features for class reusability
(c) Abstraction
(d) Use of inline functions and macros

(a) “this” pointer : When you are writing code in a member function, the “variable” this contains a pointer to the current object. Any member element, _x, can be referenced in two ways:

```
        _x = 10;
  this ->_x = 10;          // same as above.
```

References to members are usually written without this because there is no need to use it, however, there are situations where this is needed. Returning or passing a pointer to the object.

(b) Features for class reusability : Reusability is yet another important feature of OOP. It is always nice if the we could reuse something that already exists rather than trying to create the same all over again. It would not only save time and money but also reduce frustration and increase reliability. For example instance, the reuse of a class that has already been tested, debugged and used many times can save us the effort of developing and testing the same again.

Fortunately, C++ strongly supports the concept of reusability. The C++ classes can be reused in several ways. Once a class has been written and tested, it can be adapted by other programmers to suit their requirements. This is basically done by creating new classes, reusing the properties of the existing ones. The mechanism of deriving a new class from an old one is called *inheritance* (*or derivation*). The old class is referred to as the base class and the new one is called the *derived class.*

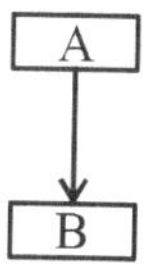

a) Single inheritance

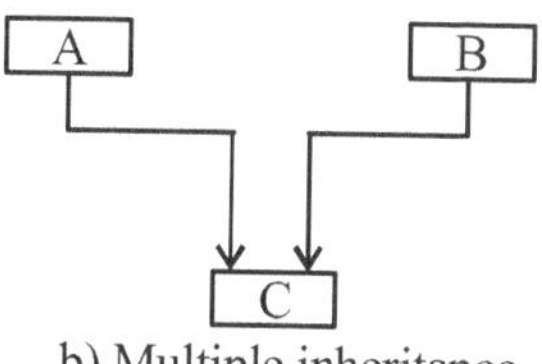

b) Multiple inheritance

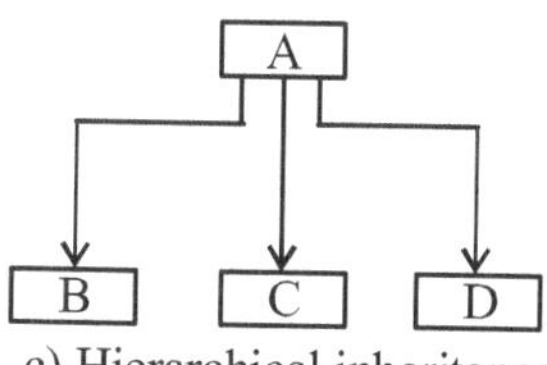

c) Hierarchical inheritance

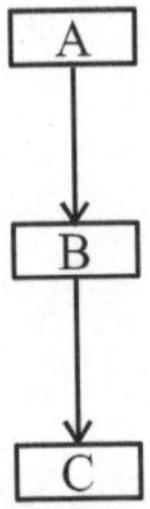

d) Multilevel inheritance

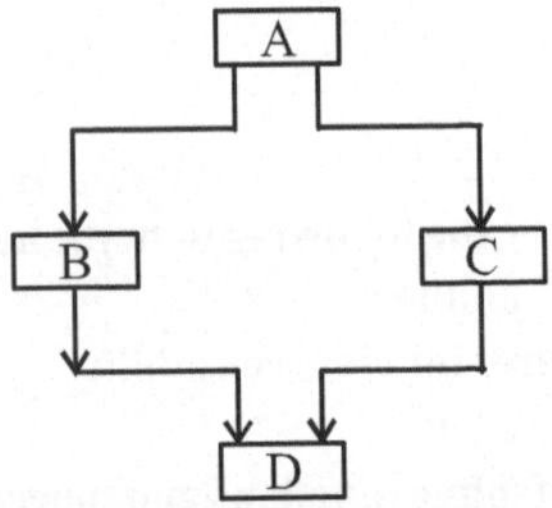

e) Hybrid inheritance

(c) Abstraction : Abstraction refers to the act of representing essential features without including the background details or explanations. Classes use the concept of abstraction and are defined as a list of abstract attributes such as size, weight and cost, and functions to operate on these attributes. They encapsulate all the essential properties of the objects that are to be created. Since the classes use the concept of data abstraction, they are known as Abstract Data Types (ADT).

(d) Use of inline function & macros.

Refer to DEC2003, Q6(i), Page no.- 171

5. Design and implement a class hierarchy for the following requirements: [10]

· The class should represent complex numbers.

· It should have overloaded operator for addition and multiplication of complex numbers.

· If an attempt is made to divide one complex number with another it generates an error message.

· The class should have suitable constructors, destructors, copy constructor and assignment operator.

Write appropriate main ( ). Make and state suitable assumptions, if any.

Refer to Study Material, Chapter-6,Q3, Page no.- 91

6(a). What is the need of friend functions? Describe the usage of friend functions with the help of an example. [4]

The concept of data encapsulation sometimes takes information hiding too far. There are situations where a rigid and controlled access leads to inconvenience and hardships.

For instance, consider a case where a function is required to operate on object of two different classes. This function cannot be made a member of both the classes. What can be done is that a function can be defined outside both the classes and made to operate on both. That is, a function not belonging to either, but able to access both. Such a function is called as a friend function. In other words, a friend function is a nonmember function, which has access to a class's private members.

Using a Friend

Using a friend function is quite simple. The following example defines a friend function to access members of two classes.

```
class Bclass;                    // Forward Declaration
class Aclass
{
public :
Aclass(int v)
{
Avar = v;
}

friend int addup(Aclass &ac, Bclass &bc);
private :
int Avar;
};

class Bclass
{
public :
Bclass(int v)
{
Bvar = v;
}

friend int addup(Aclass &ac, Bclass &bc);
private :
int Bvar;
};

int addup(Aclass &ac, Bclass &bc)
{
return( ac.Avar + bc.Bvar);
}


void main()
{
Aclass aobj;
Bclass bobj;

int total;
total = addup(aobj,bobj);
}
```

The program defines two classes - Aclass and Bclass. It also has constructors for these classes. A friend function, addup(), is declared in the definition of both the classes, although it does not belong to either. This friend function returns the sum of the two private members of the classes.

Sometimes friend functions can be avoided using inheritance and they are preferred. Excessive use of friend over many classes suggests a poorly designed program structure. But sometimes they are unavoidable.

(b) How can files be used for input/output? Discuss with the help of an example. [3]

Input/Output from Text Files

Reading a text file is very easy using an ifstream (input file stream).

1. Include the necessary headers.

2. #include <fstream>
using namespace std;

3. Declare an input file stream (ifstream) variable. For example,
ifstream myInput;

4. Open the file stream. For example,
myInput.open("C:\\temp\\datafile.txt");

Path names in MS Windows use backslashes (\). Because the backslash is also the string escape character, it must be doubled. If the full path is not given, most systems will look in the directory that contains the object program.

5. Check that the file was opened. For example, the open fails if the file doesn't exist, or if it can't be read because another program is writing it. A failure can be detected with code like that below using the ! (logical not) operator:

6. if (!myInput) {
7. cerr << "Unable to open file datafile.txt";
8. exit(1); // call system to stop
}

9. Read from the stream in the same way as cin. For example,

10. while (myInput >> x) {
11. sum = sum + x;
}

12. Close the input stream. Closing is essential for output streams to be sure all information has been written to the disk, but is also good practice for input streams to release system resources and make the file available for other programs that might need to write it.
myInput.close();

Example

The following program reads ints from a file and prints their sum.

```
#include <iostream>
#include <fstream>
using namespace std;
int main() {
  ifstream myInput;
  int x;
  int sum = 0;
  myInput.open("test.txt");
  if (!myInput) {
    cerr << "Unable to open test.txt.";
```

```
exit(1);
}
while (myInput >> x) {
sum += x;
}
cout << "total = " << sum << endl;
myInput.close();
return 0; }
```

(c) What is late binding? How is it same/different from dynamic binding? [3]

Late binding & dynamic binding mean the same. At the design level, when a software engineer is deciding what type of action is appropriate for a given object, he or she should not be concerned about how the object interprets the action (message) and implements the methods but only what the effect of the action is on the object. Object-oriented languages like C++ and Smalltalk allow a programmer to send identical messages to dissimilar but related objects and achieve identical actions while letting the software system decide how to achieve the required action for the given object. A key issue associated with polymorphism is the timing of the software system's implementations decision. If the system decides how to implement an action at compile time, this is called early binding. If the decision is made dynamically at run-time, it is called **late biding**. Generally late biding offers the advantages of flexibility and a high level of problem abstraction.

Example

```
#include<iostream.h>
class x                          //base class
{
public:
virtual void show()              //virtual function
{
cout<<"x";
}
};
class y: public x                //derived class
{
public:
void show()
{
cout<<"y";
}
};

class z:public y                 //super class
{
public:
```

```
void show()
{
cout<<"z";
}
};
```

// In this we call a function of derived class using base class pointer. One important //point is that you must declare base function with using virtual keyword.

```
void main()
{
x *xb;
x xobj;
y yobj;
z zobj;

xb=&xobj;
xb->show();                    //only x class function is called
xb=&yobj;
xb->show();                    //only y class function is called
xb=&zobj;
xb->show();                    //only z class function is called
}
```

CS-72 : C++ AND OBJECT ORIENTED PROGRAMMING

DEC2003

Note : *There are* ***six*** *questions in the Paper. Q. No.* ***1*** *is* ***compulsory*** *and carries 30 marks. Attempt any three from the rest.*

1(a). What is inheritance? What are the different types of inheritance? Give some applications of inheritance. **[5]**

Refer to Study Material, Chapter-6, Page no.- 76

(b) Design a function template to perform matrix addition of two given integer matrices, two floating point matrices and double precision value matrices separately. **[5]**

```
#include<iostream.h>
#include<conio.h>
#define SIZE 10

template<class T>
void add(T  *a,T *b,int m,int n)
{
T r[10][10];
int c=0;
for(int i=0;i<m;i++)
{
for(int j=0;j<n;j++)
if(c<=(m*n-1))
{
r[i][j]=a[c]+b[c];
c++;
}
}
cout<<"Matrix after addition :\n";
for( i=0;i<m;i++)
{
for(int j=0;j<n;j++)
cout<<r[i][j]<<"    ";
cout<<"\n";
}
}
void main()
{
int m,n,x,a[10][10],b[10][10],iterate=0;
```

```
clrscr();
cout<<"Matrix Addition Program \n";
do{
cout<<"\n Enter number of Rows";
cin>>m;
if(m>SIZE)
cout<<"\n Too many rows ! Maximum 10 allowed";
}
while(m>SIZE);
do{
cout<<"\n Enter number of Columns";
cin>>n;
if(n>SIZE)
cout<<"\n Too many columns ! Maximum 10 allowed";
}
while(n>SIZE);
do{
cout<<"\nEnter type of matrix :\n";
cout<<"1 for integer \n";
cout<<"2 for floating point or decimal \n" ;
cin>>x;
if(x<1||x>2)
cout<<"Wrong  Type";
}
while(x<1||x>2);
float a1[10][10],b1[10][10];
double a2[10][10],b2[10][10];
for(int k=1;k<=2;k++)
{
cout<<"\n Enter elements of matrix "<<k;
iterate++;
if(x==1)
{
for(int i=0;i<m;i++)
{
cout<<"\n Enter elements of row"<<i+1;
for(int j=0;j<n;j++)
{
cout<<"\n Column: "<<j+1;
if(iterate==1)
cin>>a[i][j];
else
cin>>b[i][j];
}
```

```
}
if(iterate==2)
add(*a,*b,m,n);
}

else
if(x==2)
{
for(int i=0;i<m;i++)
{
cout<<"\n Enter elements of row "<<i+1;
for(int j=0;j<n;j++)
{
cout<<"\n Column:"<<j+1;
if(iterate==1)
cin>>a1[i][j];
else
cin>>b1[i][j];
}
}
if(iterate==2)
add(*a1,*b1,m,n);
}
else
{
for(int i=0;i<m;i++)
{
cout<<"\nEnter elements of row"<<i+1;
for(int j=0;j<n;j++)
{
cout<<"\n Column :"<<j+1;
if(iterate==1)
cin>>a2[i][j];
else
cin>>b2[i][j];
}
}
if(iterate==2)
add(*a2,*b2,m,n);
}
}
                                        //outer for ends.
getch();
}
                                        //main ends
```

(c) Design and implement a class 'Itemlist' having following requirements:

- It is a linear array of size N

- Each element has Itemcode, Item Price and Quantity

- Item to be appended to the list

- Delete item from the list with the help of item code

- Print total value of stock **[10]**

```
#include<iostream.h>
#include<conio.h>
class Itemlist
{
private:
struct node
{
int itemcode;
float itemprice;
int quantity;
node*link;
}*p;
public:
Itemlist();
void append(int,float,int);
void del(int);
void total();
                                    //~Itemlist();
};

Itemlist::Itemlist()
{
p=NULL;
}
void Itemlist::append(int code,float price,int qua)
{
node*q,*t;
if(p==NULL)
{
                                    //creat first node
p=new node;
p->itemcode=code;
p->itemprice=price;
p->quantity=qua;
p->link=NULL;
}
else
{
                                    //go to last node
```

```
q=p;
while(q->link!=NULL)
q=q->link;
                                //add node at the end
t=new node;
t->itemcode=code;
t->itemprice=price;
t->quantity=qua;
q->link=t;
t->link=NULL;
}
}
void Itemlist::del(int code)
{
node*q,*r;
q=p;
                                //if node to be deleted is first node
if(q->itemcode==code)
{
p=q->link;
dclete q;
return;
}
                                //traverse
r=q;
while(q!=NULL)
{
if(q->itemcode==code)
{r->link=q->link;
delete q;
return;
}
r=q;
q=q->link;
}
cout<<"\n\nElement "<<code<< "not found\n";
}

void Itemlist::total()
{
node*q;
float t=0;
for(q=p;q!=NULL;q=q->link)
t=t+q->itemprice*q->quantity;
cout<<"\n total value of stock is:"<<t;}
```

```
void main()
{
clrscr();
Itemlist l;
cout<<"\n Value of stock :\n";
l.total();
l.append(001,1200.5,50);
l.append(002,1400.2,20);
l.append(003,1500.5,100);
cout<<"\n Value of stock :\n";
l.total();
l.del(002);
l.del(004);                    //Element 004 not present message
cout<<"\n Value of stock now";
l.total();
getch();
}
```

(d) What are the access control violations in the following program segment: **[10]**

```
Class base A
{
private;
int val;
public:
base A();
};
Class derived B : private base A
{
public :
};
Class derived C : private derived B
{
public :
};
void main ()
{
derived C obj C;
obj C. display ();
```

Class derived C	Class derived B	Class base A
Private member	private member	private member
no member	base A();	val
public member	public member	public member
no member	no member	base A()

So obj which is object of class derived c cannot call function display() as it is not member of it.

In fact, display() is not a member of any of the three classes.

2. Design and implement a class 'binsearch' for a binary search tree. It includes search, remove and add options. Make suitable assumption [10]

Refer to Study Material, Chapter-3,Q10, Page no.- 46

3(a). What is exception handler? What are the keywords used to handle the exceptions in C++? List the merits and demerits of defining an exception handler in Object Oriented Programming. [6]

Exception Handling in C++

The exception mechanism of C++ uses three new *keywords: throw, catch,* and try. Also, we need to create a new kind of entity called an *exception class.* Suppose we have an application that works with objects of a certain class. If during the course of execution of a member function of this class an error occurs, then this member function informs the application that an error has occurred. This process of informing is called *throwing* an exception. In the application we have to create a separate section of code to tackle the error. This section of code is called an *exception handler* or a *catch block.* Any code in the application that uses objects of the class is enclosed in *a try block.* Errors generated in the try block are caught in the catch block. Code that doesn't interact with the class need not be in a *try* block. The following code shows the organisation of these blocks. It is not a working program, but it clearly shows how and where the various elements of the exception mechanism are placed.

```
class sample
{
public:
//exception class
class errorclass
{
};
void fun()
{
if(some error occurs)
throw errorclass(); //throws exception
}
};
//application
void main()
{
//try block
try
{
```

```
sample s;
s.fun();
}
catch(sample::errorclass)            //exception handler or catch block
{
//do something about the error
}
}
```

Here sample is any class in which errors might occur. An exception class called *errorclass,* is specified in the *public* part of *sample.* In *main()* we have enclosed part of the program that uses *sample* in a try block. If an error occurs in *sample::fun()* we throw an exception, using the keyword *throw* followed by the constructor for the *errorclass:*

throw errorclass();

When an exception is thrown control goes to the *catch* block that immediately follows the *try* block.

Merits :

1) We can handle exceptions/errors such as 'falling short of memory', 'inability to open file', etc.

2) Leads to a safer code.

De-Merits :

1) Exceptions impose an overhead in terms of program size & time consumption.

2) A good anticipation & code study is needed to spot areas of exception which is time consuming.

(b) Explain how pointer to functions can be declared in C++. Under what conditions can two pointer variables be added, subtracted and compared? [4]

Pointer to a function is made like to an array is by using name of function (as use name of array)

if we have int a[10];

pointer to it is

int*p=a;

For a function as int display()

we will have pointer fn as

int(*fn)();

fn-display;

now we can call function display by using pointer fn.

as

(*fn(();

Note: pointer to function is used in manipulators like

endl .

1) Pointers can never be added.

2) They can be subtracted if both pointers point to same array

eg.,

int arr[]={10,20,30,45,67,56,44};

```
int*i,*j;
i=&arr[1];
j=&arr[5];
cout<<j-i          output 4
```

3) They can be compared if both pointers point to objects of same type

eg.:-

```
int arr[]={10,20,36,72,45,36};
int*j,*k;
j=&arr[4];
k=(arr+4);
if(j==k)
cout<<"Pointer point to same location";
else
cout<<"Pointer point to different location";
```

output

pointers point to same location

4. Design and develop a polymorphic class to solve a general quadratic equation $ax^2 + bx + c = 0$. **[10]**

Refer to Study Material, Chapter-6,Q10, Page no.- 100

5(a). What is a friend function? What are the pros and cons in declaring a friend class in a program? **[3]**

The concept of data encapsulation sometimes takes information hiding too far. There are situations where a rigid and controlled access leads to inconvenience and hardships.

For instance, consider a case where a function is required to operate on object of two different classes. This function cannot be made a member of both the classes. What can be done is that a function can be defined outside both the classes and made to operate on both. That is, a function not belonging to either, but able to access both. Such a function is called as a friend function. In other words, a friend function is a nonmember function, which has access to a class's private members.

Pros & Cons in declaring a friend function :

1) You increase flexibility of access but at the same time it is against the concept of data hiding.

2) This method is often desirable when there is to other option, at the first instance thereby producing an inefficient code.

(b) Explain the concept of polymorphism. How has it been implemented in C++? Give an example of its use. **[4]**

Using operators and functions in different ways depending upon what they are operated open ,is called polymorphism.

It has been implemented in C++ using Functions.

1) In function overloading we have different number of arguments & different types of arguments with same function name i.e., same form **not forming** different functions.

2) Operator overloading helps to operate on user defined data type (i.e. depending upon what they are operated on)

3)Virtual Function:- Allow same function name in different cases.

These functions can be manipulated using a single statement in **main** function.

```
e.g.- shape*arr[50];
for(i=0;i<50;i++)
arr[1]->draw();
//Different versions of draw function are
//Called depending upon arr[i] contents.
```

(c) What is meant by call by value and call by reference? Under what conditions is call by reference preferred over call by value? [3]

Call by reference : A reference provides an alias i.e. alternate name for the variable. It is useful when the values of the original variables are to be changed using a function Reference arguments are indicated by an ampersand (so) proceeding the argument e.g. int & a;

Example

```
#include<iostream.h>
#include<Conio.h>
void Swap (int &, int &)
void main ()
{

int a,b;
Cout<<"Enter any two values for a and b" <<end l;
Cin>>a;
Cin>>b;
Swap(a,b);
Cout<<"The two entered numbers are"<<"a"<<a<<" "<<",-and"<<"b"<<b<<end l.;
}
void Swap (int & a, int & b)
{
int c:
c = a;
a = b
b = c;
}
```

The above program uses call by reference method for invoking a function.

Call by value : In this method the called function creates a new set of variables and copies the value of arguments into them. The function does not have access to the original variable(actual parameters) can only work on the copies of values it created.. It is useful when the original values are not to be modified. In fact, call by value method offers insurance that the function Cannot harm the original value. The following example explain this:-

```
Calling ()
{ int passit = 90;
Called (Passit) ;
Cout<<passit;                    // unchanged value
}
Called (int receiveit)
{
receiveit = 0;
}
```

In call by References arguments that are objects, are passed by references to the called method. Any change made to the object by the called method is reflected in the calling method

```
Calling ()
{
int passit=90;
Called (Passit);
Cout<<passit;                         //changes here to 0.
}
Called (int &receiveit)
}
receiveit=0;
}
```

In a call by reference, the memory address i.e. reference of the argument's variable is passed to the called method.
When the called ()method changes the value of the argument, the change is reflected in the calling()
method.
The output-generated from the above program is "changed".

6. Describe the following with one example each : [10]
(i) Macro and Inline functions [DEC02, Q4(c)]
(ii) 'This' pointer in C++ [JUN2003,Q4(a);DEC2001,Q3(b)]
(iii) Virtual and Pure virtual functions
(iv) Scope resolution operator

(i) Macro : We can define **Macro** by using #define directive. Each time the macro is encountered, the arguments used in its definition are replaced by the actual arguments found in the program. This form of a macro is called a function-like macro.

For example :

```
#include<iostream.h>
#define ABS( a )                (a ) < 0 ? – (a ) : ( a )
int main( )
{
cont<<"abs of 1 and 1 ; "<<ABS (-1 ) <<ABS ( 1 );
return 0;
}
```

When this program is compiled, a in the macro definition will be substituted with the values 1 and 1.

The use of a function-like macro in place of real functions has one major benefit: it increases the execution speed of the code because there is no function call over-head. However, if the size of the function-like macro is very large, this increased speed may be paid for with an increase in the size of the program because of duplicate code.

Although parameterized macros are a valuable features, C++ has a way of creating inline code which uses the inline keyword.

Inline functions : In C++, we can create short functions that are not actually called; rather, their code is expanded in line at the point of each invocation. This process is similar to using a function like macro. To cause a function to be expanded in line rather than called, precede its definition with the inline instead of called :

```
#include<iostream.h>
inline int max( int a, int b)
{
return a>b.? a : b;
}
void main ()
{
cout << max(10, 20);
cout<< " "<<max(99,88 );
}
```

(ii) 'This' pointer in C++

Refer to JUN2003, Q4(a), Page no.- 188
Refer to DEC2001, Q3(b), Page no.- 234

(iii) Virtual Functions

The keyword virtual was earlier used to resolve ambiguity for a class derived from two classes, both having a common ancestor. These classes are called virtual base classes. This time it helps in implementing the idea of polymorphism with class inheritance . The function of the base class can be declared with the keyword *virtual.* The program with this change and its output is given below.

```
class Shape
{
 public :
virtual void print()
{
cout << " I am a Shape " << endl;
}
};

class Triangle : public Shape
{

 public :
void print()

{

cout << " I am a Triangle " << endl;

}
};

class Circle : public Shape
{
 public :
void print()

{
cout << " I am a  Circle " << endl;
}
};

void main()

{
Shape S;
Triangle T;
Circle C;
S.print();
T.print();
C.print();

Shape *ptr;
```

```
ptr = &S;
ptr -> print();
ptr = &T;
ptr -> print();
ptr = &C;
ptr -> print();
}
```

The **output** of the program is given below:

```
I am a Shape
I am a Triangle
I am a Circle

I am a Shape
I am a Triangle
I am a Circle
```

Pure Virtual Functions

As discussed earlier, an abstract class is one, which is used just for deriving some other classes. No object of this class is declared and used in the program. Similarly, there are pure virtual functions which themselves won't be used. Consider the above example with some changes.

```
class Shape

{
public :
virtual void print() = 0;              // Pure virtual function

};

class Triangle : public Shape

{

public :
void print()

{

cout << " I am a Triangle " << endl;

}
};
```

```
class Circle : public Shape
{
public :
void print()
{
cout << " I am a Circle " << endl;
}
};

void main()

{
Shape S;
Triangle T;
Circle C;

Shape *ptr;

ptr = &T;
ptr -> print();
ptr = &C;
ptr -> print();
}
```

The **output** of the program is given below:

```
I am a Triangle
I am a Circle
```

It can be seen from the above example that , the print() function from the base class is not invoked at all . even though the function is not necessary, it cannot be avoided, because , the pointer of the class Shape must point to its members.

(iv) The Scope Resolution Operator(::)

Global variables are defined outside any functions and thus can be used by all the functions defined thereafter. However, if a global variable is declared with the same name as that of a local variable of a function , the local variable is the one in the scope when the program executes that function . The C++ language provides the scope resolution operator (::) to access the global variable thus overriding a local variable with the same name. This operator is prefixed to the name of the global variable . The following example shows its usage.

```
int global = 10;

void main()
{
int global = 20;
```

```
printf(" Just writing global prints : %d\n", global);
printf(" Writing ::global prints : %d\n", ::global);

}
```

The output of this program will be:

Just writing global prints : 20
Writing ::global prints : 10

CS-72 : C++ AND OBJECT ORIENTED PROGRAMMING
JUNE 2004

Note : *There are* **six** *questions in the Paper. Q. No.* ***1*** *is* **compulsory** *and carries 30 marks. Attempt any three from the rest.*

Q1(a). What is abstraction? How does a class accomplish data hiding?

Abstraction : Abstraction refers to the act of representing essential features without including the background details or explanations. Classes use the concept of abstraction and are defined as a list of abstract attributes such as size, weight and cost, and functions to operate on these attributes. They encapsulate all the essential properties of the objects that are to be created. Since the classes use the concept of data abstraction, they are known as Abstract Data Types (ADT).

Data Abstraction means hiding tedious details about data from the user, and providing only the abstract view, which makes the understanding very much clear.

e.g.
```
int a;
float b;
```

A class uses above definitions to define data without concerning the user about how integers or decimals are stored/handled in memory.

Encapsulation & Data Hiding : The property of being a self-contained unit is called encapsulation. The idea that the encapsulated unit can be used without knowing how it works is called data hiding.

Encapsulation is the principle by which related contents of a system are kept together. e.g. All the resistor's properties are encapsulated in the resistor object - they are not spread out through the circuitry. It is not necessary to understand how the resistor works to use it effectively, because its data is hidden inside the resistor covering.

C++ supports the properties of encapsulation and data hiding through the creation of user-defined types, called classes. A class implements encapsulation by forming object of it. That object can call public member functions or public data of class using dot(.) operator.

Data hiding is advised using keyword private which doesn't let data to be accessible by object of the class.

e.g.
```
class A
{
int p;
float f;
public:
viod getdata()
{
cin>>p>>f;
}
};
```

```
void main()
{
A a1;
a1.getdata();          //ok (accessible)
a1.p=2;                //error (hidden)
a1.f=3.2;              //error (hidden)
}
```

Q1(b). Write a template class for linked list. It consists of the operations for inserting and deleting nodes from the list.

```
#include<conio.h>
template <class T>
class linklist
{
struct node
{
T data;
node *link;
} *p;

public :

linklist();
void addafter(T c, T num);
void append(T num);
void del(T num);
void display();
~linklist();
};
template <class T>
linklist<T>::linklist()
{
p=NULL;
}
template <class T>
void linklist<T>::append(T num)
{
node *q, *t;
if(p==NULL)                    //if list is empty
{
p=new node;
p->data=num;
p->link=NULL;
}
else
```

```
{
                              //go to last node
q=p;
while(q->link!=NULL)
q=q->link;
                              //add node at end
t=new node;
t->data=num;
t->link=NULL;
q->link=t;
}
}
template <class T>
void linklist<T>::addafter(T c, T num)
{
node *q, *t;
int i;
                              //skip to desired portion
for(i=0,q=p;i<c;i++)
{
q=q->link;
                              //if end of list is encountered
if(q==NULL)
{
cout<<endl<<"There are less than" <<c<<"elements";
return;
}
}
                              //insert new node
t=new node;
t->data=num;
t->link=q->link;
q->link=t;
}
template <class T>
void linklist<T>::del(T num)
{
node *q, *r;
q=p;
                              //if node to be deleted is first node
if(q->data==num)
{
p=q->link;
delete q;
return;
```

```
}
                    //traverse list till the last but one node is reached

r=q;
while(q!=NULL)
{
if(q->data==num)
{
r->link=q->link;
                    //free the memory occupied by node

delete q;
return;
}
r=q;
q=q->link;
}
cout<<endl<<"Element"<<num<<"not found";
}
template <class T>
linklist<T>::~linklist()
{
node *q;
if(p==NULL)
return;
while(p!=NULL)
{
q=p->link;
delete p;
p=q;
}
}
template <class T>
void linklist<T>::display()
{
node *q;
cout<<"\n";
for(q=p;q!=NULL;q=q->link)
cout<<q->data<<endl;
}

void main()
{      clrscr();
linklist<int>l1;
l1.append(11);
l1.append(22);
l1.append(33);
```

```
cout<<"\nAfter append nodes are:\n";
l1.display();

l1.addafter(1,44);
cout<<"\nAfter adding in between nodes are:\n";
l1.display();
l1.addafter(2,55);
cout<<"\nAfter adding in between nodes are:\n";
l1.display();
l1.del(44);
cout<<"\nAfter deleting 44 we have:\n";
l1.display();

getch();
}
```

Q1(c). What are the access control violation in the following program segment:

```
int glob;
class F
{

int glob;
public:
void readit ()
{cin >> glob;
}
};
class W : public F
{
public:
void test()
{
glob--;   }

};

int glob;
class F
{

int glob;
public:
void readit ()
{cin >> glob;
```

```
}
};
class W : public F
{
public:
void test()
{
glob–;  }

};
```

Although we have a global variable glob but since we are inheriting class W from F we are implicitly trying to access the members of class F, but glob has been defined as private in the class F ,so it is not accessible in class W.
Thus having global variable glob here doesn't effect inheritance although it has same name as class variable.

Q1(d). Write a C++ program with constructor, default constructor, copy constructor and destructor to read a set of lines from ' stdin' and store them in an array A: again read 2 strings S1 and S2 from 'stdin' and check whether the given string S1 is in array A. If it is , replaced S1 with S2 and print updated array e.g.
A = concatenate
S1 = cat
S2 = 123
update A is con123 enate.

```
#include <iostream.h>
#include <conio.h>
#include<string.h>
#include<stdio.h>
class string
{
char text[100];
char s1[100], s2[100];
public:
string()
{
strcpy(text," ");
}
string(char t[])
{
strcpy(text,t);
}
void getstring()
{
char ch;int i;
```

```
cout<<"Enter the string";
gets(text);

cout<<"Enter String 1";
gets(s1);

i=strlen(s1);
do
{
cout<<"\nEnter String 2";
gets(s2);

if(strlen(s2)!=i)
cout<<"Only "<<i<<" characters allowed";
}
while(strlen(s2)!=i);

}
void check()
{
int i,len,j;
char*p;
p=strstr(text,s1);
len=p-text;
if(len<=strlen(text)-strlen(s1))
for(i=len,j=0;j<strlen(s1);i++,j++)
text[i]=s2[j];
}
void print()
{
cout<<"\n The concluding string is :"<<text;
}
};
void main()
{    clrscr();
string s;
s.getstring();
s.check();
s.print();
getch();
}
```

Q2. Design and implement a class stack. using pointers. The class includes Empty-stack 'Pop' and 'Push" operations. Make suitable assumptions, if any.

```
#include <iostream.h>
#include<conio.h>
struct node
{
int data;
node *link;
};
class stack
{
node *top;
public:
stack()
{
top=NULL; }

void push(int item)
{
node *temp;
temp=new node;
if(temp==NULL)
cout<<endl<<"stack is full";
temp->data=item;
temp->link=top;
top=temp;
}
int pop()
{
if(top==NULL)
{
cout<<endl<<"stack is empty";
return NULL;
}
node *temp;
int item;
temp=top;
item=temp->data;
top=top->link;
delete temp;
return item;
}
~stack()
{
```

```
if(top==NULL)
return;
node *temp;
while(top!=NULL)
{
temp=top;
top=top->link;
delete temp;
}
}
};
void main()
{       clrscr();
stack s;
s.push(11);
s.push(13);
s.push(17);
s.push(18);
int i=s.pop();
cout<<endl<<"Item popped="<<i;
i=s.pop();
cout<<endl<<"Item popped="<<i;
getch();
}
```

Q3. Design a Polymorphic class hierarchy that prints a number and its square as well as the cube of the number.

```
#include <iostream.h>
#include<conio.h>
class number
{
protected:

int num;
public:
number(){}
number(int n)
{
num=n;
}
~number() {}
void getnumber()
{
cout<<"\n Enter the number";
```

```
cin>>num;
}
virtual void calculate()=0;
virtual void print()=0;
};
class square:public number
{
int result;
public:
void calculate()
{
result=num*num;
}
void print()
{
cout<<"\nThe square of"<<num<<"is"<<result;
}
};
class cube:public number
{
int result;
public:
void calculate()
{
result=num*num*num;
}
void print()
{
cout<<"\nThe cube of"<<num<<"is"<<result;
}
};
void main()
{    clrscr();
number *b;
square  s;
cube c;
b=&s;
b->getnumber();
b->calculate();
b->print();
b=&c;
b->getnumber();
b->calculate();
b->print();
getch();
}
```

Q4(a). What is the difference between early and late binding ? Explain with an example.

Late binding & dynamic binding mean the same. At the design level, when a software engineer is deciding what type of action is appropriate for a given object, he or she should not be concerned about how the object interprets the action (message) and implements the methods but only what the effect of the action is on the object. Object-oriented languages like C++ and Smalltalk allow a programmer to send identical messages to dissimilar but related objects and achieve identical actions while letting the software system decide how to achieve the required action for the given object. A key issue associated with polymorphism is the timing of the software system's implementations decision. If the system decides how to implement an action at compile time, this is called early binding. If the decision is made dynamically at run-time, it is called **late biding**. Generally late biding offers the advantages of flexibility and a high level of problem abstraction.

Example

```
#include<iostream.h>
class x                                 //base class
{
public:
virtual void show()                     //virtual function
{
cout<<"x";
}
};

class y: public x                       //derived class
{
public:
void show()
{
cout<<"y";
}
};

class z:public y                        //super class
{
public:
void show()
{
cout<<"z";
}
};
```

```
// In this we call a function of derived class using base class pointer. One important
// point is that you must declare base function with using virtual keyword.
void main()
{
x *xb;
x xobj;
y yobj;
z zobj;

xb=&xobj;
xb->show();                //only x class function is called
xb=&yobj;
xb->show();                //only y class function is called
xb=&zobj;
xb->show();                //only z class function is called
}
```

(b) How can you overload << function. Explain with an example.

We can overload output operator << by using istream & ostream classes along with friend functions for a better interface (same as used with cout).

Example is given below :

```
#include<iostream.h>
class de
{
public:
int a,b,c;
friend istream & operator >>(istream & os ,de &obj);
friend ostream & operator <<(ostream & os , de &obj);
};

//overloading output operator
ostream& operator <<(ostream & os,de &obj)
{
os<<obj.a<<obj.b<<obj.c;
return os;
}
void main()
{
de e;
cin>>e.a>>e.b>>e.c;
cout<<e;
getch();
}
```

(c) Is constructor overloading different from ordinary function overloading ? How?

Constructor overloading implies that we use same name of the class at two or more instances with varying number of arguments.

Whenever we have to put values in data members of a class we call different constructors by making objects & supplying arguments values whereever necessary. Depending upon number of argument constructors are called :

In function overloading same function name is used but we have :

(i) Varying number of arguments.

(ii) Different types of arguments.

We can also have varying number of arguments in constructor case but different type of arguments is not supported because data is only of one type for a single variable.

e.g. in function overloading.

```
void print(int, float);
void print(int, int);
class:classeg{
int a;
public:
classeg(int);
classeg(float);            //not possible
}
```

Also there are different cases in the limitation of number of arguments.

-In case of constructors we can have only maximum number of arguments equal to number of classes data variables normally.

-In case of function overloading we can have any number of arguments.

e.g.

```
class classeg
{
int a;
float b;
char c;
public:
classeg()
{
a=0; b=0; c='a';
}
classeg(int a1, float b1)
{
a=a1;
b=b1;
}
classeg(int a1, float b1, char c)     //maximum three arguments as we have 3
                                      //variables.
{
a=a1;
```

```
b=b1;
c=c1;
}
```

Q5. Describe the following with an example :

(a) Virtual function

Virtual Functions

The keyword virtual was earlier used to resolve ambiguity for a class derived from two classes, both having a common ancestor. These classes are called virtual base classes. This time it helps in implementing the idea of polymorphism with class inheritance . The function of the base class can be declared with the keyword *virtual.* The program with this change and its output is given below.

```
class Shape
{
public :

virtual void print()
{
cout << " I am a Shape " << endl;
}
};

class Triangle : public Shape
{
public :
void print()
{
cout << " I am a Triangle " << endl;
}
};

class Circle : public Shape
{
public :
void print()
{
cout << " I am a Circle " << endl;
}
};

void main()
{
Shape S;
Triangle T;
```

```
Circle C;
S.print();
T.print();
C.print();
Shape *ptr;
ptr = &S;
ptr -> print();
ptr = &T;
ptr -> print();
ptr = &C;
ptr -> print();
}
```

The **output** of the program is given below:

```
I am a Shape
I am a Triangle
I am a Circle

I am a Shape
I am a Triangle
I am a Circle
```

(b) I/O streams

Input/Output streams in C++

Streams :-

C++ streams are implemented as classes. The cout and cin objects are global instances of those classes, Which derive from a base class named ios and which are declared by the system.

The ostream Class

Stream output is managed by a class named ostream, which is derived from ios. The following statement :-

Cout <<"Hello, Dolly";

The cout object is an external object of the ostream class. The cout object is declared in the library, and an extern declaration of it appears in iostream.h so that is available to be used by any program that includes iosteream.h

The istream class

The istream class manages stream input in the same way that the ostream class manages output. The istream class is externally declared in iostream.h. The cin object reads data values from the standard input device.

The iostream class

The iostream class is derived from the istream and ostream classes. A program uses it for the declaration of object that do both input and output. You do not often need to deal with the iosteream class in basic input/output operations. The fstream class, which manages file input/output, derives from the iosream class.

The ofstream class

The ofstream class object are files that a program can write to. In the most elementry use of ofstream, the program declares an object an object of type ofstream, gives it a name, and writes to it. When the object goes out of scope, the file closes.

Example:-

```
#include <fstream.h>
main()
{
ofstream tfile( "test,dat");
tfile << "This is test data ";
}
```

The ifstream class

The ifstream class object are input files. A program can declare an input file stream object and read it. The following example reads a text file a one character at a time, sending each character to cout and stopping at end-of-file.

Example:-

```
#include <fstream.h>
main()
{
ifstream tfile( "test,dat");
while (!tfile.eof())
{
char ch;
tfile.getch(ch);
cout <<ch;
}
}
```

The fstream class

The fstream class supports file stream objects that a program opens for both input and output.

(c) Constructors

```
#include <iostream.h>
class integer
{
private :
int i ;
public :
void getdata()
{
cout<<endl<<"Enter any integer";
cin>>i;
}
void setdata(intj)
```

```
{
i=j;
}
integer()                    // zero argument constructor
{
}
integer(intj)                // one argument constructor
{
i=j;
}
void displaydata()
{
cout<<endl<<"value of i="<<i;
}
};
void main()
{
integer i1(100), i2, i3;
i1.displaydata();
i2.setdata(200);
i2.displaydata();
i3.getdata();
i3.displaydata();
}
```

The constructor is a special member function that allows us to set up values while defining the object, without the need to make a separate call to a member function. They have exactly the same name as the class of which they are members. No return type is used for constructors. Why not? Since the constructor is called automatically when an object is created, returning a value would not make sense.

In our program the statement

integer i1(100), i2, i3;

creates three objects of the type integer.

If you notice carefully you would find that there are two constructors with the same name integer(). Hence we call these constructors as overloaded constructors.

```
integer i2;              //calls zero-argument constructor
integer i1(100);         //calls one-argument constructor
```

(d) Significance of friend function:

The concept of data encapsulation sometimes takes information hiding too far. There are situations where a rigid and controlled access leads to inconvenience and hardships.

For instance, consider a case where a function is required to operate on object of two different classes. This function cannot be made a member of both the classes. What can be done is that a function can be defined outside both the classes and made to operate on both. That is, a function not belonging to either, but able to access both. Such a function is called as a friend function. In other words, a friend function is a nonmember function, which has access to a class's private members.

Using a Friend

Using a friend function is quite simple. The following example defines a friend function to access members of two classes.

```
class Bclass;                    // Forward Declaration
class Aclass
{
public :
Aclass(int v)
{
Avar = v;
}

friend int addup(Aclass &ac, Bclass &bc);
private :
int Avar;
};

class Bclass
{
public :
Bclass(int v)
{
Bvar = v;
}

friend int addup(Aclass &ac, Bclass &bc);
private :
int Bvar;
};

int addup(Aclass &ac, Bclass &bc)
{
return( ac.Avar + bc.Bvar);
}

void main()
{
Aclass aobj;
Bclass bobj;
int total;
total = addup(aobj,bobj);
}
```

The program defines two classes - Aclass and Bclass. It also has constructors for these classes. A friend function, addup(), is declared in the definition of both the classes, although it does not belong to either. This friend function returns the sum of the two private members of the classes.
Sometimes friend functions can be avoided using inheritance and they are preferred. Excessive use of friend over many classes suggests a poorly designed program structure. But sometimes they are unavoidable.

Q6(a). What is inheritance ? Discuss its various forms.
The new dimension of OOP uses a method called inheritance to modify a class to suit one's needs. Inheritance means deriving new classes from the old ones. The old class is called the *base class* or *parent class or super class* and the class which is derived from this base class is called as *derived class* or *child class or sub class.* Deriving a new class from an existing one, allows redefining a member function of the base class and also adding new members to the derived class and this is possible without having the source also. In other words, a derived class not only inherits all properties of the base class but also has some refinements of its own. The base class remains unchanged in the process. In other words, the derived class "is a " type of base class, but with more details added.

Derived class

A singly inherited derived class id defined by writing :

1) The keyword *class.*
2) The name of the derived class.
3) A single colon (:).
4) The type of derivation (private, protected, or public).
5) The name of the base, or parent class.
6) The remainder of the class definition.

E.g.

```
class A
{
public :
int public_A;
void public_function_A();

private :
int pri_A;
void private_function_A();

protected :
int protected_A;
void protected_function_A();
};
class B : private A
{
public :
```

```
int public_B;
void public_function_B();

private :
int pri_B;
void private_function_B();
};
class C : public A
{
public :
int public_C;
void public_function_C();

private :
int pri_C;
void private_function_C();
};
class D : protected A
{
public :
int public_D;
void public_function_D();

private :
int pri_D;
void private_function_D();
};
```

A derived class always contains all of the members from its base class. you cannot "subtract" anything from a base class. However, accessing the inherited variables is a different matter. Just because you happen to derive a class does not mean that you are automatically granted complete and unlimited access privileges to the members of the base class. To understand this you must look at the different types of derivation and the effect of each one.

Private derivation

If no specific derivation is listed, then a private derivation is assumed. If a new class is derived privately from its parent class , then :

* The private members inherited from its base class are inaccessible to new member functions in the derived class. This means that the creator of the base class has absolute control over the accessibility of these members, and there is no way that you can override this.

* The public members inherited from the base class have private access privilege. In other words, they are treated as though they were declared as new private members of the derived class, so that new member functions can access them. However, if another private derivation occurs from this derived class, then these members are inaccessible to new member functions.

Public derivation

Public derivations are much more common than private derivations. In this situation:

* The private members inherited from the base class are inaccessible to new member functions in the derived class.

* The public members inherited from the base class may be accessed by new member functions in the derived class and by instances of the derived class.

E.g.

```
class base
{
private :
int number;
};

class derived : public base
{
public :
void f()
{
++number;                    // Private base member not
accessible
}
};
```

The compiler *error* message is

' base :: number ' is not accessible in the function derived::f();

Here, only if the number is public then you can access it.

Note : *However example 2 and 3 in the above section works here if you derive them as "public".*

Protected derivation

In addition to doing private and public derivations, you may also do a protected derivation. In this situation:

- The private members inherited from the base class are inaccessible to new member functions in the derived class.(this is exactly same as if a private or public derivation has occurred.)
- The protected members inherited from the base class have protected access privilege.
- The public members inherited from the base class have protected access.

Thus, the only difference between a public and a protected derivation is how the public members of the parent class are inherited. It is unlikely that you will ever have occasion to do this type of derivation.

(b) What is meant by static data member of a class ? Explain its characteristics.

All the objects of the class have different data members but invoke the same member functions. However, there is an exception to this rule. If the data member is declared with the keyword *static,* then only one such data item is created for the entire class, no matter how many objects it has. Static data members are useful, if all objects of a class must share a common data item. Whereas, the visibility of this data item remains same, the duration of this variable is for entire lifetime of the program. For example, such a variable can be particularly useful if an object requires to know how many objects of its kind exist.

```
class counter
{
public :
counter ();
int getcount();
private:
static int count;
};
counter::counter ()
{
count++;
}

int counter::getcount()
{
return ( count );
}
int counter :: count = 0;                //initialization of static member
void main()
{
counter c1,c2;

cout << " Count = " << c1.getcount() << endl;
cout << " Count = " << c2.getcount() << endl;

counter c3;

cout << " Count = " << c3.getcount() << endl;

counter c4,c5;

cout << " Count = " << c4.getcount() << endl;
cout << " Count = " << c5.getcount() << endl;
}
```

Output:

```
Count = 2          //not 1 because 2 objects are already created.
Count = 2
Count = 3
Count = 5
Count = 5
```

In the above example, the class counter demonstrates the use of static data members. It contains just one data member count. *Notice the initialization of this static class member*. For some compilers it is mandatory.

(c) How are exception handled in C++ ? Explain its need.

Exception Handling in C++

The exception mechanism of C++ uses three new *keywords: throw, catch,* and try. Also, we need to create a new kind of entity called an *exception class.*

Need : Suppose we have an application that works with objects of a certain class. If during the course of execution of a member function of this class an error occurs, then this member function informs the application that an error has occurred. This process of informing is called *throwing* an exception. In the application we have to create a separate section of code to tackle the error. This section of code is called an *exception handler* or a *catch block.* Any code in the application that uses objects of the class is enclosed in *a try block.* Errors generated in the try block are caught in the catch block. Code that doesn't interact with the class need not be in a *try* block. The following code shows the organisation of these blocks. It is not a working program, but it clearly shows how and where the various elements of the exception mechanism are placed.

```
class sample
{
public:
//exception class
class errorclass
{
};
void fun()
{
if(some error occurs)
throw errorclass(); //throws exception
}
};
//application
void main()
{
//try block
try
{
```

```
sample s;
s.fun();
}
catch(sample::errorclass)          //exception handler or catch block
{
                                   //do something about the error
}
}
```

Here sample is any class in which errors might occur. An exception class called *errorclass,* is specified in the *public* part of *sample*. In *main()* we have enclosed part of the program that uses *sample* in a try block. If an error occurs in *sample::fun()* we throw an exception, using the keyword *throw* followed by the constructor for the *errorclass:*

throw errorclass();

When an exception is thrown control goes to the *catch* block that immediately follows the *try* block.

CS72 : C++ AND OBJECT ORIENTED PROGRAMMING
DEC 2004

Note : *There are six questions in the paper, Q. No. 1 is* **compulsory** *and carries 30 marks. Attempt any* **three** *from the rest.*

1(a) What is a friend class ? How is it declared ? Explain its use with an example. **[5]**

A class can be made friend of other class. To grant friendship to another class, write the keyword friend followed by the class name. The keyword class is optional. Note that this declaration also implies a forward declaration of the class to which the friendship is being granted. The implication of this declaration is that all of the member functions of the friend class are friend functions of the class that bestows the friendship.

```
class Aclass
{
public :
      :
      :
      :

friend class Bclass;                    // Friend declaration.
private :
int Avar;
};

class Bclass
{
public :
      :
      :
void fn1(Aclass ac)
{
Bvar = ac. Avar;                        //Avar can be accessed.
}
private :
int Bvar;
};

void main()
```

```
{
Aclass aobj;
Bclass bobj;
bobj.fn1(aobj);
}
```

The program declares class Bclass to be a friend of Aclass. It means that all member functions of Bclass have been granted direct access to all member functions of Aclass.

(b) Define the terms 'data abstraction', 'encapsulation' and 'data hiding'. List the differences among them. **[5]**

Abstraction :- Abstraction refers to the act of representing essential features without including the background details or explanations. Classes use the concept of abstraction and are defined as a list of abstract attributes such as size, weight and cost, and functions to operate on these attributes. They encapsulate all the essential properties of the objects that are to be created. Since the classes use the concept of data abstraction, they are known as Abstract Data Types (ADT).

Data Abstraction means hiding tedious details about data from the user, and providing only the abstract view, which makes the understanding very much clear.

e.g.

```
int a;
float b;
```

A class uses above definitions to define data without concerning the user about how integers or decimals are stored/handled in memory.

Encapsulation & Data Hiding :- The property of being a self-contained unit is called encapsulation. The idea that the encapsulated unit can be used without knowing how it works is called data hiding.

Encapsulation is the principle by which related contents of a system are kept together. e.g. All the resistor's properties are encapsulated in the resistor object - they are not spread out through the circuitry. It is not necessary to understand how the resistor works to use it effectively, because its data is hidden inside the resistor covering.

C++ supports the properties of encapsulation and data hiding through the creation of user-defined types, called classes. A class implements encapsulation by forming object of it. That object can call public member functions or public data of class using dot(.) operator.

Data hiding is advised using keyword private which doesn't let data to be accessible by object of the class.

e.g.

```
class A
{
```

```
int p;
float f;
public:
void getdata()
{
cin>>p>>f;
}
};
void main()
{
A a1;
a1.getdata();            //ok (accessible)
a1.p=2;                  //error (hidden)
a1.f=3.2;                //error (hidden)
}
```

(c) What is inheritance ? What are the three different ways of deriving a class from a single base class ? Explain each with help of an example. Describe the access control for there inherited classes. [10]

OOP uses a method called inheritance to modify a class to suit one's needs. Inheritance means deriving new classes from the old ones. The old class is called the *base class* or *parent class or super class* and the class which is derived from this base class is called as *derived class* or *child class or sub class*. Deriving a new class from an existing one, allows redefining a member function of the base class and also adding new members to the derived class and this is possible without having the source also.

E.g.

```
class base
{
public :
int number;
};
class derived : private base
{
public :
void f()
{
++number;
}};
```

E.g.

```
class base
{
private :
int number;
};

class derived : public base
{
public :
void f()
{
++number;    // Private base member not accessible
}
};
```

Protected derivation :- In addition to doing private and public derivations, you may also do a protected derivation. In this situation:

- ➢ The private members inherited from the base class are inaccessible to new member functions in the derived class.(this is exactly same as if a private or public derivation has occurred.)
- ➢ The protected members inherited from the base class have protected access privilege.
- ➢ The public members inherited from the base class have protected access.

Thus, the only difference between a public and a protected derivation is how the public members of the parent class are inherited. It is unlikely that you will ever have occasion to do this type of derivation.

Figure : Depicts these accesses.

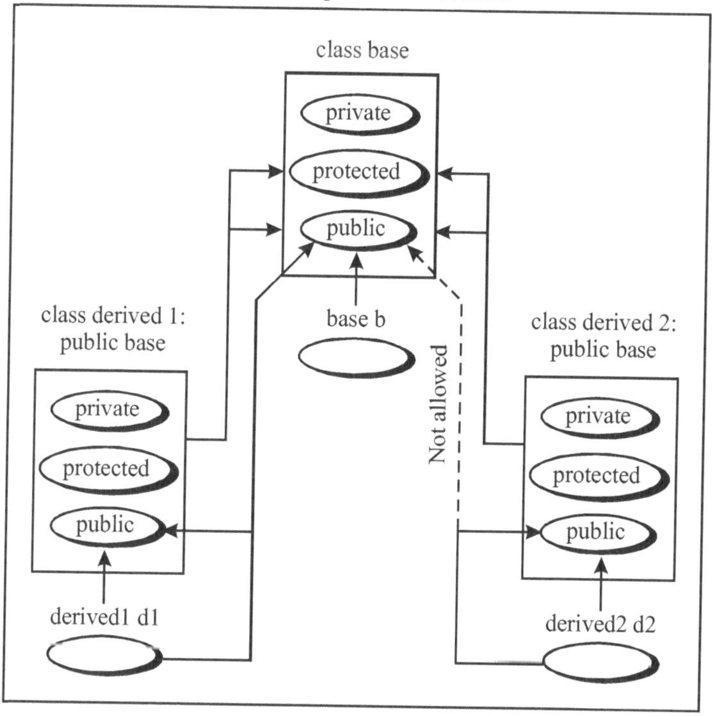

(d) Design and implement a polymorphic class hierarchy of closed shapes such as circle, rectangle and triangle. Also, write a polymorphic function that calculates the perimeter of these shapes. Write an appropriate main() function to demonstrate the polymorphism in the function above. **[10]**

```
#include<iostream.h>
#include<conio.h>
class shapes
	{
	public:
	virtual void param()=0;
	virtual void getdata()=0;
	};
class circle:public shapes
	{
	int rad;
	public:
	void getdata()
```

```
{
cout<<"Enter the radius of the circle";
cin>>rad;
}
void param()
{
cout<<"The paramater is"<<2*3.14*rad<<endl;
}
};
class rect:public shapes
{
int l,b;
public:
void getdata()
{
cout<<"Enter the length and breadth of rectangle";
cin>>l>>b;
}
void param()
{
cout<<"The parameter is"<<2*(l+b)<<endl;
}
};
class triangle:public shapes
{
int a,b,c;
public:
void getdata()
{
cout<<"Enter the three sides of the triangle";
cin>>a>>b>>c;
}
void param()
{
cout<<"The parameter is"<<a+b+c;
}
};
void main()
{
clrscr();
shapes *p[2];
```

```
circle c;
rect r;
triangle t;

p[0]=&c;
p[1]=&r;
p[2]=&t;

for(int i=0;i<=2;i++)
{
p[i]->getdata();
cout<<endl;
p[i]->param();
cout<<endl;
}
getch();
}
```

Q2. Design and implement a class "linked list" using pointers. The class should include functions of insertion, deletion and search for an element. Make assumptions, if required. [10]

```
#include<iostream.h>
#include<conio.h>

class linklist
{
        struct node
        {
        int data;
        node *link;
        }*p;

        public:

        linklist()
        {
        p=NULL;
        }

        void insert(int num)
        {
```

```
node*q,*t;
        if(p==NULL)
        {
        //create first node
        p=new node;
        p->data=num;
        p->link=NULL;
        }
        else
        {
        //go to last node
        q=p;
        while(q->link!=NULL)
        q=q->link;

        //add node at end
        t=new node;
        t->data=num;
        t->link=NULL;
        q->link=t;
        }
}

void del(int num)
{
node *q,*r;
q=p;
//if node to be deleted is first
        if(q->data==num)
        {
        p=q->link;
        delete q;
        return;
        }

//traverse till last but one node is reached
r=q;
        while(q!=NULL)
        {
                if(q->data==num)
                {
```

```
                r->link=q->link;
                delete q;
                return;
                }
        r=q;
        q=q->link;
        }
cout<<"\n"<<"Element"<<num<<"not found";
}

void search(int num)
{
node*q;
int c=0;
        for(q=p;q!=NULL;q=q->link)
        {
        c++;
                if(num==q->data)
                {
                cout<<"\nData present at position:"<<c;
                return;
                }
        }
cout<<"\nData not present\n";
}

void display()
{
node*q;
int c=0;
        for(q=p;q!=NULL;q=q->link)
        cout<<endl<<q->data;
}
~linklist()
{
node*q;
        if(p==NULL)
        return;

        while(p!=NULL)
        {
```

```
                q=p->link;
                delete p;
                p=q;
                }
        }
};

void main()
{
clrscr();
linklist ll;

ll.insert(11);
ll.insert(22);
ll.insert(33);
ll.insert(44);
ll.insert(55);
ll.insert(66);
cout<<"After insertion list is:\n";
ll.display();

ll.del(300);
ll.del(66);
cout<<"\n\nAfter deletion of 66 list is:\n";
ll.display();


ll.search(22);
ll.search(30);
getch();
}
```

3(a) What are the two main differences between a constructor and simple member function of class ? What are parameterised constructors ? How are they related to a polymorphism ? [5]

Constructor	Simple member function
(1) Name of constructor must be same as that of class name. It's a strict syntax.	Name of member function is not. Same as that of class. It is a strict restriction.
(2) Constructor is called every time you create an object of the class. It is implicit calling.	Member functions have to be called explicitly by using (.) dot operator with the object of the class.

Parameterised Constructor :- A constructor that carries arguments with it is called parametrised. It is used to assign default value to class data members as soon as an object is created that means you don't have to create an explicit member function in the class only for the purpose of assigning default values to data members. for eg:

Example : -

```
#include <iostream.h>

class integer
{
        private

                int i ;

        public

                void getdata ( )
                {
                        cout << endI << "Enter any integer" ;
                        cin >> i ;
                }

                void setdata (int j)
                {
                        i = j ;
                }
                integer (.) // zero argument constructor
                }
                {
```

```
                integer (int j) // one argument constructo
                {
                        i = j ;
                }

                void displaydata( )
                {
                cout << endI << "value of i =" << i ;
                }
} ;

void main( )
{
        integer  i1 (100), i2, i3 ;
i1.displaydata( ) ;
i2.setdata (200) ;
i2. displaydata( ) ;
i3.getdata( ) ;
i3.displaydata( );
}
```

The constructor is a special member function that allows us to set up values while defining the object, without the need to make a separate call to a member function.

They have exactly the same name as the class of which they are members.

No return type is used for constructors. Why not? Since the constructor is called automatically when an object is created, returning a value would not make sense.

In our program the statement

Integer i1 (10)m i2, i3 ;

Creates three objects of the type integer.

If you notice carefully, you would find that there are two constructors with the same name *integer ( )*. Hence we call these constructors as *overloaded constructors.*

Integer i2 ; // calls zero-argument constructor

Integer i1 (100) ; // calls one-argument constructor

In the above eg. we saw constructors with same name as that of class. That are overloaded constructors i.e. same name but called according to zero arguments or one argument, i.e.. They are exhibiting polymorphism.

(b) What are three different ways of using the keyword "const" in C++? Explain with the help of one example each. **[5]**

(1) The keyword const (for constant), if present, precedes the data type of a variable. It specifies that the value of the variable will not change throughout the program. Any attempt to alter the value of the variable defined with this qualifier will result into an error message from the complier. *const* is usually used to replace *#defined* constants.

The following program shows the usage of const.

```
#include <iostream.h>
void main( )
{
        float r, a ;
        const float PI = 3.14 ;

        cin >> r ;
        a = PI * r * r ;
        cout << endI << “Area of circle =”  << a ;
}
```

If a *const* is placed inside a function its effect would be localized to that function, whereas, if it is placed outside all functions then its effect would be global. We cannot exercise such finer control while using a *#define.*

(2) We have met the const keyword already as a way of defining a constant value which can be used in place of a raw number within your program. The const keyword has several other uses in C++, particularly in relation to function definitions. Consider the function definition:

```
int ConstArgs(const int &Arg1, const float &Arg2) {....}
```

The const keyword before each argument tells the compiler that although these arguments are being passed by reference, they are not allowed to be modified within the function body. They become, in essence, ‘read-only objects: their values may be accessed but not altered. Thus, the following function definition would give rise to a compile-time error:

```
int ConstArgs(const int &Arg1, const float &Arg2)
{
Arg1 *= 2;
}
```

A general rule is: if you agree with those people who tell you to pass arguments by reference whenever possible, you should carefully consider whether each variable should be changed within the function to which it is being passed. If not, you should ensure that it is declared as a const parameter in the function definition. Thus is purely a safeguard against subtle errors; if your program is written correctly, it won’t make any difference whether the const is there or not, but if you make a mistake and attempt to alter a variable within a function where it shouldn’t be altered, the prefix const just might save you hours or debugging.

(3) Another use of the const keyword is *after* a function declaration in a class. Constant member functions are used in classes to protect changes to class's data.
For example, in the class definition:

```
Class ConstClass
{
private:
declarations
public:
int ConstFunc(args) cosnt;
};
```

The const after the declaration of ConstFunc( ) states that ConstFunc( ) is not allowed to change any fields of the object that calls it. For example, with the code fragment:

```
ConstClass Object;
Object.ConstFunc( );
```

The call to ConstFunc ( ) must not alter any of the values of any of the data fields of Object. This is another safety feature in C++ designed to help you catch programming errors early. If you declare a function as const in this fashion and then inadvertently insert some statements into the definition of that function that alter some of the fields of the object calling the function, the compiler will flag an error. It is therefore a good idea to think carefully about whether or not a function should be allowed to alter data fields and, if not, declare it as const.

4(a) Write a program to read two matrices and multiply them. Use operator overloading so that the statement for multiplication of the matrices may be written as Z = X * Y, where X and Y are matrices. [7]
We can only multiply two **matrices** iff the number of **columns** in first matrix is equal to number of rows in second matrix.

$$\begin{bmatrix} \underbrace{a_1 a_2 a_3 a_4}_{\text{no. of columns} = 4} \end{bmatrix} \quad \begin{bmatrix} \left.\begin{matrix} b_1 \\ b_2 \\ b_3 \\ b_4 \end{matrix}\right\} \text{no. of rows} = 4 \end{bmatrix} \quad a_1*b_1+a_2*b_2+a_3*b_3+a_4*b_4$$

```
#include<conio.h>
#include<stdio.h>
#include<iostream.h>
```

```
#include<iomanip.h>
class matrix
{
private:
int maxrow,maxcol;
int *ptr;
public:

matrix(int r, int c)
{
maxrow=r;
maxcol=c;
ptr=new int[r *c];
}

void getmat()
{
int i,j,mat_off,temp;
cout<<endl<<"Enter Elements matrix : "<<endl;
for(i=0;i<maxrow;i++)
{
for(j=0;j<maxcol;j++)
{
mat_off=i*maxcol+j;
cin>>ptr[mat_off];
}
}
}

void printmat()
{
int i,j,mat_off;
for(i=0;i<maxrow;i++)
{
cout<<endl;
for(j=0;j<maxcol;j++)
{
mat_off=i*maxcol+j;
cout<<setw(3)<<ptr[mat_off];
}
```

```
}
}

matrix operator * (matrix b)
{
matrix c(b.maxcol,maxrow);
int i,j,k,mat_off1,mat_off2,mat_off3;

for(i=0;i<c.maxrow;i++)
{
for(j=0;j<c.maxcol;j++)
{
mat_off3=i*c.maxcol+j;
c.ptr[mat_off3]=0;
for(k=0;k<b.maxrow;k++)
{
mat_off2=k*b.maxcol+j;
mat_off1=i*maxcol+k;
c.ptr[mat_off3]+=ptr[mat_off1]*b.ptr[mat_off2];
}
}
}
return(c);
}};
void main()
{
int rowa,cola,rowb,colb;

cout<<endl<<"Enter dimensions of A";
cin>>rowa>>cola;
matrix a(rowa,cola);
a.getmat();
cout<<endl<<"Enter dimensions of matrix B";
cin>>rowb>>colb;
matrix b(rowb,colb);
b.getmat();

matrix d(rowa,colb);
d=a*b;
cout<<endl<<"The product of two matrices = ";
d.printmat(); } }
```

(b) "The assignment operator can not be overloaded through a friend function." Is this true ? Justify your answer. [3]

It is true that assignment operator cannot be overloaded through a friend function. The reason is derived from the fact that (1) Writing an expression involving assignment operator in a program will tend to invoke copy constructor or overloaded assignment operator if operation involves objects of same class.

(2) If operation involves objects of different class where use of friend function could be meaningful, then also compiler only searches for a copy constructor or a conversion routine. That conversion can be as a conversion function or in the destination data class i.e. as a constructor.

e.g.

```
class A {
};
class B {
};
void main()
{
A a;
B b;
a=b;   ← source object (b)
       → destination object (a)
```

Q5. Define the following term giving one example each : [10]

(a) Default parameter passing

(b) Exception handling in C++

(c) Static data and static member function

(d) Macros

(a) Default parameter passing :- A C++ function prototype can declare that one or more of the function's parameters have default values. What a call to the function omits the corresponding arguments, the compiler inserts the default values where it expects to see the arguments.

We can declare default values for arguments in a C++ function prototype in the following way:

```
Void myfunc(int=5,double=1.23);
```

The expression declare default values for the arguments. The C++ compiler substitutes the default values if you omit the arguments when you call the function. We can call the function by using any of the following ways:

```
myfunc(12,3.45);        // overrides both defaults
myfunc(3);              // effectively func(3, 1.23);
myfunc();               // effectively func(5,1.23);
```

To omit first parameter in these examples, you must omit the second one; however, you can omit a parameter unless you omit the parameters to its right.

Here is the example:

```
#include<iostream.h>
void show(int=1,float=2.3,long=4);
main()
{
show(); //all three parameters default
show(5);        //provide 1st parameter
show(6,7.8);    //provide all three parameters
}
void show(int first, float second, long third)
{
cout<<"\nfirst= "<<first;
cout<<"second="<<second;
cout<<"third="<<third;
}
```

(b) Exception handling in C++ :- The extensibility of C++ can increase substantially the number and kind of errors that can occur. The feature enable There are many popular means of dealings with errors. Most commonly, error handling.

The advantage of this approach is that a programmer reading code can see the error processing in the immediate vicinity of the code and determine if the proper errors checking has been implemented.

Use of exception handling :- Exception handling is used in situations is which the system can recover from the error causing the exception. The recovery procedure is called an exception handler.

The exception mechanism of C++ uses three new *keywords: throw, catch,* and try. Also, we need to create a new kind of entity called an *exception class.* Suppose we have an application that works with objects of a certain class. If during the course of execution of a member function of this class an error occurs, then this member function informs the application that an error has occurred. This process of informing is called *throwing* an exception. In the application we have to create a separate section of code to tackle the error. This section of code is called an *exception handler* or a *catch block.* Any code in the application that uses objects of the class is enclosed in *a try block.* Errors generated in the try block are caught in the catch block. Code that doesn't interact with the class need not be in a *try* block. The following code shows the organisation of these blocks. It is not a working program, but it clearly shows how and where the various elements of the exception mechanism are placed.

```
class sample
{
public:
//exception class
class errorclass
{
};
void fun()
{
if(some error occurs)
throw errorclass(); //throws exception
}
};
//application
void main()
{
//try block
try
{
sample s;
s.fun();
}
catch(sample::errorclass) //exception handler or catch block
{
//do something about the error
}
}
```

Here sample is any class in which errors might occur. An exception class called *errorclass,* is specified in the *public* part of *sample*. In *main()* we have enclosed part of the program that uses *sample* in a try block. If an error occurs in *sample::fun()* we throw an exception, using the keyword *throw* followed by the constructor for the *errorclass:*

throw errorclass();

When an exception is thrown control goes to the *catch* block that immediately follows the *try* block.

(c) Static data and static member function :- If the data member is declared with the keyword *static,* then only one such data item is created for the entire

class, no matter how many objects it has. Static data members are useful, if all objects of a class must share a common data item. Whereas, the visibility of this data item remains same, the duration of this variable is for entire lifetime of the program.
For example, such a variable can be particularly useful if an object requires to know how many objects of its kind exist.

```
class counter
{
public :
counter ();
int getcount();
private:
static int count;
};
counter::counter ()
{
count++;
}

int counter::getcount()
{
return ( count );
}
int counter :: count = 0;   // INITIALIZATION OF STATIC MEMBER.

void main()
{
counter c1,c2;
cout << " Count = " << c1.getcount() << endl;
cout << " Count = " << c2.getcount() << endl;

counter c3;

cout << " Count = " << c3.getcount() << endl;
counter c4,c5;

cout << " Count = " << c4.getcount() << endl;
cout << " Count = " << c5.getcount() << endl;
}
```

Output:

```
Count = 2        //not 1 because 2 objects are already created.
Count = 2
Count = 3
Count = 5
Count = 5
```

In the above example, the class counter demonstrates the use of static data members. It contains just one data member count.

The example above demonstrates how to keep track of all the objects of a class which are in existence. However, this function uses existing objects to invoke a member function getcount(), which returns the value of the static data member. *What if the programme does not want to use objects to invoke this function and still the programme would like to know how many objects have been created? If there is no object how the member function is invoked?* Further, as can be seen from the previous output, the number of objects (count) remains same at a given instance no matter which object is used to invoke the member function. In fact, the use of existing objects, like in the above example, is not an effective way to access the value of the static data member. A specific object should not be used to refer to this member, since it does not belong to that object; it belongs to the entire class. C++ gives a facility to define static function members, for the same. That is, to invoke such a function, an object is not required. It can be invoked with the name of the class. The programme given below illustrates its use.

```
class counter
{
public :
counter ();
static int getcount();

private:
static int count;
};
counter::counter ()
{
count++;
}

int counter::getcount()
```

```
{
return ( count );
}
int counter :: count = 0;   // INITIALIZATION OF STATIC MEMBER.

void main()
{
counter c1,c2;

cout << " Count = " << counter :: getcount() << endl;
cout << " Count = " << counter :: getcount() << endl;

counter c3;

cout << " Count = " << counter :: getcount() << endl;

counter c4,c5;

cout << " Count = " << counter :: getcount() << endl;
cout << " Count = " << counter :: getcount() << endl;
}
```

Output:

Count = 2
Count = 2
Count = 3
Count = 5
Count = 5

(d) Macros :- We can define **Macro** by using #define directive. Each time the macro is encountered, the arguments used in its definition are replaced by the actual arguments found in the program. This form of a macro is called a function-like macro.

For example :-

```
#include<iostream.h>
#define ABS( a )                    (a ) < 0 ? – (a ) : ( a )
int main( )
{
cont<<"abs of 1 and 1 ; "<<ABS (-1 ) <<ABS ( 1 );
return 0;
```

}

When this program is compiled, a in the macro definition will be substituted with the values 1 and 1.

The use of a function-like macro in place of real functions has one major benefit: it increases the execution speed of the code because there is no function call overhead. However, if the size of the function-like macro is very large, this increased speed may be paid for with an increase in the size of the program because of duplicate code.

Although parameterized macros are a valuable features, C++ has a way of creating inline code which uses the inline keyword.

6(a) What is the purpose of class-diagrams ? Explain with the help of an example. **[4]**

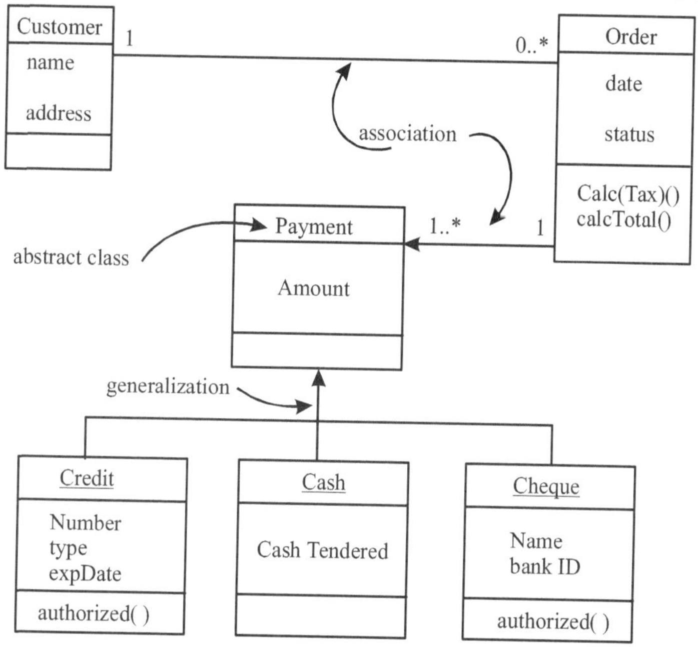

Class diagram for order processing

Class diagrams serve the purpose of pictorial representation of data members & function in the class & relationships among the class is e.g. inherited classes or classes at base level that have logical relationships.

Inheritance - also called generalization

Relationships – also called associations

e.g. The above classes diagram

For order processing classes credit,
Cash & cheque are inherited from class payment.
Class customer has 1 to many relation with class order & class order has 1 to many (start at 1.) relation with class payment.

(b) What is the advantage of using templates ? Write a template class for the stack. [6]

Templates are a mechanism that make it possible to use one function or class to handle many different data types. By using templates, we can design a single class/function that operates on data of many types, instead of having to create a separate class/function for each type. When used with functions they are known as *function templates,* whereas when used with classes they are called *class templates*, We would first look at function templates and then go on to class templates.

Two advantage of Templates

1) Rewriting the program body (function class) for different types is a resided.
2) Program consumes less disk space.

```
#include<iostream.h>
#include<stdio.h>
#include<conio.h>
#include<process.h>
template <class t>
class st
{
public :
t stack[20];
int top;
t val;
int choice;
st()
{top=-1;
}
int pop(t stack[ ],int &top);
void push(t stack[ ],int &top,t val,int n);
void display(t stack[ ],int top);
};
//Insert in stack
template <class t>
void st<t>::push(t stack[ ],int &top,t val,int n)
{
```

```
if(top < n)
{
top++;
stack[top]=val;
}
else
cout<<"Stack is full";
}
//deletion in stack
template <class t>
int st<t>::pop(t stack[ ],int &top)
{
int delvalue;
if(top>=0)
{
delvalue=stack[top];
top--;
return delvalue;
}
else
{
cout<<"\n Stack is empty";
return(-9999);
}
}
//Display in stack
template <class t>
void st<t>::display(t stack[ ],int top)
{
int i;
if(top>=0)
{
cout<<"\n";
for(i=top;i>=0;i--)
{
cout<<stack[i];
}
getch();
fflush(stdin);
}
}
void main()
```

```
{
st<char> obj;
do
{
cout<<"\n         Menu      ";
cout<<"\n 1 ==> Push    2 ==> Pop";
cout<<"\n 3 ==> Display  4 ==>Quit ";
cout<<"Enter your choice";
cin>>obj.choice;
switch(obj.choice)
{
case 1: cout<<"Enter the value to pushed";
cin>>obj.val;
obj.push(obj.stack,obj.top,obj.val,30);
break;
case 2: obj.val=obj.pop(obj.stack,obj.top);
if(obj.val!=-9999)
cout<<"\n the popped last value of stack  is "<<obj.val;
break;
case 3: obj.display(obj.stack,obj.top);
break;
case 4: exit(0);
default:
cout<<"wrongh value ";
        }
      }while(obj.choice!=4);
}
}
```

CS-72 : C++ AND OBJECT ORIENTED PROGRAMMING
JUNE 2005

Note : *There are six questions in this paper. Question 1 is* ***compulsory*** *and carries 30 marks. Attempt any* ***three*** *from the rest.*

Q1(a) Explain the paradigm of Object Oriented Programming (OOP). Give an example of a problem that is suitable to be programmed using an OOP language. Justify your answer. [5]

Object Oriented Programming :- is a programming methodology where the main emphasis is given on the object or the data and not on the functions or operations that operate on data. Data is undervalued in procedural programming. Here, the design puts data upfront & organization of data is significant area. Access rights are reserved as well to protect data from accidental changes by an intruder.

Advantages :-

(i) Promotes organization in programming style.

(ii) Offers reusability i.e. the work done in the past can be put into use as such in future.

(iii) One function can have many forms that permits widening of area of application.

Disadvantages :-

(i) OOP is a high level concept so takes more time to execute as many routines run behind at the time of execution

(ii) Offers less number of functions as compared to low level programming which interacts directly with hardware.

(iii) Increased burden on part of OOP developer.

Problem best suited to be programming using an OOP language is that of a game having players acting as objects as in cricket.

The different players have common functions but associated data such as fielding points may vary. Common functions include catching, throwing & batting.

A team may represent a class having players as objects.

The idea behind object-oriented programming is that a computer program is composed of a collection of individual units, or *objects*, as opposed to a traditional view in which a program is a list of instructions to the computer. Each object is capable of receiving messages, processing data, and sending messages to other objects.

Object-oriented programming is claimed to give more flexibility, easing changes to programs, and is highly suitable for large scale software engineering.

Furthermore, proponents of OOP claim that OOP is easier to learn for those new to computer programming than previous approaches, and that the OOP approach is often simpler to develop and to maintain, lending itself to more direct analysis, coding, and understanding of complex situations and procedures than other programming methods.

(b) Define the terms *Object* and *Class*. Give an example of each. [5]

The fundamental idea behind object-oriented languages is to combine both data and the functions that operate on that data into a single unit called ***an object***. An object's functions, called member functions in C++ typically provide the only way to access its data. If you want to read a data item in an object, you call only way to access its data.

Thinking in terms of object, rather than functions has a surprisingly helpful effect on how easily programs can be designed. This results from the close match between objects in the programming sense and objects in the real world. Below are some examples :

Physical objects

Automobiles in a traffic-flow simulation

Electrical components in a circuit-design program

Countries in an economics model

Aircraft in an-traffic-control system

Elements of the computer-user environment

The mouse and the keyboard

Windows

Menus

Graphics object (lines, rectangles, circles)

In OOP we say that objects are members of classes. Almost all computer languages have built-in data types. For instance a data type int. Meaning integer, is predefined in C++ . You can declare as many variables of types int as you need in your program:

int marks;

int no_of_assignments;

int no_of_papers;

In a similar way you can make objects of the same class, as shown in the following figure.

A Class and Its Objects

Sales Department

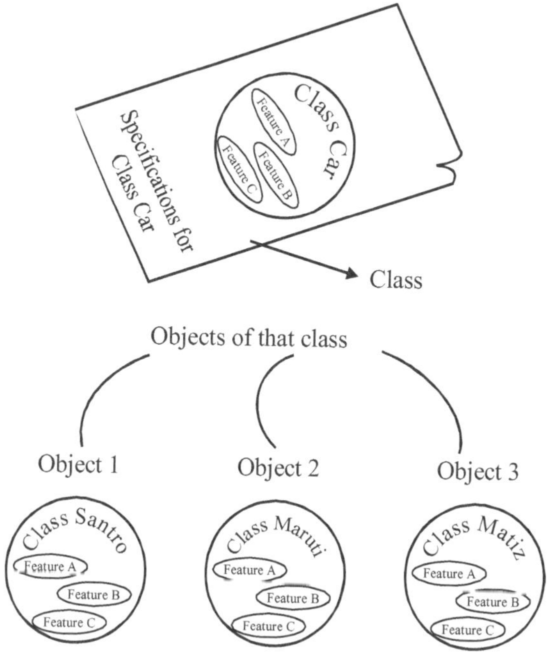

A class serves as a plan, or template. It specifies what data and what functions will be included in object of that class. Defining the class doesn't create any abject, just as the mere existence of a type int doesn't create any variables. A class is thus a collection of similar objects. This fits our nontechnical understanding of the class of mountaineers. There is no one person called "mountaineers" but specific people with specific names are members of this class if they posses certain characteristics.

(c) Define a class *employee*. The class should consist of member variables and the names of member functions. There is no need to specify the body of member functions. Make necessary assumptions. [5]

```
#include<iostream.h>
#include<conio.h>
#include<string.h>
class employee
{
protected:
```

```
int no;
char name[15];
char deptname[25];
char desig[25];
public:
void getdata()
{
cout<<"Enter No:";
cin>>no;
cout<<"\nEnter Name:";
cin>>name;
cout<<"\nEnter Department name:";
cin>>deptname;
}
void putdata()
{
cout<<"No="<<no;
cout<<"\nName="<<name<< "\n";
cout<<"Dept Name="<<deptname<<"\n";
}
};
class Fulltimeemp:public employee
{
protected:
float salary;
public:
void getdata()
{
employee::getdata();
cout<<"\nEnter salary:";
cin>>salary;
}
void putdata(void)
{
employee::putdata();
cout<<"Salary ="<<salary<<"\n";
}
};
class parttime:public employee
{
```

```
protected:
float salary;
public:
void getdata()
{
employee::getdata();
cout<<"\nEnter fees:";
cin>>salary;
}
void putdata(void)
{
employee::putdata();
cout<<"Salary ="<<salary<<"\n";
}
};
int main()
{
int ch,i=0,j=0,n,k;
do
{
clrscr();
cout<<"1.FullTimeEmployee\n";
cout<<"2.PartTimeEmployee\n";
cout<<"3.Exit\n";
cout<<"Enter choice(1/2/3):";
cin>>ch;
switch(ch)
{
case 1: Fulltimeemp ob1[10];
ob1[i++].getdata();
break;
case 2:parttime ob2[10];
ob2[j++].getdata();
break;
case 3:if(i!=0||j!=0)
{
n= i;
int k=0;
```

```
for(;k<n;k++)
ob1[k].putdata();
n=j;
k=0;
for(;k<n;k++)
ob2[k].putdata();
getch();
}
}
}while(ch!=3);
return 0;
}
```

(d) Define Multiple Inheritance. Give an example of it. State two problems related to the implementation of multiple inheritance. [5]

Multiple Inheritance : Multiple inheritance, as the name suggests, is deriving a class from more than one class. The derived class inherits all the properties of all its base classes. Consider the following example:

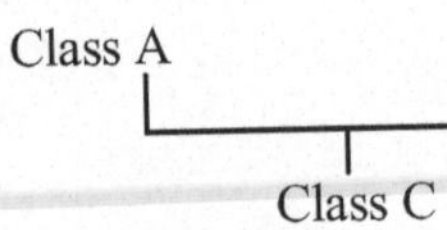

Multiple Inheritance

```
class Aclass
{
:
:
};

class  Bclass
{
:
:
};

class Cclass : public Aclass, public Bclass
{

private :
:
:
```

```
public :

Cclass(...) : Aclass (...), Bclass(...)
{
};
};
```

The class Cclass in the above example is derived from two classes - Aclass and Bclass - therefore the first line of its class definition contains the name of two classes, both publicly inherited. Like with normal inheritance, constructors have to be defined for initializing the data members of all classes. The constructor in Cclass calls constructors for base classes. The constructor calls are separated by commas.

Problems With Multiple Inheritance

The following example presents a problem with multiple inheritance.

```
class Aclass
{
public :
void put()
{
:
}
};


class  Bclass
{
public :
void put()
{
:
}
};

class Cclass : public Aclass , public Bclass
{
public :
:
:

};
```

```
void main()
{
A objA;
B objB;
C objC;

objA.put();                    // From Class A
objB.put();                    // From class Bs
objC.put();                    //AMBIGUOUS -RESULTS IN ERROR
}
```

The above example has a class C derived from two classes A and B. Both these classes have a function with the same name - put(), which assume, the derived class does not have. The class C inherits the put() function from both the classes. When a call to this function is made using the object of the derived class, the compiler does not know which class it is referring to. In this case, the scope resolution operator has to be used to specify the correct object. Its usage is very simple. The statement giving an error from the above example has to be replaced with the following:

```
objC.A::put();    // for class A
objC.B::put();    // for class B
```

Multiple inheritance with a common base (Hybrid Inheritance)

Inheritance is an important and powerful feature of OOP. Only the imagination of the person concerned is the limit. There are many combinations in which inheritance can be put to use. For instance, inheriting a class from two different classes, which in turn have been derived from the same base class .

Hybrid Inheritance

```
class base
{
:
:
};

class  Aclass : public base
{
:
:
};

class  Bclass : public base
{
```

```
:
:
};

class derived : public Aclass, public Bclass
{
:
:
};
```

Aclass and Bclass are two classes derived from the same base class. The class derived has a common ancestor - class base. This is multiple inheritance with a common base class. However, this type of inheritance is not all that simple. One potential problem here is that both, Aclass and Bclass, are derived from base and therefore both of them, contain a copy of the data members of base class. The class derived is derived from these two classes. That means it contains two copies of base class members - one from Aclass and the other from Bclass. This gives rise to ambiguity between the base data members. Another problem is that declaring an object of class derived will invoke the base class constructor twice. The solution to this problem is provided by virtual base classes.

Virtual Base Classes :- This ambiguity can be resolved if the class derived contains only one copy of the class base. This can be done by making the base class a virtual class. This keyword makes the two classes share a single copy of their base class. It can be done as follows :

```
class base
{
:
:
};

class Aclass : virtual public base
{
    :
    :
};

class Bclass : virtual public base
{
    :
    :
};
```

```
class derived : public Aclass, public Bclass
{
    :
    :
};
```

This will resolve the ambiguity involved.

(e) Write at least 5 operators of C++ that can be overloaded. Show operator overloading of any one of these operators with the help of an example. **[5]**

By overloading operators we can give additional meaning to operators like +, *, -, <=, >=, etc. which by default are supposed to work only on standard data types like *ints, floats* etc.

Here is the program which implements complex number addition and multiplication using overloaded operators rather than through member functions like *add_complex()* and *mul_complex()*.

```
#include <iostream.h>
class complex
{
        private
            float real, imag ;
        public :
            complex()
            {
            }

           complex (float r, float i)
           {
                 real = r ;
                 imag = i ;
           }
           void getdata()
           }
                 float r, i;
                 cout << endI << "Enter real and imaginary that" ;

                 cin >> r >> i ;
                 real = r ;
                 imag = i ;
           }

           void setdata (float r, float)
           {
```

```
        real = r ;
        imag = i ;
    }
    void displaydata( )
    {
        cout << endI << "real=" << real ;
        cout << endI << "imaginary=" << imag ;
    }
    complex operator + (complex c)
    {
        complex t ;
        t.real = detail on this real
        t.imag = imag + c.imag ;
    }
    complex operator * (complex c)
    {
        complex t ;

        t.real = real * c.real - image * c.image ;
                t.imag = real * c.imag + c.real * image ;
        }
    };
    void main( )
    {
        complex c1, c2 (1.5, -2.5), c3, c4 ;
        c1. setdata (2.0, 2.0) ;
        c3. displaydata( ) ;

        c4.getdata( ) ;
        complex c5 (2.5, 3.0), c6 ;
        c6. c4 * c5 ;
        c6.displaydata( ) ;
    }
```

Let us examine the call and the definition of the overloaded '+' operator more closely.

```
\\definition
complex operator + (complex c)
{
```

```
        complex t ;
        t.real = real +c.real ;
        t.imag = imag + c.imag ;
        return t ;
}
```

// call
c3 = c1 + c2

When the *operator +( )* function is called, the object *c2* is passed to it and is collected in the object c. As against this, the object *c1* gets passed to it automatically. This becomes possible because the statement *c3 = c1 + c2* is internally treated by the compiler as

c3 = c1. operator + (c2) ;

That should give you an idea why the first operand in case of a overloaded binary operator function becomes available automatically, whereas, the second operand needs to be passed explicitly.

It the definition of the overloaded + operator function when we use the statement
st.real = real + c.real ;

real refers to the one that belongs to the object using which the operator function has been called.

(f) Given the following instances, which C++ construct would you use to ensure that it happens, and why ?
(i) A member function does not alter the contents of a class and its parameters.
(ii) A member function returns a pointer to itself. **[5]**

(i) The member function should be defined followed by keyword const to avoid it changing contents of class.
To avoid changing of parameters, the parameters must be preceded by keyword const.

```
eg.     class   sample
                {
                    private:
                            int data;
                    public:
                            :
                            :
                    void add (sample const s, sample const t) const
```

```
                {
                data = s.data + t.data ;
                }
        }
```

(ii) Member function returns pointer to itself when it returns its own name.
e.g

```
int (*)   add (sample S, sample t)
          (
              :
              :
     return add;
             }
```

Q2(a). Define the terms Loading and Linking. Give an example of each. **[2]**

Loading :- is the process of placing a program from hard disk to RAM for a process to begin. This is done at start of the process.

Linking :- is the process of accessing a program or chunk of it from disk in between a process. This is done while a process is in continuation.

Taking example of Java Language, during the loading process, the virtual machine must parse the stream of binary data that represents the type and build internal data structures. At this point, certain checks will have to be done just to ensure the initial act of parsing the binary data won't crash the virtual machine. During this parsing, implementations will likely check the binary data to make sure it has the expected overall format. Parsers of the Java class file format might check the magic number, make sure each component is in the right place and of the proper length, verify that the file isn't too short or too long, and so on. Although these checks take place during loading, before the official verification phase of linking, they are still logically part of the verification phase. The entire process of detecting any kind of problem with loaded types is placed under the category of verification.

Another check that likely occurs during loading is making sure that every class except Object has a superclass. This may be done during loading because when the virtual machine loads a class, it must also make sure all of the class's superclasses are loaded also. The only way a virtual machine can know the name of a given class's superclass is by peering into the binary data for the class. Since the virtual machine is looking at every class's superclass data during loading anyway, it may as well make this check during the loading phase.

Another check—one that likely occurs after the official verification phase in most implementations—is the verification of symbolic references. The process of dynamic linking involves locating classes, interfaces, fields, and methods referred to by symbolic references stored in the constant pool, and replacing the symbolic references with direct references. When the virtual machine searches for a symbolically referenced entity (type, field, or method), it must first make sure the entity exists. If the virtual machine finds that the entity exists, it must further check that the referencing type has permission to access the entity, given the entity's access permissions. These checks for existence and access permission are logically a part of verification, the first phase of linking, but most likely happen during resolution, the third phase of linking. Resolution itself can be delayed until each symbolic reference is first used by the program, so these checks may even take place after initialization.

(b) Can any two matrices be multiplied? Give reasons for your answer. Further, write a program in C++ for the multiplication of two matrices. Apply the concept of operator overloading for this. Define necessary classes, member functions and the main () function. [8]

We can only multiply two **matrices** iff the number of **columns** in first matrix is equal to the number of rows in second matrix.

$$\begin{bmatrix} \underbrace{a_1 a_2 a_3 a_4}_{\text{no. of columns} = 4} \end{bmatrix} \quad \begin{bmatrix} \left.\begin{matrix} b_1 \\ b_2 \\ b_3 \\ b_4 \end{matrix}\right\} \text{no. of rows} = 4 \end{bmatrix} \quad a_1{*}b_1{+}a_2{*}b_2{+}a_3{*}b_3{+}a_4{*}b_4$$

```
#include<conio.h>
#include<stdio.h>
#include<iostream.h>
#include<iomanip.h>
class matrix
{
private:
int maxrow,maxcol;
int *ptr;
public:

matrix(int r, int c)
{
maxrow=r;
maxcol=c;
ptr=new int[r *c];
}
```

```
void getmat()
{
int i,j,mat_off,temp;
cout<<endl<<"Enter Elements matrix : "<<endl;
for(i=0;i<maxrow;i++)
{
for(j=0;j<maxcol;j++)
{
mat_off=i*maxcol+j;
cin>>ptr[mat_off];
}
}
}
void printmat()
{
int i,j,mat_off;
for(i=0;i<maxrow;i++)
{
cout<<endl;
for(j=0;j<maxcol;j++)
{
mat_off=i*maxcol+j;
cout<<setw(3)<<ptr[mat_off];
}
}
}

matrix operator * (matrix b)
{
matrix c(b.maxcol,maxrow);
int i,j,k,mat_off1,mat_off2,mat_off3;

for(i=0;i<c.maxrow;i++)
{
for(j=0;j<c.maxcol;j++)
{
mat_off3=i*c.maxcol+j;
c.ptr[mat_off3]=0;
for(k=0;k<b.maxrow;k++)
{
mat_off2=k*b.maxcol+j;
```

```
mat_off1=i*maxcol+k;
c.ptr[mat_off3]+=ptr[mat_off1]*b.ptr[mat_off2];
}
}
}
return(c);
}};

void main()
{
int rowa,cola,rowb,colb;

cout<<endl<<"Enter dimensions of A";
cin>>rowa>>cola;
matrix a(rowa,cola);
a.getmat();
cout<<endl<<"Enter dimensions of matrix B";
cin>>rowb>>colb;
matrix b(rowb,colb);
b.getmat();

matrix d(rowa,colb);
d=a*b;
cout<<endl<<"The product of two matrices = ";
d.printmat(); } }
```

Q3(a). Draw a comparative chart with respect to any 5 features of an Object Oriented Programming language for C++ and Java. [5]

C++	JAVA
1) Pointers are used extensively.	1) Pointers are not used to avoid security breach.
2) Package concept is not present.	2) Packages are used intensively.
3) Virtual functions are present.	3) No Virtual functions as pointer concept is not present.
4) Its not necessary that program name be same as classname in it.	4) It is necessary that program name be same as class name in it.
5) It is not platform independent.	5) It is platform independent.

(b) What is meant by Type conversion ? Explain implicit and explicit type conversions, with an example of each. [5]

Type conversion is converting data of one type to another type. E.g. 'float' to 'double', 'int' to 'long.

It is normally done to accommodate data to higher type.

Implicit type conversion.

where data type are automatically converted to higher data types

```
Eg      int     a=5 ; float     b = 10 ;
                float c ;
                C = a * b;
                    ▼   ▼
                int * float——►float
```

integer multiplied by float then int is automatically converted to float type.

Explicit type conversion

We can **convert** any data type to other data type.

This is also called type **casting.**

```
Fg    int     a = 5, b = 10 ;
      float C ;

      C = a / float (b);

        ▼   ▼
      Int / float ——►float
```

Here after explicit conversion by statement float (b). Implicit conversion of int/float = float takes places where 'int' is promoted to float & then division takes place.

Q4(a). Write a program in C++ for binary search. **[4]**

```
#include<iostream.h>
#include<conio.h>
void main()
{
int arr[50],n,mid,beg=0,end,i,j,temp,data;
clrscr();
cout<<"Enter the no: of elements:";
cin>>n;

end=n-1;

cout<<"Enter the elements:";
for(i=0;i<n;i++)
cin>>arr[i];

cout<<"Enter data to be searched:" ;
cin>>data;
```

```
for(i=0;i<n-1;i++)
for(j=0;j<n-1-i;j++)
if(arr[j]>arr[j+1])
{temp=arr[j];
 arr[j]=arr[j+1];
 arr[j+1]=temp;
}
mid=(beg+end)/2;

while(arr[mid]!=data)
{
if(data>arr[mid])
beg=mid+1;
else
if(data<arr[mid])
end=mid-1;

if(beg==end)
break;

mid=(beg+end)/2;
}

if(arr[mid]==data)
cout<<"The no: is present";
else
cout<<"The no: is not present";

getch();

}
```

(b) Describe the three ways to inherit a class in C++, with the help of a diagram. **[6]**

Private derivation :- If no specific derivation is listed, then a private derivation is assumed. If a new class is derived privately from its parent class, then :

➢ The private members inherited from its base class are inaccessible to new member functions in the derived class. This means that the creator of the base class has absolute control over the accessibility of these members, and there is no way that you can override this.

➢ The public members inherited from the base class have private access privilege. In other words, they are treated as though they were declared as new private members of the derived class, so that new member functions can access them. However, if another private derivation occurs from this derived class, then these members are inaccessible to new member functions.

Public derivation :- Public derivations are much more common than private derivations. In this situation:

- The private members inherited from the base class are inaccessible to new member functions in the derived class.
- The public members inherited from the base class may be accessed by new member functions in the derived class and by instances of the derived class.

Protected Derivation :- In addition to doing private and public derivations, you may also do a protected derivation. In this situation :

- The private members inherited from the base class are inaccessible to new member functions in the derived class. (this is exactly same as if a private or public derivation has occurred.)
- The protected members inherited from the base class have protected access privilege.
- The public members inherited from the base class have protected access.

Thus, the only difference between a public and a protected derivation is how the public members of the parent class are inherited. It is unlikely that you will ever have occasion to do this type of derivation.

Figure : Depicts these accesses.

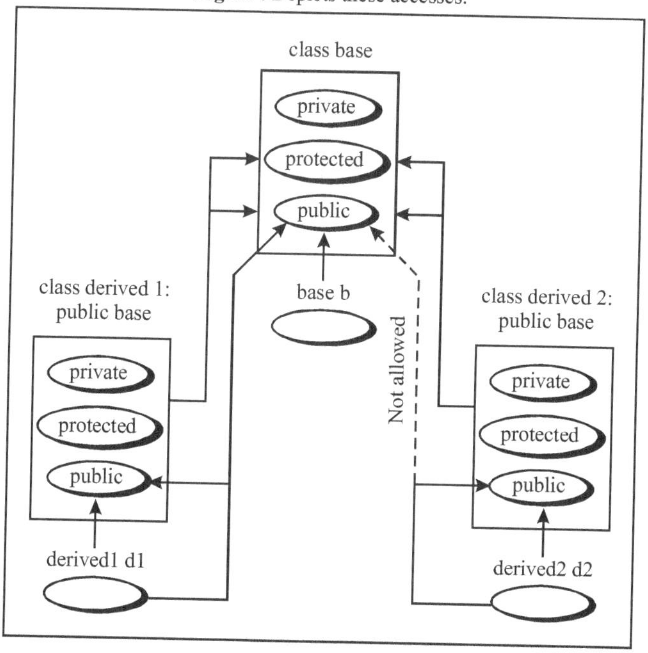

Q5(a). Define the term *Template*. Write at least two advantages of templates. **[3]**

Templates are a mechanism that make it possible to use one function or class to handle many different data types. By using templates, we can design a single class/function that operates on data of many types, instead of having to create a separate class/function for each type. When used with functions they are known as *function templates,* whereas when used with classes they are called *class templates*, We would first look at function templates and then go on to class templates.

Two advantage of Templates

1) Rewriting the program body (function class) for different types is a resided.
2) Program consumes less disk space.

(b) Write a program in C++ for the concatenation of two strings. **[7]**

```
# include<string.h>
# include<iostream.h>
class string
{
char *p;
int len;
public :
string( ) {len = 0; p = 0 ;}                    ///create null string
string ( const char * s) ;                      /// create string from array s
string (const string & s) ;                     ///copy constructor
~string ( ) {delete p ;}                        /// destructor
friend string operator + (const string & s, const string & t);
friend int operator <= (const string & s, const string & t);
friend void show (const string s) ;
string &operator=(string &c)
{strcpy(p,c.p);
return *this; }
};

string :: string (const char * s)
{
len = strlen (s);
p = new char [len + 1];
strcpy (p,s);
}
string :: string (const string & s)
{
```

```
len = s.len;
p = new char[len + 1];
strcpy (p, s.p);
{
//................OVERLOADING + operator ..............................
string operator + (const string & s, const string & t)
{
string temp;
temp.len = s.len + t.len;
temp.p = new char [temp . len + 1];
strcpy (temp.p, s.p);
strcat (temp.p, t.p);
return (temp);
}
//..................OVERLOADING <=  operator ............................
Int operator <= (const string & s, const string & t)
{
int m = strlen (s . p);
int n = strlen (t.p);
if (m <= n) return (1);
else return (0);
}
void show (const string s)
{
cout << s.p;
}
main ( )
{
string s1 = "New";
string s2 = "York";
string s3 = "Delhi"
string t1, t2, t3, t4;

t1 = s1;
t2 = s2;
t3 = s1+s2;
t4 = s1 + s3 ;

cout << "\nt1 = "; show (t1);
cout << "\nt2 = "; show (t2);
cout << "\n";
```

```
cout << "\nt3 = "; show (t3);
cout << "\nt4 = "; show (t4);
cout << "\n\n";
if (t3 < = t4)
{
show (t3);
cout << " smaller than";
show (t4);
cout << "\n";
}
else
{
show (t4);
cout << "smaller than";
show (t3) ;
cout << "\n";
}
}
/////////////////////////////////////////////// < PROGRAM >//////////////////////////////////////////
```

The following is the output of Program

t1 = New
t2 = York
t3 = New York
t4 = New Delhi
New York smaller than New Delhi.

CS-72 : C++ AND OBJECT ORIENTED PROGRAMMING
DEC-2005

Note: Question number 1 is compulsory. Attempt any three questions from the rest.

1(a). What is dynamism in the context of the object-oriented programming paradigm ? What are the different types of dynamism existing in the object-oriented programming paradigm? Explain each type with the help of an example **[6]**

The basic idea of dynamism is to move the burden of decision-making regarding resources allocation and code properties from compile time and link time to run time. The underlying philosophy is to allow the control of resources indirectly rather than putting constraints on their actions by the demand of the computer language and the requirements of the complier and linker. In other words, freeing the world of users from the programming environments.

There are three kinds of dynamism for object-oriented design these are:

1) Dynamic typing: that is, to determine the class of an object at run time.
2) Dynamic binding: That is, the decision object involving a function in response to a call is moved to run time.
3) Dynamic loading: that is, adding new components to a program as it is getting executed.

1) Dynamic Typing: Dynamic typing is the basis of dynamic binding. It allows associations between object to be determined at run time, rather than fixing them to be encoded in state compile time.
For example, a message could pass an object as an argument without declaring exactly the type/class of that object. The message receiver may then send a message to the object again without ascertaining the class of the object. Because the receiver uses the object to do some of its own work, which is in sense customised by the object of indeterminate type (indeterminate in source code, but, not at run time).
2) Dynamic Binding: Dynamic binding means that delaying the decision of exactly which method to perform until the program is running Dynamic binding is not supported by all object oriented languages. It can easily be accomplished through messaging. You do not need to go through the indirection of declaring a pointer and assigning values to it. You also need not assign each alternative

procedure a different name.

Dynamic binding is possible even if dynamic typing does not exist in a programming language but it is not very useful. For e.g., the benefits of waiting until run time to match a method to a message when the class of the receiver is already fixed and known to the compiler are very little. The compiler could just as well find the method itself; such results well not be different from run time binding results. However, in case of the type/ class of the receiver is dynamic, the compiler cannot, determine which method to invoke. The method can be bound only after the class of the receiver is bounded at run time. Thus, Dynamic typing, entails dynamic binding.

Dynamic typing opens the possibility that a message might have a very different results depending on the class of the receiver because the run time data may influence the outcome of a message.

Dynamic typing and binding opened the possibility of sending messages to objects that have not yet been designed. If object types need not be decided until run time, you can give more freedom to designers to design their own class and name their own data types, and still your code may send messages to their objects. All you need to decide jointly is the message, that is, the interfaces of the objects and not the data types.

3). Dynamic Loading: dynamic loading encourages modular development with an added flexibility that the entire program may not be developed before a program can be used, the program can be delivered in pieces and you can update one part of it at any time. You can also create program that groups many different tools under a single interface and load just the tools desired by the user.

One of the important benefits of dynamic loading is that it makes applications extensible.

(b). For each of the statements labeled (i), (ii), (iii), and (iv), point out the errors, if any. If there is no error in a statement, indicate its effect. **[4]**

```
Class base

{
        int i;
        public :
                void set_i (int num){i=num;}
                int get_i ( ) {return i;}
```

```
Class derived : public base
{
        int j;
        public :
                void set_j (int num) {j=num;}
                int get_j ( ) {return j; }
}
void main ( )
{
        base *bp;
        derived d;
bp = &d;
bp → set_i (10);                        (i)
bp → set_j (20)                         (ii)
cout << bp → get_i{ };                  (iii)
cout << bp → get_j{ };                  (iv)
}
class base
{
int i;
public:
void set_i(int num)
{
i=num;
}
int get_i()
{
return i;
}
}

class derived:public base
{
int j;
public : void set_j(int num)
{
j=num;
}
int get_j()
{
return j;
```

```
}
}
void main()
{
base *bp;
derived d;
bp=&d;
bp->set_i(10);
bp->set_j(20);  \\wrong
cout << bp->get_i();
cout << bp->get_j();      \\wrong
}
```

In function main, we create a pointer that point to objects of class base (bp). Then we assign references to d to this pointer, and because this is object of class derived from base, both are valid assignations.
The only limitation in using *bp instead of d is that bp is of type base* and therefore we can only use this pointer to refer to the members that derived inherits from base. For that reason when we call the get_j() and set_j() members at the end of the program we have to use directly the object d instead of the pointer bp.

In order to use get_j() and set_j() with the pointer to class base, this member should also have been declared in the class base, and not only in its derived classes, therefore we cannot implement it in the base class. This is when virtual members become handy:

(c). What is inheritance ? What are its advantages? Explain any two types of inheritance with the help of an exemplar diagram. [5]

Refer to Dec-04, Q.No-1(c), Page No.275

(d). What is UML? What are the benefits of UML for system designers? List types of UML diagrams. [5]

The Unified Modeling Language (UML) is a language for specifying, visualizing, constructing, and documenting the artifacts of software systems, as well as for business modeling and other non-software systems the UML represents a collection of best engineering practices that have proven successful in the modeling of large and compiler system.

Benefits of UML are as follows:

1) Provide users with a ready-to-use expensive visual modeling language so that they can develop and exchange meaningful models

2) Provide extensibility and specialisation mechanisms to extend the user concepts.
3) Be independent of particular programming languages and development processes.
4) Provide a formal basis for understanding the modeling language.
5) Encourage the growth of the OO tools markets.
6) Support higher-level development concepts such as collaborations, frameworks, patterns and components.
7) Integrate best practices

The UML define various types of diagrams

1) Use case Diagrams: Use cases are used in almost every project they are helpful in exposing requirements and planning the project.
2) Class diagrams: Class diagrams are widely used to describe the types of objects in a system and their relationships class diagrams model class structure and contents using design elements such as classes, packages and objects. They describe three different perspectives when designing a system, conceptual, specification, and implementation. These perspectives become evident as the diagram is created and help solidify the design.
3) Interaction Diagrams: Interaction diagrams model the behaviour of use cases by describing the way groups of objects interact to complete the task. They are used when you want to model the behaviour of several objects in a use case. They demonstrate now the objects collaborate for the behaviours.
4) State Diagrams: State diagrams are used to describe the behaviour of a system in the state and response of a class. They describe the behaviour of a class in response to external stimuli. State diagrams describe all the possible states of an object as events occur. Each diagram usually represents objects of a single class and tracks the different states of its objects through the system.

(e) Design a template class that is used to create a doubly linked list of integers or floats. Implement 'insert' and 'delete' operations along with the printing of elements. Also, check whether the linked list is null or not. **[10]**

Refer to June-04, Q.No-1(b), Page No.138

2. Design and implement a class 'string' using an array, with a maximum size of 20 characters. The class should contain the necessary constructors, destructor, overloaded assignment operator and a friend function for concatenation of two strings. Make suitable assumptions if required. Also write main ( ) for the above. **[10]**

Refer to Chapter-3, Q.No-.8, Page No-41

3(a). What is the need of a virtual functions ? Describe this with the help of a suitable example using C++. What is a pure virtual function? [6]

Refer to Chapter-6, Page No-86

(b). What is an inline function? In which situations would you make a function inline? Give two example of inline functions [4]

Refer to Chapter-4, Page No-58

4. Design and implement a class 'stack' using pointers. The class should include necessary constructors and destructor and the functions for addition and deletion of elements. It should also check whether a stack is full or empty. Make any assumption, if required. [10]

Refer to June-03, Q.No-3, Page No-186

5. Define the following terms, with an example of each? [10]

(a) Scope resolution operator

Refer to Dec-03, Q.No-6(iv), Page No-171

(b) Macros

Refer to Dec-03, Q.No-6(i), Page No-171

(c) 'this' pointer

Refer to Dec-03, Q.No-6(ii), Page No-171

(d) iostreams

Refer to June-04, Q.No-5(b), Page No-151

CS-72 : C++ AND OBJECT ORIENTED PROGRAMMING
JUNE-2006

Note: Question number 1 is compulsory. Attempt any three questions from the rest.

1(a). Explain the concepts of encapsulation and information hiding in an object oriented paradigm, with the help of an example in C++. [5]

In computer science, the principle of information hiding is the hiding of design decisions in a computer program that are most likely to change, thus protecting other parts of the program from change if the design decision is changed. Protecting a design decision involves providing a stable interface which shields the remainder of the program from the implementation (the details that are most likely to change). In modern programming languages, the principle of information hiding manifests itself in a number of ways, including encapsulation (given the separation of concerns) and polymorphism.

The term encapsulation is often used interchangeably with information hiding, while some make distinctions between the two.

Information hiding serves as an effective criterion for dividing any piece of equipment, software or hardware, into modules of functionality. For instance a car is a complex piece of equipment. In order to make the design, manufacturing, and maintenance of a car reasonable, the complex piece of equipment is divided into modules with particular interfaces hiding design decisions. By designing a car in this fashion, a car manufacturer can also offer various options while still having a vehicle which is economical to manufacture. For instance, a car manufacturer may have a luxury version of the car as well as a standard version. The luxury version comes with a more powerful engine than the standard version. The engineers designing the two different car engines, one for the luxury version and one for the standard version, provide the same interface for both engines. Both engines fit into the engine bay of the car which is the same between both versions. Both engines fit the same transmission, the same engine mounts, and the same controls. The differences in the engines are that the more powerful luxury version has a larger displacement with a fuel injection system that is programmed to provide the fuel air mixture that the larger displacement engine requires.

With all of these changes, most of the car is the same between the standard version and the luxury version. The engineers design the car by dividing the task up into pieces of work which are assigned to teams. Each team then designs their component to a particular standard or interface which allows the sub-team flexibility in the design of the component while at the same time ensuring that all of the components will fit together. As can be seen by this example, information hiding provides flexibility. This flexibility allows a programmer to modify functionality of a computer program during normal evolution as the computer program is changed to better fit the needs of users. When a computer program is well designed decomposing the source code solution into modules using the principle of information hiding, evolutionary changes are much easier because the changes typically are local rather than global changes.

C++ supports the properties of encapsulation and information hiding through the creation of classes. A class implements encapsulation by forming object of it. That object can call public member functions or public data of class using dot (.) operator.

Information hiding is advised using keyword private which doesn't let data to be accessible by object of the class.

e.g.

```
class A {
int p;
float f;
public: void getdata()
{
cin>>p >>f ;
}
};
void main()
{
A a1;
a1.getdata();       //accessible
a1.p=2; //error (hidden)
a1.f=3.2;           //error (hidden)
}
```

Here, a1 (object) is an encapsulated unit, containing attributes and functionality together.

(b). Explain 'dynamic binding', with the help of an example. Give its advantages and disadvantages. **[5]**

When designing a system it is often the case that developers:

1.know what class interface they want, without precisely knowing the most suitable representation.

2. know what algorithms they want, without knowing how particular operations should be implemented.

In both cases, it is often desirable to delay certain decisions as long as possible Dynamic binding provides a dynamic place-holder i.e. defer certain decisions until run-time without disrupting existing code structure.

Refer to Chapter-6, Q.No-11, Page No.102

Disadvantages:

1. Dynamic binding is less powerful than pointers to functions, but more comprehensible and less error prone i.e. since the compiler performs type checking at compile time.

2. There may be some additional time and space overhead from using dynamic binding.

3. Dynamically bound objects are difficult to store in shared memory.

4. It is less efficient than static binding.

Advantages

1. Dynamic binding facilitates more flexible and extensible software architectures e.g.

a). Not all design decisions need to be known during the initial stages of system development, they may be postponed until run time.

b). Complete source code is not required to extend the system i.e. only headers and object code.

2. This aids both flexibility and extensibility

a). Flexibility – easily recombine existing components into new configurations.

b). extensibility- easily adds new components.

(c). Differentiate between function and operator overloading. Also give one example each. **[5]**

Function overloading is the practice of declaring the same function with different signatures. The same function name will be used with different number of parameters and parameters of different type. But overloading of functions with different return types is not allowed.

```
#include<iostream.h>
//prototype declaration for overloading function volume()
int volume(int);
double volume(double, int);
long volume(long,int,int);

void main()
{
cout<<volume(10) <<endl;
cout<<volume(2.5,8) <<endl;
```

```
cout<<volume(100L,75,15) <<endl;
}

int volume(int s) //cube
{
return(s*s*s);
}
double volume(double r,int h)      //cylinder
{
return(3.14519*r*r*h)
}
long volume(long l,int b,int h)//rectangular box
{
return(l*b*h)
}
```

The output is:
1000
157.2595
112500

Operator Overloading

Operator overloading is extremely powerful and useful feature of Object Oriented programming

In C++, you can overload any of the built-in operators, such as + or * to suit particular applications.

example:

Imagine that you're running a restaurant and you want to write a program to handle your billing, print your menus, and so on. We create a MenuItem class:

```
class MenuItem
{
private:
float price;
char name[ 40 ];

public:
MenuItem::MenuItem( float itemPrice, char *itemName );
float MenuItem::GetPrice( void );
};
```

Your program could define a MenuItem object for each item on the menu. When someone orders, you'd calculate the bill by adding together the price of each MenuItem like this:

```
MenuItem chicken( 8.99, "Chicken Jalfrezi" );
MenuItem wine( 2.99, "Rioja" );

float total;

total = chicken->GetPrice() + wine->GetPrice();
```

This particular diner had the chicken and a glass of wine. The total is calculated using the member function GetPrice().

Operator overloading provides an alternative way of totaling up the bill.

```
total = chicken + wine;
```

by adding the price of chicken to the price of wine.

Note: Currently, the compiler would complain if you tried to use a nonintegral type with the + operator.

In C++, You can "reprogram" this operation by giving the + operator a new meaning. To do this, we need to create a function to overload the + operator:

```
float operator+( MenuItem item1, MenuItem item2 )
{
return( item1.GetPrice() + item2.GetPrice() );
}
```

Notice the name of this new function. Any function whose name follows the form:

operator<C++ operator>

is said to overload the specified operator. When you overload an operator, you're asking the compiler to call your function instead of interpreting the operator as it normally would.

Calling an Operator Overloading Function

When the compiler calls an overloading function, it maps the operator's operands to the function's parameters. For example, suppose the function

```
float operator+( MenuItem item1, MenuItem item2 )
{
return( item1.GetPrice() + item2.GetPrice() );
}
```

is used to overload the + operator. When the compiler encounters the expression chicken + wine it calls operator+(), passing chicken as the first parameter and wine as the second parameter. operator+()'s return value is used as the result of the expression.

It is important to note that:

The number of operands taken by an operator determines the number of parameters passed to its overloading function.

For example, a function designed to overload a unary operator takes a single parameter; a function designed to overload a binary operator takes two parameters.

(d). What are public and private inheritance? Why do we need different access specifiers? [5]

Inheritance is an important feature of classes; in fact, it is integral to the idea of object oriented programming. Inheritance allows you to create a hierarchy of classes, with various classes of more specific natures inheriting the general aspects of more generalized classes. In this way, it is possible to structure a program starting with abstract ideas that are then implemented by specific classes. For example, you might have a class Animal from which class dog and cat inherent the traits that are general to all animals; at the same time, each of those classes will have attributes specific to the animal dog or cat.

Public inheritance:

The most open level of data hiding is public. Anything that is public is available to all derived classes of a base class, and the public variables and data for each object of both the base and derived class is accessible by code outside the class. Functions marked public are generally those the class uses to give information to and take information from the outside world; they are typically the interface with the class. The rest of the class should be hidden from the user using private or protected data (This hidden nature and the highly focused nature of classes is known collectively as encapsulation).

The syntax for public is:

public:

Everything following is public until the end of the class or another data hiding keyword is used.

```
class base{
private: int number;
};
class derived :public base{
public: void f()
{
++number;     //private base member not accessible
}
};
```

The compiler error message is

'base::number ' is not accessible in the function derived::f();

Here ,only if the number is public then you can access it.

Private inheritance::

Private is the highest level of data-hiding. Not only are the functions and variables marked private not accessible by code outside the specific object in which that data appears, but private variables and functions are not inherited (in the sense that the derived class cannot directly access these variables or functions). The level of data protection afforded by protected is generally more flexible than that of the private level. On the other hand, if you do not wish derived classes to access a method, declaring it private is sensible. The syntax for private is:

private:

```
class base{
public: int number;
};
class derived :private base{
public: void f()
{
++number;     //public base member  accessible
}
};

class derived 2:private derived{
public: void g()
{
++number;     //  access to number is prohibited
}
};
```

The compiler error message is

'base::number ' is not accessible in the function derived2::g();

Since public members of a base class are inherited as private in the derived class, the function derived::f() has no problem accessing it. However, when another class is derived from the class derived, this new class inherits number but cannot access it. If derived::g()
were to call upon derived::f(),there is no problem since derived::f() is public and inherited into derived2 as private.

Ie. In derived2 we can write,

```
void g() {
f();
}
```

We need different access specifiers:

Any class can inherit from any other class, but it is not necessarily good practice to do so. Inheritance should be used when you have a more general class of objects that describes a set of objects. The features of every element of that set (of every object that is also of the more general type) should be reflected in the more general class. This class is called the base class. Base classes usually contain functions that all the classes inheriting from it, known as derived classes, will need. Base classes should also have all the variables that every derived class would otherwise contain.

Let us look at an example of how to structure a program with several classes. Take a program used to simulate the interaction between types of organisms, trees, birds, bears, and other creatures inhabiting a forest. We have base classes for the animals and the plants. Then we want classes for specific types of animals: pigeons and vultures, bears and lions, and specific types of plants: oak and pine, grass and flower.

Classes share data. A derived class has access to most of the functions and variables of the base class. There are, however, ways to keep a derived class from accessing some attributes of its base class. The keywords public, protected, and private are used to control access to information within a class. It is important to remember that public, protected, and private control information both for specific instances of classes and for classes as general data types. Variables and functions designated public are both inheritable by derived classes and accessible to outside functions and code when they are elements of a specific instance of a class. Protected variables are not accessible by functions and code outside the class, but derived classes inherit these functions and variables as part of their own class. Private variables are neither accessible outside the class when it is a specific class nor are available to derived classes

(e). Explain the utility of the friend function, using an appropriate example **[5]**

Refer to June-04, Q.No-5(d), Page No.153

(f). Write a String class in C++ which should include the member function to calculate the length of the string. **[5]**

```
#include<iostream.h>
#include<conio.h>

class Stringlt
{
char name[25];
public:
```

```
int x;
void getname()
{
cin.getline(name,25);
}
void getlength()
{
 x=0;
while(name[x]!='\0')
{
  x++;
}
}
void putlength()
{
cout<<"The length is"<<x;
}
};
void main()
{
Stringlt st;
st.getname();
st.getlength();
st.putlength();
getch();
}
```

2(a). If a base class and derived class each include a member function with the same name, which member function will be called by an object of a derived class, and why ? [3]

```
#include <iostream.h>
class base
{
public:
virtual void display()
{
  cout<<"\nBase";
}
};
class derived : public base
```

```
{
public:
void display()
{
cout<<"\nDerived";
}
};

void main()
{

base *ptr = new derived();
ptr->display();
}
```

In the above example, the pointer is of type base but it points to the derived class object. The method display() is virtual in nature. Hence in order to resolve the virtual method call, the context of the pointer is considered, i.e., the display method of the derived class is called and not that of the base. If the method was non virtual in nature, the display() method of the base class would have been called.

(b). Write a program to read and display information about employees and managers. Employee is a class that contains employee_no, name and address. Manager class contains all the information of the employee class and the list of employees working under the manager. **[5]**

```
#include<iostream.h>
class employee
{
public:
 char *name;
char *address;
int *no;
employee(char *n, char *d, int *l)
{
name=n;
address=d;
no=l;
}
vitual void print();
};
```

```
void employee::print()
{
cout<<"name:"<<name;
cout<<"address"<<address;
cout<<"emp no"<<no;
}

class manager:public employee
{
public:
short position:
manager(char *n ,char *d int *l,short p):employee(n,d,l)
{
name=n;
address=d;
no=l;
position =p;
}

void print()
{
cout<<"name:"<<name;
cout<<"address"<<address;
cout<<"emp no"<<no;
cout<<"position"<<p;
}

void main()
{
employee *e("john","noida",3);
manager *m("james","delhi",2,4);
e->print();
m->print();
}
```

3(a). Define a class template. What are its advantages ? **[3]**

Refer to June-05, Q.No-5(a), Page No.270

(b) Write a template function for exchanging (swapping) the values between two variables. Use this function in main ( ) for int, double and char type of variables. **[4]**

```
#include<iostream.h>
#include<conio.h>

template <class T>
void swap(T &x ,T &y)
{
T temp=x;
x=y;
y=temp;
}

void main()
{
clrscr();
int a=2,b=4;
double c=55.2,d=999.09;
char e='f',f='k';

cout<<"values of the variables before swapping"<<endl;
cout<< "a= "<<a <<"   b= "<<b<<endl;
cout<< "c= "<<c <<"   d= "<<d<<endl;
cout<< "e= "<<e <<"   f= "<<f<<endl;

swap(a,b);
swap(c,d);
swap(e,f);

cout<<"values of the variables after swapping"<<endl;
cout<< "a= "<<a <<"   b= "<<b<<endl;
cout<< "c= "<<c <<"   d= "<<d<<endl;
cout<< "e= "<<e <<"   f= "<<f<<endl;

getch();
}
```

Output of the program is:

```
values of the variables before swapping
a= 2 b=4
c= 55.2 d=999.09
```

e= f f=k

values of the variables after swapping

a= 4 b=2

c= 999.09 d=55.2

e= k f=f

4(a). What is an interaction diagram? Explain the steps involved in drawing such a diagram, with the help of example. [5]

Interaction Diagrams

Interaction diagrams model the behavior of use cases by describing the way groups of objects interact to complete the task. The two kinds of interaction diagrams are sequence and collaboration diagrams.

When to Use: Interaction Diagrams

Interaction diagrams are used when you want to model the behavior of several objects in a use case. They demonstrate how the objects collaborate for the behavior. Interaction diagrams do not give a in depth representation of the behavior.

How to Draw: Interaction Diagrams

Sequence diagrams, collaboration diagrams, or both diagrams can be used to demonstrate the interaction of objects in a use case. Sequence diagrams generally show the sequence of events that occur. Collaboration diagrams demonstrate how objects are statically connected. Both diagrams are relatively simple to draw and contain similar elements.

Sequence diagrams:

Sequence diagrams demonstrate the behavior of objects in a use case by describing the objects and the messages they pass. The diagrams are read left to right and descending. The example below shows an object of class 1 start the behavior by sending a message to an object of class 2. Messages pass between the different objects until the object of class 1 receives the final message.

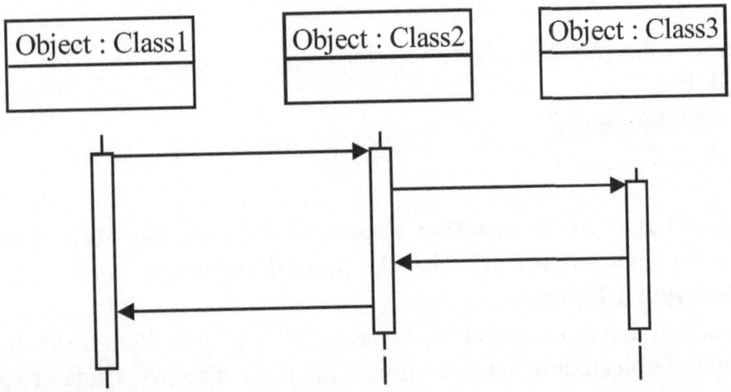

Collaboration diagrams:

Collaboration diagrams are also relatively easy to draw. They show the relationship between objects and the order of messages passed between them. The objects are listed as icons and arrows indicate the messages being passed between them. The numbers next to the messages are called sequence numbers. As the name suggests, they show the sequence of the messages as they are passed between the objects. There are many acceptable sequence numbering schemes in UML. A simple 1, 2, 3... format can be used, as the example below shows, or for more detailed and complex diagrams a 1, 1.1 ,1.2, 1.2.1... scheme can be used.

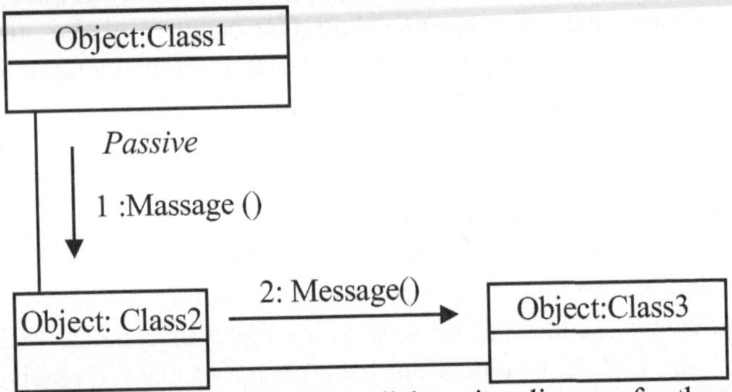

The example below shows a simple collaboration diagram for the placing an order use case. This time the names of the objects appear after the colon, such as :Order Entry Window following the objectName:className naming convention. This time the class name is shown to demonstrate that all of objects of that class will behave the same way

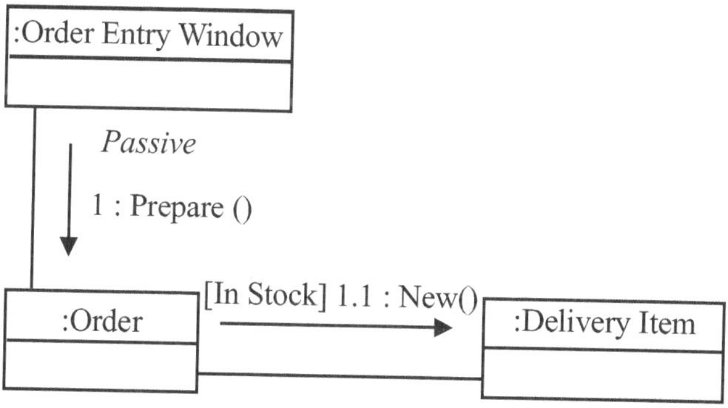

(b). Explain the concept of virtual functions. Give three examples of the use of such functions. **[5]**

In object-oriented programming (OOP), a virtual function or virtual method is a function whose behavior, by virtue of being declared "virtual", is determined by the definition of a function with the same signature furthest in the inheritance lineage of the instantiated object on which it is called. This concept is a very important part of the polymorphism portion of object-oriented programming (OOP).

The concept of the virtual function solves the following problem:

In OOP when a derived class inherits from a base class, an object of the derived class may be referred to (or cast) as either being the base class type or the derived class type. If there are base class functions overridden by the derived class, a problem then arises when a derived object has been cast as the base class type. When a derived object is referred to as being of the base's type, the desired function call behavior is ambiguous.

The distinction between virtual and not virtual is provided to solve this issue. If the function in question is designated "virtual" then the derived class's function would be called (if it exists). If it is not virtual, the base class's function would be called.

For example, a base class Animal could have a virtual function eat. Subclass Fish would implement eat() differently than subclass Wolf, but you can invoke eat() on any class instance referred to as Animal, and get the eat() behavior of the specific subclass.

This allows a programmer to process a list of objects of class Animal, telling each in turn to eat (by calling eat()), with no knowledge of what kind of animal may be in the list. You also do not need to have knowledge of how each animal eats, or what the complete set of possible animal types might be.

The following is an example in C++:

```
#include <iostream>
```

```
class Animal
{
public:
  virtual void eat() { std::cout << "I eat like a generic Animal.\n"; }
};

class Wolf : public Animal
{
public:
  void eat() { std::cout << "I eat like a wolf!\n"; }
};

class Fish : public Animal
{
public:
  void eat() { std::cout << "I eat like a fish!\n"; }
};

class OtherAnimal : public Animal
{
};

int main()
{
Animal *anAnimal[4];
anAnimal[0] = new Animal();
anAnimal[1] = new Wolf();
anAnimal[2] = new Fish();
anAnimal[3] = new OtherAnimal();

for(int i = 0; i < 4; i++)
anAnimal[i]->eat();
}
```

Output with the virtual method eat:
I eat like a generic Animal.
I eat like a wolf!
I eat like a fish!
I eat like a generic Animal.
Output without the virtual method eat:
I eat like a generic Animal.
I eat like a generic Animal.

I eat like a generic Animal.
I eat like a generic Animal.

```
class Window // Base class for C++ virtual function example
{
public:
virtual void Create() // virtual function for C++ virtual function example
{
cout <<"Base class Window"<<endl;
}
};

class CommandButton : public Window
{
public:
void Create()
{
cout<<"Derived class Command Button "<<endl;  //Overridden C++ virtual
function
}
};

void main()
{
Window *x, *y;

x = new Window();
x->Create();

y = new CommandButton();
y->Create();
}
```

The output of the above program will be,
Base class Window
Derived class Command Button

Here when we remove virtual.
The output of the above program will be,
Base class Window
Base class Window

Refer to June-04, Q.No-5(a), Page No.150

5. Explain the following with the help of an example each : [10]

(i) Static data member

Refer to June-04, Q.No-6(b), Page No.158

(ii) Object Oriented Programming

Refer to Chapter-1, Page No.1

(iii) File streams in C++

Refer to Chapter-7, Page No.115

(iv) Exception handling.

Refer to Dec-04, Q.No-5(b), Page No.290

CS-72 : C++ AND OBJECT ORIENTED PROGRAMMING
DEC-2006

Note: Question number 1 is compulsory. Attempt any three questions from the rest.

1(a). Explain any five advantages of object oriented programming. [5]

The following are the basic advantages of object-oriented programming:

1. Modular Design: The software built around OOP are modular, because they are built an objects and we know objects are entity in themselves, whose internal working is hidden from other objects and is decoupled from the rest of the program.
2. Simple approach: the objects, model real world entities, which results in simple program structure.
3. Modifiable: Because of its inherent properties of data abstraction and encapsulation, the internal working of objects is hidden from other objects thus, any modification made to them should not affect the rest of the system.
4. Extensible: The extension to the existing program for its adaptation to new environment can be done by simple adding few new objects or by adding new features in old classes/ types.
5. Reusable: Objects once made can be reused in more than one program.

(b). Explain the need of inheritance and list any three Advantages of it. [5]

Inheritance is the OOPS feature which allows derivation of the new objects from the existing ones. It allows the creation of new class, called derived class, from the existing classes called as base class the concept of inheritance allows the features of base class to be accessed by the derived class, which in turn have their new features in addition to the old base class features. The original base class is also called the parent or super class and the derived class is also called as sub-class.

Advantages of Inheritance

1. Reuse of existing code and program functionality: The programmer does not have to write and re-write the same code for logically same problems. They can derives the existing features from the existing classes and add the required characterizes to the new derived classes.

2. Less Labour intensive: The programmer do not have to rewrite the same long similar programs just because the applications to be developed has slightly different requirements.

3. Well Organised: The objects are well oganised in a way that they fellow some hierarchy.

(c). Explain the purpose of the following with the suitable example of each: [6]

(i) Use Case Diagram

Use case Diagrams describe the functionality of a system and users of a system. These diagrams contain the following items:

Actors- Which are users of system, including human beings and other system components.

Use Cases- Which includes services provided to users of the system.

An actor represents a user or another system that well interact with the system you are modeling. A use case is an external view of the system that represents some action the user might perform in order to complete a task.

Use case are used in almost every project they are helpful in exposing requirements and planning the project. During the initial stage of a project, most use cases should be defined, but as the project contains more might become visible.

Example: A user placing an order with a sales company might follow these steps:

1) Browse catalog and select items.
2) Call sales representation
3) Supply shipping information
4) Supply payment information
5) Receive confirmation number from salesperson

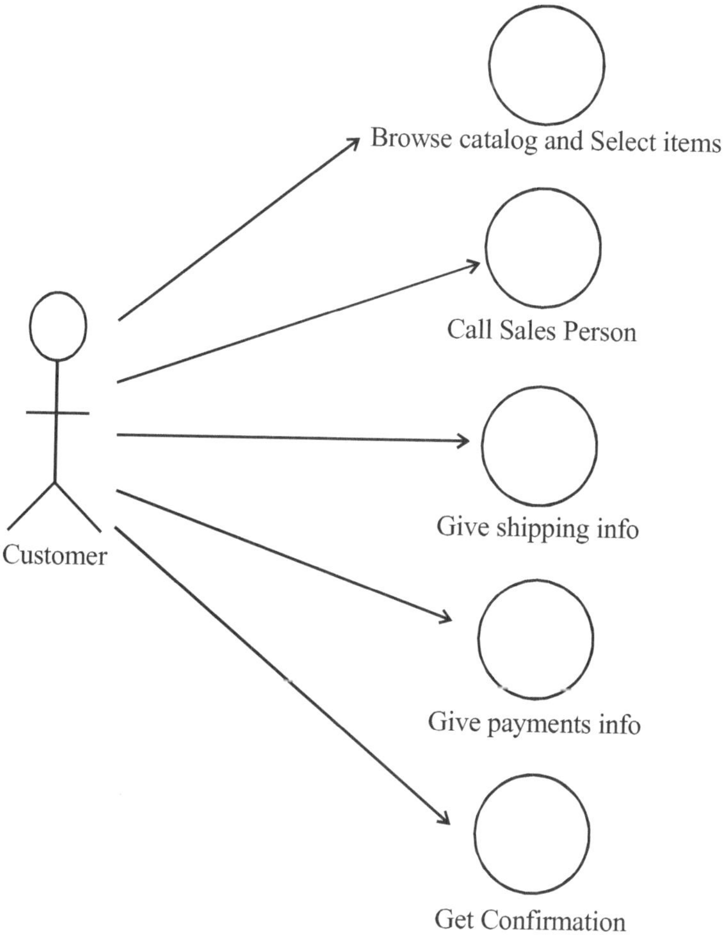

(ii) Interaction Diagram

Interaction diagram model the behaviour of use cases by describing the way groups of objects interact to complete the task. The two kinds of interaction diagrams are sequence and collaboration diagrams.

Interaction diagrams are used when you want to model the behaviour of several objects in a use case. They demonstrate how the objects collaborate for the behaviours. They do not give a in-depth representation of the behaviour. Sequence diagrams generally show the sequence of events that occur. Collaboration diagrams demonstrate have objects are statically connected.

The following example shows a simple collaboration diagram for placing an order use case.

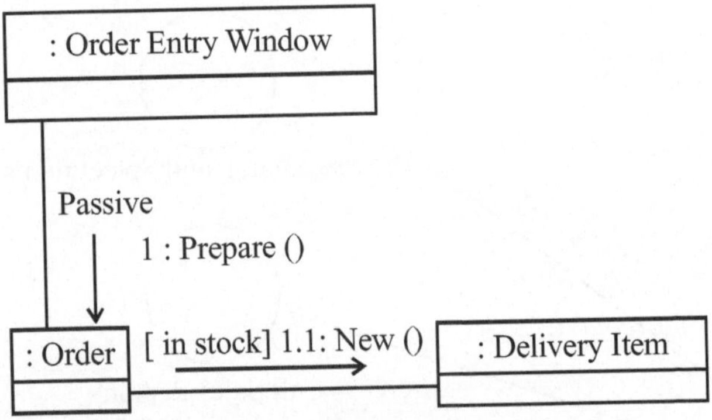

(d). Write C+ + code to create a class date. Using this class. Calculate the age of a person as on the current date. [5]

```
#include "CDate.h"
#include <cstdlib>
#include <ctype.h>
#include <sstream>
#include <cstring>
#include <ctime>
using namespace cdate;
using namespace std;

#include <iostream>

CDate::CDate()
: _formatStr(NULL)
{
 time_t ltime;
 time (&ltime);

 char today[10] = { 0 };
 strftime(today, 10, "%Y%m%d", localtime(&ltime));

 StringToDate(today, "YYYYMMDD");
}

CDate::CDate(int totalDays)
: _daycount(totalDays), _formatStr(NULL)
{
 CalcMDY();
```

```
}

CDate::CDate(const CDate &rhs)
: _daycount(rhs._daycount),
  _m(rhs._m), _d(rhs._d), _y(rhs._y),
  _formatStr(NULL)
{
}

CDate::CDate(int m, int d, int y)
: _m(m), _d(d), _y(y), _formatStr(NULL)
{
  CalcDayCount();
}

CDate::CDate(const char *date, const char *fmt)
: _formatStr(NULL)
{
  StringToDate(date, fmt);
}


CDate::~CDate() {
  if (_formatStr != NULL)
    delete [] _formatStr;
}

void CDate::StringToDate(const char *date, const char *fmt) {
  int len = strlen(fmt);

ostringstream d, m, y;

const char *mfmt = strchr(fmt, 'm');
const char *tmp = strchr(fmt, 'M');
if (mfmt == NULL || (tmp < mfmt && tmp != NULL))
mfmt = tmp;

bool moByName = mfmt != NULL;
if (moByName)
 moByName = strnicmp(mfmt, "MMM", 3) == 0;
```

```
for (int i = 0; i < len; ++i) {
switch (toupper(fmt[i])) {
case 'Y':
 y << date[i];
break;

case 'M':
m << date[i];
break;

case 'D':
d << date[i];
break;
}
}

if (!moByName)
  _m = atoi(m.str().c_str());
else {
  _m = 0;
for (int i = 0; i < 12; ++i) {
 if (!strnicmp(MONTH_NAMES[i], m.str().c_str(), m.str().length())) {
  _m = i + 1;
 break;
  }
 }
 }

  _d = atoi(d.str().c_str());
 _y = atoi(y.str().c_str());

 CalcDayCount();
 }

 const char* CDate::Format(const char *fmt, char *recvBuf) const {
 ostringstream ostr;

 ostringstream d, m, y;
 m << _m;
 d << _d;
  y << _y;
```

```
int dlen = d.str().length();
int mlen = m.str().length();
int ylen = y.str().length();
int days = 0;
int mos = 0;
int yrs = 0;

bool moByName = false;
int moNameLen = strlen(MONTH_NAMES[_m - 1]);
int moFmtLen = 0;

int i;

int len = strlen(fmt);
for (i = len - 1; i >= 0; —i) {
switch (toupper(fmt[i])) {
case 'Y':
if (yrs < ylen) {
ostr << y.str()[ylen - yrs - 1];
++yrs;
}
else
ostr << '0';
break;

case 'M':
if (!moByName && mos == 0) {
// if there at least 3 in a row, user wants the name of the month
moByName = strnicmp(fmt + i - 2, "MMM", 3) == 0;
if (moByName) {
mlen = 0;
for (int j = i; j >= 0; —j)
if (toupper(fmt[j]) == 'M')
++mlen;
else
break;

moFmtLen = mlen;
if (mlen > moNameLen)
mlen = moNameLen;
}
```

```
}

if (mos < mlen || (moByName && mos < moFmtLen)) {
if (moByName) {
if ((moFmtLen - mos - 1) >= moNameLen) {
ostr << ' ';
++mlen;
}
else {
if (fmt[i] == 'm')
ostr << static_cast<char>(tolower(MONTH_NAMES[_m - 1][mlen - mos -
1]));
else
ostr << static_cast<char>(toupper(MONTH_NAMES[_m - 1][mlen - mos -
1]));
}
}
else
ostr << m.str()[mlen - mos - 1];

++mos;
}
else {
if (moByName)
ostr << ' ';
else
ostr << '0';
}
break;

case 'D':
if (days < dlen) {
ostr << d.str()[dlen - days - 1];
++days;
}
else
ostr << '0';
break;

default:
```

```
ostr << fmt[i];
break;
}
}

ostr << ends;

int j = 0;
bool prevspace = false;
for (i = len - 1; i >= 0; —i) {
char ch = ostr.str()[i];

if (!prevspace || ch != ' ') {
recvBuf[j] = ch;
recvBuf[++j] = NULL;
}

prevspace = ch == ' ';
}

return recvBuf;
}

const char* CDate::Format(const char *fmt) {
if (_formatStr != NULL)
delete [] _formatStr;

int len = strlen(fmt);
_formatStr = new char[len + 1];
return Format(fmt, _formatStr);
}

void CDate::CalcMDY() {
_y = static_cast<int>((_daycount * 100) / ((DPY + 0.25) * 100));

bool isleapyear = (_y % 4) == 0;

int daysintoyear = _daycount - static_cast<int>((_y * ((DPY + 0.25) * 100))
/ 100);

if (isleapyear)
```

```
++daysintoyear;

_m = 1;

int days = 0;

if (daysintoyear <= 31) {
 _d = daysintoyear;
}
else {
for (unsigned i = 1; i <= 12; ++i) {
int next;

if (i == 2) {
next = isleapyear ? 29 : 28;
}
else if ((i % 2) == 1) {
if (i <= 7)
next = 31;
else
next = 30;
}
else {
if (i < 7)
next = 30;
else
next = 31;
}

 _m = i;

 if ((days + next) >= daysintoyear)
 break;

 days += next;
 }

 _d = daysintoyear - days;
 }

 if (_d == 0)
```

```
_d = 1;
}

void CDate::CalcDayCount() {
if (_y > 0)
_daycount = (DPY * _y) + static_cast<int>((_y - 1) / 4);
else
_daycount = 0;

bool isleapyear = (_y % 4) == 0;

for (unsigned i = 1; i < _m; ++i) {
if (i == 2) {
 _daycount += isleapyear ? 29 : 28;
}
else if ((i % 2) == 1) {
if (i <= 7)
 _daycount += 31;
else
_daycount += 30;
}
else {
if (i < 7)
 _daycount += 30;
else
_daycount += 31;
}
}

_daycount += _d;
}

int CDate::GetDayOfWeek() const {
int y, m, d;

if (_m < 3) {
y = _y - 1;
m = _m + 12;
d = _d;
}
else {
```

```
y = _y;
m = _m;
d = _d;
}

return (((13 * m + 3) / 5) + d + y + (y / 4) - (y / 100) + (y / 400) + 1) % 7;
}

int CDate::operator-(const CDate &rhs) const {
  return _daycount - rhs._daycount;
}

const CDate CDate::operator+(int count) const {
CDate cd = *this;
cd._daycount += count;
cd.CalcMDY();
return cd;
}

const CDate CDate::operator-(int count) const {
CDate cd = *this;
cd._daycount -= count;
cd.CalcMDY();
return cd;
}

CDate& CDate::operator+=(int count) {
_daycount += count;
CalcMDY();
return *this;
}

CDate& CDate::operator-=(int count) {
_daycount -= count;
CalcMDY();
return *this;
}

const CDate CDate::operator++(int) {
CDate cd = *this;
operator++();
```

```
return cd;
}

const CDate CDate::operator—(int) {
CDate cd = *this;
operator—();
return cd;
}

CDate& CDate::operator++() {
return operator+=(1);
}

CDate& CDate::operator—() {
return operator-=(1);
}

CDate::operator const char*() const {
static char buf[9];// 9 because DEF_FORMAT is 8 chars long
return Format(cdate::DEF_FORMAT, buf);
}
```

(e). Last the various restrictions with operator overloading. Write a C++ program to illustrate the overloading of Increment operator. [9]

In operator overloading, though the meanings are redefined, their precedence cannot be changed. At the same time a unary operator cannot be redefined as a binary operator.

The operator functions namely operator=, operator [], operator () and operator ? Must be non-static member functions. Due to this, their first operands will be values. An operator function should be either a member or take at least one class object arguments. The operators new and delete need not follow the rule. Also, an operator function which needs to accept a basic type as its first argument, cannot be a member function.

Overloading of increment operator.

Since ++ can use as postfix as well a prefix operator, we can have two different overloaded functions.

The following is a program, which uses an operator function of ++ for prefix application

```
# include < iostream .h>
class increment
```

```
{
int i, j, k;
public:
increment ()
{
i=5;
j=6;
k=7;
}
void operator ++ U
{
cout <<(++i) <<(++j) <<(++k);
}
};
void main ()
{
increment in;
++ in;
}
```

the following is an example of an operator function of ++ for postfix application

```
# include <iostream .h>
class increment
{
int i, j, k,;
public:
increment ()
{
i=5;
j=6;
k=7;
}
void operator ++ (int)
{
cout << (i++) <<(j++) <<(k++);
}
};
void main ()
{
increment in ;
 in ++;
}
```

2(a). Define the term exception handling. Write a program to raise an exception if an attempt is made to divide divide a number by zero. [6]

Refer to Dec-02, Q.No-3(a) Page No-201

(b). Give output of the following: [4]

```
{       int a = 10, b = 20, d:
         d = b+ +:
        cout <<d<<b:
         d = + + a:
        cout <<d<<a:          }
```

d=20 b=21
d=11 a=11

3(a). Explain the purpose of function overloading. Write a C+ + program that uses a function to check whether a given number is divisible by another number or not give proper comments whether the denominator number is a prime number or not. [8]

First Refer to Chapter-5, Page No-71

```
#include<iostream.h>
#include<conio.h>
void check(int,int);
void main()
{
int no1,no2;
clrscr();
cout<< "enter2 no";
cin>>no1;
cin>> no2;
check(no1,no2);
                    //to check whether no2 is prime no or not
if(no2==1 ||no2==2)
cout<<" denominator is a prime no";
for(int i=2;i<no2;i++)
{       if(no2%i == 0)
{
cout<<" \n not prime";
break;
} else
{       cout<<" denominator is a prime no";
        break;          }       }
getch();                }
```

```
void  check(int x ,int y)
{
int no1,no2;
no1=x;
no2=y;
if( no1%no2 == 0)
{
cout<<"The no is divisible";
} else   {
cout<<"The no is not divisible";
        }      }
```

(b). Explain briefly static data members. **[2]**

Refer to June-04, Q.No-6(b), Page No-158.

4(a). Define a friend function. Explain the relation of friend function with respect public, if given numbers is 121345 then the output is 1+2+3+4+5 = 15). **[5]**

Refer to Chapter-4, Page No-56

(b). Write a C + + program to find the sum of all digit in a five digit number.(For example, if given number is 12345 then the output is 1+2+3+4+5 = 15) **[5]**

```
# include < iostream.h>
# include <conio.h>
void main ()
{       int num, sum =0, var;
        cout<<"enter number",
        cin>>num;
        while (num ≥ 1)          {
                                 var =num %10;
                                 num =num/10;
                                 sum =sum +var;          }
 cout <<"the sum of digits is "<<sum;        }
```

5. Define the following with an example of each : **[10]**

(i) This pointer Refer to Dec-03, Q.No-6(ii), Page No-171

(ii) Destructor Refer to Chapter 3, Page No-23

(iii) Typecasting Refer to June -05, Q.No-3(b), Page No-266

(iv) Abstract class

Ans. An abstract class is one that is not used to create object. An abstract class is designed only to act as a base class (to be inherited by other class). It is a design concept in program development and provides a base upon which other class may be built.

(v) Parameterized Constructor Refer to Dec-04, Q.No-3(a), Page No-283

CS-72 : C++ AND OBJECT ORIENTED PROGRAMMING
June, 2007

Note : Question no. 1 is **compulsory**. Answer any **three** questions from the rest.

1. (a) Mention the difference between C and C++. Why is necessary to include header files in a program written in these languages?
Refer to Chapter-2, Page No.-12 to 16

(b) Discuss the basic data types of C++. Suggest appropriate data type for the following :
(i) Someone's height in meters
(ii) An exclamation mark
(iii) The number of students in a university
Ans. Basic data types of C++
char – to store an ASCII character and uses bits can also be used to store integer between –128 to 127.
int – to store integer and occupy 4 bytes of memory.
float – to store single precision floating point numbers and occupy 4 bytes of memory.
double – to store double precision floating point numbers and occupy 8 bytes of memory.
void – to represent generic data type.
(i) Float, **(ii)** Char, and **(iii)** Int

(c) What is the purpose of information hiding?
Ans. Refer to June-2006, Q.No.-1(a), Page No.-305

(d) Write a program which will accept a string of maximum 10 characters from the keyboard, and count the occurrences of each of the 5 vowels in the string. The output should be in tabbed format as shown below :

A E I O U
0 1 0 0 1

Ans.
```
# include <iostream.h>
#include <string.h>
void main ()
{
char str [11];
int a = 0, e = 0, i = 0, o = 0, u = 0, j, len;
```

```
cout ("\n Enter anything:");
cin >> str
if (strlen (str) < 10)
str [11] = '\0';
len = strlen (str);
for (j = 0, j < len'; j++)
{
switch (str[j])
{ case 'a': a++;
break;
case 'e': e++;
break;
case 'i': i++;
break;
case 'o': o++'
break;
case 'u': u++;
break;  }        }
cout <<"\n A\tE\tI\to\tU\n";
cout <<a<<'\t'<<e<<'\t'<<i<<'\t'<<o<<'\t'<<u;            }
```

2. (a) Difference between operator and function overloading with the help of suitable example.

Ans. Refer to Chapter-5, Page No.-71 to 74

(b) Explain the concept of a destructor in a class. What is its role in terms of cleanup of unwanted objects?

Ans. Refer to Chapter-3, Page No.-23 to 24

3. (a) How is the exception handling performed in C++? Write a program that throws an arithmetic exception as and when a number input is greater than 9999.

Ans. Exception handling in C++ is performed using three keywords:

(a) throw

(b) try

(c) catch

throw throws an exception and catch catches the exception. Catch block contains the exception handling routine. Both throw and catch are included in the try block.

```
#include <iostream.h>
void main ()
```

```
{ int num;
try
{
cout <<"\n Enter any number";
cin >> num;
if (num > 9999)
throw num;
catch (int)
{ cout <<"\n Number is greater than 9999"; }    }    }
```

(b) Write a C++ template function, called exchange ( ) that accepts two arguments of generic type and swaps their contents.

Ans.

```
temptate <class T>
void swap (T & x, T & y)
{
T temp;
temp = x;
x = y;
y = temp;
}
```

4. (a) Write a C++ program to print reverse of a 5–digit number.

Ans.

```
#include <iostream.h>
void main ()
{
int num, rev = 0, rem, temp;
cout <<"Enter any number";
cin >> num.;
temp = num;
while (temp > 0)
{ rem = temp % 10;
temp = temp / 10;
rev = rev * 10 + rem;    }
cout <<"Reverse of" <<num<<"is"<<rev;    }
```

(b) Explain the concept of metadata.

Ans. Data about data is called as "metadata". Metadata describes the data. For example (i) A class is a metadata which defines the instances. (ii) A table structure is also a metadata which defines the each record of the table.

5. Define the following :

(i) Polymorphism

Ans. Refer to Chapter-1, Page No.-8

(ii) Typecasting

Ans. Refer to June-2005, Q.No.3(b), Page No.-266

(iii) Class and instance

Ans. A class is a vehicle to implement the OOP features in the C++ language. Once a class is declared, an object of that type can be defined. An object is said to be a specific instance of a class.

```
class player {
char name;
public :
void getstats();
void showstats();         }
```

Once a class has been defined several objects of that type can be declared. For instance, an object of the class defined above can be declared with the following statement:

player Sachin, Dravid, Mohan; [Or] class player Sachin, Dravid, Mohan;
where Sachin and Dravid are two objects of the class player. Both the objects have their own set of member variables. Once the object is declared, its public members can be accessed using the dot operator with the name of the object. We can also use the variable no_player in the public section with a dot operator in functions other than the functions declared in the public section of the class.

```
E.g.  Sachin.getstats();
      Dravid.showstats();
      Mohan.no_player = 10;
```

(iv) Containership

When an object class contains another object class is called as containership.

For example:

```
class A
{
.....
class B {.....} b;
.....
}
```

(v) Abstract class

Refer to Dec-2001, Q.No.-6(c), Page No.-237

CS-72 : C++ AND OBJECT ORIENTED PROGRAMMING
December, 2007

Note : Question no. 1 is **compulsory**. Answer any **three** questions from the rest.

1. (a) Differentiate between Procedural Programming and Object Oriented Programming. List and explain the components of OOP. Also explain any five characteristics of OOP.

Ans. Refer to Chapter-1, Q.No.-1, Page No.-1

(b) What is Inheritance? Explain, with examples, the various types of inheritance. Explain any four advantage of inheritance.

Ans. **Refer to Page No.-76**

Types of Inheritance:

(1) Single Inheritance - Refer to June-2001, Q.No.-1(d), Page No.-239

(2) Multiple Inheritance - Refer to June-2001, Q.No.-1(d), Page No.-239

(3) Multilevel Inheritance - Refer to Chapter-6, Page No.-81

(4) Hybrid Inheritance - Refer to Chapter-6, Page No.-84

Advantages of Inheritance:

(1) Inheritance allows the redefining a member function of the base class and also adding new members to the derived class.

(2) Inheritance is used in C++ for class modification and extension.

(3) Inheritance is a powerful feature in C++ for code reusability.

(4) Inheritance imposes a hierarchical relationship among classes in which a child class inherits from its parent.

(c) What are templates? Write their syntax and usage. Design a function template in C++ to sort an array.

Ans. Refer to Chapter-2, Page No.-10

Syntax of Class Templates : Refer to Chapter-7, Page No.-114

Syntax of Function Template: Refer to Chapter-7, Page No.-113to114

Usage of Templates: Templates are used for advance applications in C++ where we want to use the same class or same function with different parameters.

Function template in C++ to sort an array

```
template <class T>
sort (T a[ ], int n)
{
for(int i = 0; i < n – 1; i++)
```

```
for(int j = n – 1; i < j; j—)
if(a[j] < a[j – 1])
{ T temp = V[j];
V[j] = V[j – 1];
V[j – 1] = temp; }
```

We can invoke this sort function just like any ordinary function in C++. Suppose if iArray and fArray are given as array of int and array of float, then we can apply same sort function to each array as:

```
sort(iArray);     //Sort the array of int
sort(fArray);     //Sort the array of float
```

(d) What is the significance of function overloading? Explain the various methods for overloading functions, giving examples of each.

Ans. Refer to June-2001, Q.No.-5(d), Page No.-244

2. (a) Justify the need of the scope resolution operator for accessing global variables, with an example.

Ans. Refer to Dec-2003, Q.No.-6(iv), Page No.-175

(b) What are friend function and friend class? Write a program to add 2 distances using friend function expressed in meters & cm and feet & inches.

Ans. Friend Function and Friend Class : Refer to June-2002, Q.No.6(a), Page No.-222

```
//Program to add two distances using friend function
# include <iostream.h>
class distance
{ private:
int feet;
double inches;
int meters;
double centimeters;
public:
distance(void);
~distance(void);
distance(int f, int m, double inch, double cm);
void get_distance(void);
void show_distance(void);
void set_distance(int f, int m, double inch, double cm);
Friend operator + (distance d);
};
distance:: distance(void) {        }
distance::~distance(void) {        }
distance::distance(int f, int m, double inch, double cm)
{ feet = f;
meters = m;
```

```
inches = inch;
centimeters = cm;          }
void distance::get_distance(void)
{ cout <<"Enter feet:";
cin>>feet;
cout <<"Enter meters:";
cin>>meters;
cout <<"Enter inches:";
cin>>inches;
cout <<"Enter centimeters:";
cin>>centimeters;          }
void distance::set_distance(int f, int m, double inch, double cm)
{ feet = f;
inches = inch;
meters = m;
centimeters = cm;          }
void distance::show_distance(void)
{ cout<<feet <<"\"<<inches <<"\"\n";
cout<<meter <<"\"<<centimeters <<"\"\n";          }
operator + (distance d)
{ double inch1 + = d.inches + 12.0*d.feet;
double cm1 = d.centimeters + 100*d.meters;
return(inch1, cm1);          }
void main(void)
{ distance d1;
cout <<"Enter the data::\n";
d1.get_distance( );
cout <<"distance = ";
d1.show_distance( );          }
```

3. (a) What is Operator Overloading? Overload the '+' operator for adding two-complex numbers.

Ans. Refer to June-2005, Q.No.-1(e), Page No.-260

(b) What is Polymorphism ? How do we attain Run time Polymorphism? Explain with an example.

Ans. Refer to June-2003, Q.No.-6(c), Page No.-192

4. (a) What are Streams? Explain the input and output streams. Write a program to demonstrate the application of either the input or output operator for user defined types.

Ans. Refer to Dec-2001, Q.No.-4(a), Page No.-234

(b) What are Macros? Explain their advantages and usage with an example.

Ans. Refer to Dec-2004, Q.No.-5(d), Page No.-294 & Dec-2003, Q.No.-6(i), Page No.-171to172

5. Write short notes on the following with a suitable examples for each.

(a) SIZEOF operator

Ans. SIZEOF operator: The sizeof( ) operator is a compile time operator and when used with an operand returns the number of bytes the operand occupies. The operand may be a variable constant or a data type quantifier. Example: sizeof(int) or sizeof(num) etc.

If a is an integer type variable then

cout<<sizeof(a); //It will give 2 as output as integer occupies 2 bytes in memory.

(b) Bitwise operator

Ans. BITWISE operator: They are used for manipulating the data at bit level. These operators are used for testing the bits or shifting them right or left. Bitwise operators are applicable to integer datatypes only and Bitwise operators are not applicable to float or Double datatypes.

Bitwise Operators	Meaning
&	Bitwise Logical AND
|	Bitwise Logical OR
^	Bitwise Logical XOR
<<	Left Shift
>>	Right Shift
~	One's Complement

(c) Use Case Diagram

Ans. Refer to Dec-2006, Q.No.-1(c)(i), Page No.-324

(d) Nested Classes

Ans. Nested Classes: If the class contain objects of other classes as its members, then this type of class is known as nested class.

Example: class alpha {————};
class beta {————};
class gamma {
alpha a; //object of alpha class
beta b; //object of beta class
———— };

Here gamma class is a nested class as it contains the objects a and b of alpha and beta classes.

(e) Copy constructor

Ans. Copy Constructor: A copy constructor is used to declare and initialize an object from another object of the same class.

Example: If I1 is the first object of integer class and I2 is the second object of integer then the statement.

integer I2 = I1 //It is the way a copy constructor is implemented in C++.

CS – 72: C++ AND OBJECT ORIENTED PROGRAMMING
June, 2008

*Note: (i) Question number 1 is **compulsory**.*
*(ii) Attempt any **three** questions from the rest.*

Q1. (a) State whether the following are true or false:
(i) The object oriented programming cannot be used for client server application.
(ii) The kernel of LINUX operating system is implemented in C++.
(iii) One of the advantages of object oriented database management system is that it reduces development cost.
(iv) Object Oriented Programming C++ is slower than procedural programming.
(v) Error handling cannot be done in object oriented programming.
Ans. **(i)** False, **(ii)** True, **(iii)** True, **(iv)** False, **(v)** False

(b) Write a program that accepts two strings as argument and reports whether the first string is part of second or not. In case first string occurs multiple times in second string, it reports the number of times it occurs in second.

Ans.
```
#include <iostream.h>
#include<conio.h>
#include<string.h>
int substring(char *,char *);
void main()
{ clrscr ( );
char s1[50],s2[20];
int i,j,f=0;
⇒ cout<<"enter main string" ;
gets(s1);
cout<<("Enter substring to be searched in main string : ";
gets(s2);
if(substring(s1,s2)!=0)
cout<<"Found";
else
cout<<"Not found";
getch ( ); }

int substring(char *s1,char *s2)
```

```
{ int f=0;
for(;*s1!=`\0`;)
{ if(*s2= =`\0`)
break;
for(;*s2!=`\0`;)
{ if(*s1= =*s2)
{ f=1;
s1+ +;
s2 + +;
} else {
f=0;
s1 + +;
break;
} } }
if(f = = 0)
return 0;
else
return 1;
getch( ); }
```

(c) Differentiate between dynamic loading and late binding.

Ans. Late Binding is also known as Dynamic Binding.

Refer to Page-299, Dec-2005, Q.No.-1(a)

(d) What are various viability modes in C++? Explain each of them with suitable examples.

Ans. Various visibility modes in C++ are: Private, Public and Protected.

Public Mode: In this mode all members in C++ class are public members that can be accessed by any function, whether member function of a class or non-member function of a class.

Example:

```
class X
{ public:
int a;
int sqr(int a)
{ return a * a; }
};
X obj1;
void main( )
{ int b;
obj1.a = 10;                //valid as public member
```

```
b = obj1.sqr(15);          //valid as public member
}
```

Private Mode: In private mode all the class member are private members and are hidden from outside world. The private members implement the OOP concept of data hiding. The private members of a class can be used only by member functions and friend functions of the class in which it is declared.

Protected Mode: In this mode all members are protected members that can be used only by the member functions and friends of the class in which it is declared. The protected members are similar to private members that cannot be accessed by non-member functions. The difference between protected and private members is that private members can be inheritable but private members are not inheritable.

(e) Differentiate between class diagram and interaction diagram. Also list their applications.

Ans. Class Diagram: Refer to Page-295, Dec-2004, Q.No.-6(a)

Interaction Diagram: Refer to Page-317, June-2006, Q.No.-4(a)

Q2. (a) Write a C++ program to accept a 5 digit number and report whether it is divisible by 3, 5, 7, 9 or not.

Ans.

```
#include <iostream.h>
#include <conio.h>
void main( )
{ int num;
cout<<"Enter a five digit number";
cin>>num;
if(num % 3 = = 0)
cout<<num<<"is divisible by 5";
if(num % 7 = = 0)
cout<<num<<"is divisible by 7";
if(num % 9 = = 0)
cout<<num<<"is divisible by 9; }
```

(b) Define the following:

(i) Operator overloading Refer to Page-260, June-2005, Q.No.-1(e)

(ii) Function overloading Refer to Page-307, June-2006, Q.No.-1(c)

(iii) Friend function Refer to Page-169, Dec-2003, Q.No.-5(a)

Q3. (a) What is UML? List primary goals of UML. Why do we use UML?

Ans. UML: Unified Modelling Language is a language for specifying, visualizing, constructing and documenting the artifacts of software systems, as well as business modeling and UML is an open method that offers a standard way to write a system's blueprints including conceptual components and concrete things.

Primary Goal of UML: It provides a formal basis which includes various types of diagrams such as Use Case Diagram, Class Diagram, Interaction Diagram and State Diagram for understanding the modeling languages, which can encourage the growth of object oriented tools markets.

Why do we use UML? We use UML because of the various benefits of UML which are as follows:

1. It provides user with a ready-to-use experience visual modeling language so that they can develop and exchange meaningful models.

2. Provides extensibility and specialization mechanisms to extend the user concepts.

3. Be independent of particular programming languages and development processes.

4. Integrate best practices.

5. It automatically transform to other representations (e.g. Java).

6. It can model concurrent and distributed system.

(b) Differentiate between modular programming and object oriented programming.

Ans. Object Oriented Programming: Refer to Chapter-1, Q.No.-1

Modular Programming: The technique of hierarchical decomposition of a procedural program, to specify the various modules or tasks that are to be completed in an order to solve a problem, is known as Modular Programming.

Modular Programming

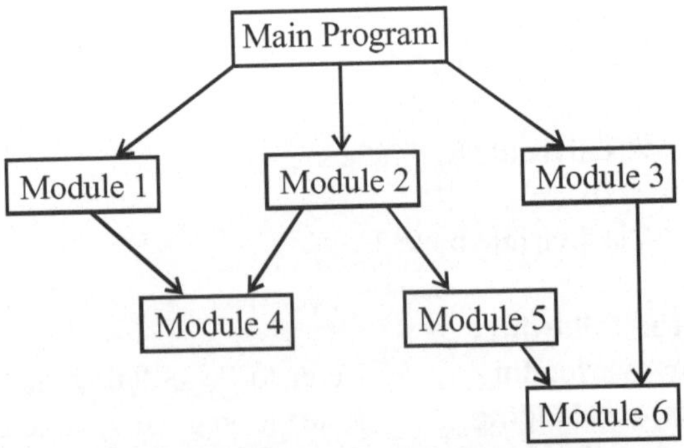

Fig : Typical Structure of Modular Programming

Main Characteristics of Modular Programming are:

1. Emphasis is given on algorithms.

2. Large programs are divided into smaller modules.

3. Most of the modules share global data.
4. Modules transforms data from one form to another.
5. Employs a top-down approach in program design.
6. Data move openly around the system from one form to another.

Q4. (a) What is meant by exception handling? Write a C++ program that throws an arithmetic exception whenever the result of arithmetic computation becomes odd.

Refer to Page-184, June-2003, Q.No.-2(a)

(b) Explain the concept of polymorphism with the help of suitable example.

Ans. Polymorphism: Using Operators and Functions in different ways by same name is called polymorphism. The word polymorphism means existing in different forms. Polymorphism can by implemented in C++ through:

(a) Function Overloading and **(b)** Operator Overloading

Example of Polymorphism: Refer to Page-277, Dec-2004, Q.No.-1(d)

Q5. Define the following :

(i) Activity diagram (ii) Python (iii) Source code reuse (iv) Macros (v) Comma operator in C++

Ans. (i) Activity Diagram: Activity diagram represents the business and operational step by step work flows of components in a system. We make activity diagram to emphasize the behaviour of a system.

(ii) Python: Python is an object-oriented scripting language used for writing system utilities and Internet scripts. It is also used as a glue language for integrating components in C and C++. Python is an interpreted language that compiles to byte code and requires a "Virtual Machine" for runtime execution.

(iii) Source Code Reuse: Refer to Page-188, Dec-2003, Q.No.-4(b)

(iv) Macros: Refer to Page-171, Dec-2003, Q.No.-6(i)

(v) Comma Operator in C++: Comma operator is simple operator in C++ which comes at the end position of operators precedence table in C++. We can use comma operator in the following manners:

Example 1:

int num1, num2, num3;

Here comma operator is used to declare three variables num1, num2 and num3 of same data type i.e. integer.

Example 2:

ans = (a = 10, b = 20, a + b);

Here ans = 30 using comma operator.

CS – 72: C++ AND OBJECT ORIENTED PROGRAMMING
December, 2008

Note: (i) Question number 1 is ***compulsory.***
(ii) Attempt any ***three*** *questions from the rest.*

Q1. (a) What are public and private inheritance? Why do we need different access specifiers for inheritance.

Refer to June-2006, Q.No.-1(d)

(b) What are the applications of use case diagram and interaction diagram? Give an example of each.

Refer to Dec-2006, Q.No.-1(b)

(c) How are objects created and initialized? Explain with the help of an example.

Ans. Object Creation and Initialization in C++: A class description will not reserve any space in the memory. It provides only a template or a blue print to create data objects. To create actual data, objects are created. Object reserves memory for individual data members.

Values can be assigned to individual data members using objects. Objects are created in C++ with following syntax:

```
classname      objectname;              //object declaration and creation//
```

Here class becomes the datatype for object. A class has same relationship with an object as that of a datatype to a variable.

The member functions of the class are invoked using object as:

```
objectname.member Function( );
```

Two scopes of declaration of objects in C++ are:

1. Global Object: If objects are declared outside all function bodies in a class. This object is globally available to all functions in the program i.e. object can be used anywhere in the class.

Example:

```
class X
{ public:
int a;
void fun(void);
};
X obj1;
int main( )
{ obj1.a = 10;                    //creation and initialization of object//
obj1.fun( );                      //object obj1 is global//
............
}
void fun1(void)
{ obj1.a = 20;                    //object obj1 is global//
obj1.fun( );
............
}
```

2. Local Object: An object is said to be a local object if it is declared with in a function, which means that this object is locally available to the function that declares it and it cannot be used outside the function declaration.

(d) Write a program which will accept a string from the user, reverse it and find whether the string is a palindrome or not.

Ans.
```
#include <string.h>
#include <stdio.h>
#include <conio.h>
void main( )
{ char str[80], rev[80];
int i, j, k, ans = 0;
cout <<"\n Enter any string (up to 79 character)";
gets(str);
for(i = 0; str[i] != '\0'; ++i);
for(j = i – 1, k = 0; j >= 0; —j; ++k)
rev[k] = str[j];
rev[k] = '\0';
cout <<"\n Reverse String is:";
puts(rev);
ans = strcmp(str, rev);
if(ans = = 0)
cout <<"String is a palindrome";
else
cout <<"String is not a palindrome";
getch( );
}
```

(e) Explain the concepts of operator overloading and function overloading with the help of an example of each.

Refer to June-2006, Q.No.-1(c)

Q2. (a) What is exception handling? How is it performed in C++? Explain with the help of an example.

Refer to June-2007, Q.No.-2(a)

(b) Write a C++ template function that accepts two arguments of any numeric type and finds the larger of them.

Ans. Template Function to Find Larger of Two Arguments
```
template <class T>
void Greater (T & x, T & y)
{ T res;
if(x >= y)
res = x;
else
res = y;
cout <<"Greater of two number is" <<res;
}
```

Q3. (a) How are arrays declared in C++? How can pointers manipulate

array elements? Give an example.

Ans. Array Declaration in C++: Array is a named list for a finite number n of similar data elements. Each of the data elements can be referenced respectively by a set of consecutive numbers, usually 0, 1, 2, 3 … n.

Array declaration can be done in C++ as: datatype arrayname[size];

Example: int arr[10];

Here arrayname is arr and its size is 10 elements each of type int.

Array can be one dimensional, two dimensional or multi dimensional.

Array elements can be manipulated using pointers.

C++ treats the name of an array as a pointer i.e. the base memory address of array elements i.e. C++ interprets array name as the address of its first element.

Example: A C++ program showing relations between array and pointers i.e. How array elements can be accessed and manipulated using pointers.

```
#include <iostream.h>
void main(void)
{ int num[10] = {2, 4, 6, 8, 10, 12, 14, 16, 18, 20};
cout <<"Value of num =" <<num <<endl;
cout <<"Value of num[0] =" <<num[0] <<endl;
cout <<"Value of &num[0] =" <<&num[0] <<endl;
cout <<"Value of num[5] =" <<num[5] <<endl;
cout <<"Value of *(num + 5) =" <<*(num + 5) <<endl;
int *ptr;
ptr = num;
cout <<"Value of *(ptr + 3)=" <<*(ptr + 3) <<endl;
cout <<"Value of ptr[3] =" <<ptr[3] <<endl;
cout <<"Value of num[3] =" <<num[3];
cout <<"\n Value After Increment" <<endl;
ptr = ptr + 1;
cout <<"Value of *(ptr + 3)" <<*(ptr + 3);
cout <<"Value of ptr[3] =" <<ptr[3];
cout <<"Value of num[3] =" <<num[3];
}
```

(b) Explain the concept of virtual functions with the help of an example.

Refer to June-2006, Q.No.-4(b)

Q4. (a) Define a friend function. Explain the access rights of a friend function with respect to public and private data members of a class with the help of an example.

Refer to June-2002, Q.No.-6(a)

(b) What is abstraction in object oriented languages? Explain its importance with the help of an example. Refer to Dec-2002, Q.No.-1(a)

Q5. Design and represent a queue of integers as a class. Also, illustrate the use of insert and delete operations for the queue. Make any assumptions that are required.

Refer to June-2002, Q.No.-1(b)

CS – 72: C++ AND OBJECT ORIENTED PROGRAMMING

June, 2009

Note: Question number **1** is **compulsory**. Attempt any **three** questions from the rest. All examples must be in C++ programming language only.

Q1. (a) Explain the use of inheritance with the help of an example. List three advantages of inheritance.

Refer to Page-161, Q. No.-1(a), now refer to Page-343, Q.No.-1(b)

(b) What is a friend function and a friend class? Write a program using friend function to add two objects representing heights expressed in feet and inches and meters and centimeters respectively.

Refer to Page-344, Q.No.-2(b)

(c) Explain the concept of constructors and destructors in a class with the help of an example.

Refer to Page-22, 23

(d) What is UML? List six goals of UML.

Refer to Page-349, Q. No.-3(a)

(e) Explain the significance of virtual function with the help of an example. What is a pure virtual function?

Refer to Page-86-87

(f) How would you make a library of user-defined functions? Explain it with the help of an example.

Refer to Page-18 2nd Heading.

Q2. (a) Design and implement a stack as a class template. Write the main ( ) function to show the use of stack template for data types, integer and float.

Refer Page-296, Q. No.-6 (b)

(b) Design a class complex representing complex numbers. Overload '<<' operator for this class complex.

Ans. Class A

```
{
public:
```

```
int x;
int y;
};
A operator+ (const A& x, const A& y)
{
        A retObj;
        retObj.y = x.y + y.y;
        return retObj;
}
ostream& operator<<(ostream& out, A& x )
        {
        out << x.x << " " << x.y << endl;
        return out;
                }

        int main()
                {
        A a,b,c;
        a.x = 5;
        a.y = 10;
        b.x = 4;
        b.y      = 15;
        c=a+b;
        cout << c;
        cout << a+b;
                }
```

Q3. (a) How is exception handling performed in C++ ? Write a program that throws an exception when an input number is greater than 1000.

Refer to Page-290, Q.No. 5 (b)

Now refer www.gullybaba.com/ignou/bca/cs72.html

(b) What are macros? Explain their advantages with the help of an example.

Refer to Page-294, Q. No.-1 (d)

Q4. (a) Write program in C++ that maintains the list of students enrolled in different courses alongwith their personal details in a file. Write code for creating, reading and updating this file.

Now refer www.gullybaba.com/ignou/bca/cs72.html

(b) Explain the significance of the scope resolution operator for accessing global variables, with the help of an example.

Refer to Page-175, Q.No.6 (iv)

Q5. Explain the following with the help of a suitable example:

(a) Containership

Refer to Page-342, Q. No. 5 (iv)

(b) Abstract class

Refer to Page-237, Q. No. 6 (c)

(c) Interaction diagram

Refer to Page-317, Q.No. 4 (a)

(d) Command Line arguments

Ans. Command Line Arguments:- the command line arguments are typed by the user and are delimited by the user and are delimited by a space.

The first argument is always the filename and contains the program to be executed.

The main() functions which we have been using up to now without any arguments can take two argumets

main(int argc, char*argv[]).

the first argument argc represents the number of arguments in the command line. The second argument argv is an array of char type pointers that points to the command line arguments. The size of this array will be equal to the value of argc.

(e) 'This' pointer

Refer to Page-188, Q.No.- 4 (a)

CS – 72: C++ AND OBJECT ORIENTED PROGRAMMING
December-2009

Note: Question number **I** is **compulsory**. Attempt any three questions from the rest.

Q1. (a) Define operator Overloading and function overloading. Write a C++ program to overload "+" operates to concatenate two strings and add two complex numbers.

Ans. Operator overloading and function overloading :

Refer to Chapter-5, Page-71

C++ program to overload '+' oater to concatenate two string and add two complex numbers. :-

Refer to Page-260-270

(b) What are pointers? What are the advantages of using pointers in programming? What are the differences between passing parameters by value and passing by reference (using pointers)? Give an examples of each.

Ans. In C++ a pointer is a variable that points to or references a memory location in which data is stored. Each memory cell in the computer has an address that can be used to access that location so a pointer variable points to a memory location we can access and change the contents of this memory location via the pointer.

Pointer declaration: A pointer is a variable that contains the memory location of another variable. The syntax is as shown below. You start by specifying the type of data stored in the location identified by the pointer. The asterisk tells the compiler that you are creating a pointer variable. Finally you give the name of the variable.

type * variable name

Example:

```
int *ptr;
float *string;
```

Now Refer to Page-51

(c) Explain the different forms of polymorphism in C++ with the help of an example.

Refer to Chapter -5, Page-71-74.

(d) Design and implement a class 'polynomial' of degree two that adds and subtracts two polynomials. Write the necessary constructors, destructors and overloaded functions for input-output.

Ans. Class Polynomial

```
{
        public:
                Polynomial();
                Polynomial(int numer, int denom = 1);
                void Insert(ostream &sout);
        void Extract(istream &sin);
                Polynomial Add(const Polynomial &Q) ;
                Polynomial Subtract(const Polynomial &Q);
                int Degree();
                double Coefficient(int I);
                double Evaluate(double Value);
                Polynomial Compose(const Polynomial &P);
        private:
                int degree;
                double coefficients[1000];
};
Polynomial operator+(const Polynomial &P,const Polynomial &R);
Polynomial operator-(const Polynomial &P,const Polynomial &Q);
ostream& operator<<(ostream &sout, const Polynomial &Q);
istream& operator>>(istream &sin, Polynomial &P);
#endif
#include <iostream>
#include "polynomial.h"
Polynomial::Polynomial()
{
}
Polynomial::Polynomial()
{
}
void Polynomial::Insert(ostream &sout)
{
        sout << Coefficient(I) << "x^" << Degree;
        return;
}
void Polynomial::Extract(istream &sin)
{
}
Polynomial Polynomial::Add(const Polynomial &Q)
{
}
Polynomial Polynomial::Subtract(const Polynomial &Q)
```

```
{
}
int Polynomial::Degree()
{
}
double Coefficient(int I)
{
}
double Evaluate(double Value)
{
}
Polynomial Compose(const Polynomial &P)
{
}
Polynomial operator+(const Polynomial &P,const Polynomial &Q)
{
        return P.Add(Q);
}
Polynomial operator-(const Polynomial &P,const Polynomial &Q)
{
        return P.Add(-Q);
}
ostream& operator<<(ostream &sout, const Polynomial &Q)
{
        Q.Insert(sout);
        return sout;
}
istream& operator>>(istream &sin, Polynomial &P)
{
        P.Extract(sin);
        return sin;
}
#include <iostream>
#include "polynomial.h"
using namespace std;

int main()
{
        Polynomial degree;
        cout << "Enter the highest degree of your polynomial: ";
        cin >> degree;
        Polynomial coefficients[degree];
```

```
for(int i = 0; i <= degree; i++){
cout << "Enter each coefficient individually, starting with the one with the highest degree(press enter after each)";
cin >> s;
}
```

Q2. (a) How are dynamic objects created and destroyed? Explain it with the help of an example.

Ans. Objects are dynamically created (allocated) and deleted (destroyed or deallocated) using operators *new* and *delete.* These operators are intended as replacements for the C storage allocation functions such as *malloc* and the storage deallocation function *free*, which are also available in C++. There are several advantages to using operators *new* and *delete* instead of using the functions *malloc* and *free*. For example,

(i) *new* does not require specification of the object size; it computes that automatically from the specified type.

(ii) *new* returns a pointer of the correct type. The pointer returned by *malloc* must typically be coerced to the desired pointer type. In ANSI C, the pointer returned by *malloc* is a *void* pointer which is automatically coerced to the desired pointer type.

(iii) Operators *new* and *delete,* respectively, invoke the appropriate constructor and the destructor to initialize the newly created object and to cleanup prior to deleting the object.

Operators *new* and *delete* call the global operator functions *new* and *delete,* or if defined class-specific operator functions with the same names to allocate and deallocate objects. Most programmers usually do not write their own customized storage allocation and deallocation operator functions (which are invoked by the operators *new* and *delete*) because they find the global functions to be adequate. Occasionally, programmer may have to write such functions to meet system design requirements (e.g., execution speed and storage allocation from a specific memory pool).

(b) Define a friend function. Explain the relation of friend function with respect to public, private and protected data members of the class.

Ans. Refer to Chapter-4, Page-56

Q3. (a) What is a class template? Define a class template for sorting an array.

Refer to Chapter -7, Page-114 and
Now Refer to December-2007,Q.No.-1(a), Page-343

(b) What are exceptions? Create an exception for checking division by zero.

Ans. Refer to Chapter-8, Q.No.-1,Page-134 and now

Create an exception for checking division by zero:- A program in c++:

```
#include<iostream.h>
#include<conio.h>
        class DivideByZero
        {
        public:
        double divisor;
        DivideByZero(double x);
        };
DivideByZero::DivideByZero(double x) : divisor(x)
        {
        }
        int divide(int x, int y)
        {
        if(y==0)
        throw DivideByZero(x);
        }
        try
        {
        divide(12, 0);
        }
        catch (DivideByZero divZero)
        {
          cerr<<"Attempted to divide "<<divZero.divisor<<" by zero";
        }
```

(c) Explain difference between dynamic binding and late binding with the help of an example.

Refer to June-2003, Q.No.-6.(c), Page-192

Q4. (a) Write a C++ program that will accept a string of maximum of 20 characters from keyboard and display the count of vowels in the string.

Ans. Refer to Q.No.-1 (d), Page-339

(b) What is a class diagram? Explain the steps involved in drawing a class diagram, with the help of an example.

Refer to December-2009, Q.No.-6(a), Page-295

Q5. Explain the following with the help of a suitable example:

(a) SIZEOF operator - Refer to December-2007, Q.No.-5(a), Page-346

(b) Copy constructor - Refer to December-2007, Q.No.-5(e), Page-346

(c) Inheritance visibility nodes or modes - Refer Page-81 to 84

(d) Pure virtual function - Refer Page-87

(e) Nested classes - Refer to December-2007, Q.No.-5(d), Page-346

CS-72: C++ AND OBJECT ORIENTED PROGRAMMING
June, 2010

Note: *Question number 1 is* ***compulsory****. Attempt* ***any three*** *from the rest. All examples must be in C++ programming language only.*

Q1. (a) What is an object? Explain its significance with the help of an example. Explain any three basic characteristics of any object oriented programming language.

Ans. Refer to Page No.-1 to 5, Q.No.1, Chapter-1

(b) Write a program in C++ to overload the '+' operator to concatenate two string variables using the simple expression x3 = xl + x2
Where xl, x2 and x3 are three string objects. Make suitable assumptions, if any.

Ans. Refer to Page No.-41, Q.No.-8

(c) What are Templates? How are templates defined? Differentiate between class and function templates with the help of an example of each.

Ans. Refer to Page No.-10, Chapter-2, Third Point,
Now Refer to Page No.-112-114

(d) Explain the following with the help of an example each :

(i) Scope Resolution Operator

Ans. Refer to Page No.-175, Dec-03, Q.No.-6(iv)

(ii) Protected inheritance

Ans. This allows derived classes of derived classes to know about the inheritance relationship. Thus your grand kids are effectively exposed to your implementation details. This has both benefits (it allows derived classes of the protected derived class to exploit the relationship to the protected base class) and costs (the protected derived class can't change the relationship without potentially breaking further derived classes). Protected inheritance uses the : protected syntax.

(iii) Private and public member functions

Ans. Member functions can be private or public, just as member variables are. Public member functions can be accessed anywhere in the program, even outside the class. Private member functions are for the sole use of the class itself. Usually member data are made private while functions (or methods) are made public. There might be instances where you might want to make certain functions private (i.e. you may not want the user to directly access these functions). Private functions can only be called from within public member functions. These functions are also called 'helper functions'.

Q2. (a) What are Bitwise operators? Explain the working of any one bitwise operator giving suitable examples.

Ans. Refer to Page No.-346, Dec-07, Q.No.-5(b)

Left shift and right shift operator : The bitwise left shift (<<) shifts operator bits to the left. For example, consider the number 3, which is binary 0011. Left shifting by 1 (3 << 1) changes 0011 to 0110, which is decimal 6. Note how each bit moved 1 place to the left. Left shifting by 2 (3 << 2) changes 0011 to 1100, which is decimal 12. Left shifting by 3 (3 << 3) changes 0011 to 1000. Note that we shifted a bit off the end of the number! Bits that are shifted off the end of the binary number are lost.

The bitwise right shift (>>) operator shifts bits to the right. Right shifting by 1 (3 >> 1) changes 0011 to 0001, or decimal 1. The rightmost bit shifted off the end and was lost!

Although our examples above are shifting literals, you can shift variables as well:

view source

print?

```
unsigned int nValue = 4;
nValue = nValue << 1; // nValue will be 8
```

Rule: When dealing with bit operators, use unsigned variables.

Programs today typically do not make much use of the bitwise left and right shift operator in this capacity. Rather, you tend to see the bitwise left shift operator used with cout in a way that doesn't involve shifting bits at all! If << is a bitwise left shift operator, then how does cout << "Hello, world!"; print to the screen? The answer is that cout has overridden (replaced) the default meaning of the << operator and given it a new meaning.

(b) What is the difference between arguments passed by value or passed as reference? Explain the difference with the help of an example.

Ans. Refer to Page No.-62, Q.No.-4

Q3. (a) Define the terms constructor and destructor. Give an example of each. What is copy constructor? Give an example to illustrate its use.

Ans. Refer to Page No.-22-23 & Page No.-346, Q.No.-5(e)

(b) Explain the purpose of macros in C++ with the help of an example.

Ans. Refer to Page No.-67, Q.No.-8

Q4. (a) What is Dynamism? Explain any three kinds of dynamism for object-oriented design with an example for each.

Ans. Refer to Page No.-299, Dec-05, Q.No.-1(a),

Example Dynamic Binding : Page No.-14,15

(b) Consider the following class hierarchy.

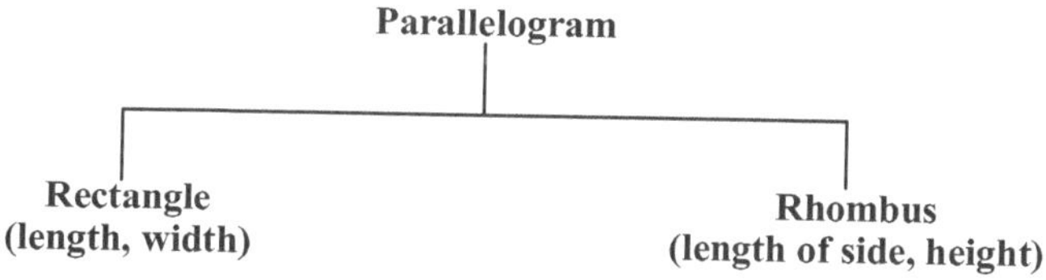

Create the class hierarchy using C++, having at least one constructor for each class. Assuming that all parallelograms are either rectangles or rhombuses, write a polymorphic function to calculate the areas of the figures.

Ans. Class parallelogram

```
{ int length;
 public:
    Parallelogram () {length = 0;}
          long area () = 0;
};
Class Rectangle : public parallelogram
{ int width;
   Public;
     Rectangle () {length = 0; width = 0;}
     long area ()
     { return length*width;
     }
    void input () { cin >> length >> width; }
};
Class Rhombus : public parallelogram
{ int height;
     public:
      Rhombus () {length = 0; height = 0; }
      void input () {cin >> length >> height;}
      long area ()
     { return length*height;}
};
```

Q5. (a) How is exception Handling implemented in C++? Write a program in C++ that raises an exception when a number is divided by zero and prints a suitable error message.

Ans. Refer to Page No.-167 Dec-03, Q.No.-3(a),
Now Page No.-361, Q.No.-3(b)

(b) What are friend functions? Explain the utility of friend functions with the help of an example.

Ans. Refer to Page No.-169, Q.No.-5(a) & Page No.-189, Q.No.-6(a)

CS-72: C++ AND OBJECT ORIENTED PROGRAMMING
December, 2010

Note: *Question number 1 is* **compulsory**. *Attempt* **any three** *from the rest. All examples must be in C++ programming language only.*

Q1. (a) What is UML? Why is UML used? What are Interaction diagrams and why are they used? Explain types of Interaction diagrams

Ans. UML: Refer to Page No.-349, June-09, Q.No.-3(a),
Interaction diagrams: Refer to Page No.-317, June-06, Q.No.-4(a) and;

(b) What is Inheritance? Explain the two main types of Inheritance giving examples of each.

Ans. Refer to Page No.-343, Dec-07, Q.No.-1(b)

(c) Explain the utility of 'this' pointer with the help of an example.

Ans. Refer to Page No.-188, June-03, Q.No.-4(a)

(d) What are Macros? How are they different from in-line function? Explain with the help of examples.

Ans. Refer to Page No.-67, Chapter-4, Q.No.-8

(e) Write a menu-driven program in C++ to add, modify and search a student record in a file.

Ans.
```
#include <iostream.h>
#include <string.h>
class student
{  int rollno;
    char name [25]
   public:
     void input ( )
     { cout << "\n Enter roll no.";
      cin >> roll no;
      cin << "\n enter name:";
      cin >> name;
     }
     int getroll no ( ) { return rollno.
      void setname (char, *n) {strcpy (name, n);}
     void display"( )
     { cout << "\n Roll no: " << roll no << " Name: "
               << name ; }
```

```
};
int main ( )
{ student s;
      char n [25];
  int ch=0; rollno;
fstream file ("student. dat:, ios:: in | ios:: app);
do {
   cout << "\n 1. Add";
   cout << "\n 2. Modify:'
   cout << "\n 3. Search":
   cout << "\n 4. Exit";
   cout << "\n Enter your choice:";
   cin >> ch;
     switch (ch)
     { case 1: s.input ( );
              file.write ((char) & s, size of (s));
              break;
      case 2: cout << "\n enter roll no:";
              cin >> roll no:
              file. seekg(0);
              do { file.read ((char )&s, size of (s)):
              if (file.oof ( )) {cout << "Not found"; break;}
              else if (s.getroll no ( ) == roll no)
              {  s.input ( );
                     file.write ((char *)& s, size of (s));
                     break;
              }
          }
        break;
   case 3: cout << "\n Enter roll no:";
           cout >> roll no;
           file.seek g(o);
           do{file.read ((char*)s, size of (s));
           if (file. Of (1) { cout << "not found"; break)
           else if (s. get roll no ( ) = = roll no.)
           {  s.display ( ) ; break ;}
           :
   case 4: break;
           otherwise: cout "((" in invalid choice, try again";
  }while (ch; = 4);
return 0;
}
```

Q2. (a) What are Virtual Functions? Explain their utility with an example. Explain pure virtual function.

Ans. Refer to Page No.-86-87, Chapter-6

(b) Explain any five disadvantages of the C programming language as compared to C++.

Ans. Refer to Page No.-9-10

Q3. Explain the following terms with suitable examples.

(a) Size of operator

Ans. Refer to Page No.-364, Q.No.-5(a), December-2007

(b) && and | |

Ans. The logical operators && and || are used when evaluating two expressions to obtain a single relational result. The operator && corresponds with Boolean logical operation AND. This operation results true if both its two operands are true, and false otherwise. The following panel shows the result of operator && evaluating the expression a && b:

&& OPERATOR

a	b	a && b
true	true	true
true	false	false
false	true	false
false	false	false

The operator || corresponds with Boolean logical operation OR. This operation results true if either one of its two operands is true, thus being false only when both operands are false themselves. Here are the possible results of a || b:

|| OPERATOR

a	b	a || b
true	true	true
true	false	true
false	true	true
false	false	false

E.g. ((5 == 5) && (3 > 6)) // evaluates to false (true && false).
((5 == 5) || (3 > 6)) // evaluates to true (true || false).

(c) ++i and i++

Ans. Both i++ and ++i exist since both can only be used to add one and both are the same length. The reason for the two alternatives is that these are not really intended to be used as stand alone statements but are really designed to be able to be incorporated into more complex statements where you actually update more than one variable in the one statement.

Probably the simplest such statement is as follows:

```
j = i++;
```

This statement updates the values of both of the variables i and j in the one statement. The thing is that while ++i and i++ do the same thing as far as updating i is concerned they do different things with regard to updating other variables. The above statement can be written as two separate statements like this:

```
j = i;
i += 1;
```

Note that combining them together means we have eight characters instead of 13. Of course the longer version is much clearer where it comes to working out what value j will have. Now if we look at the alternative:

```
j = ++i;
```

This statement is the equivalent of the following:

```
i += 1;
j = i;
```

This of course means that j now has a different value to what it had in the first example. The position of the ++ either before or after the variable name controls whether the variable gets incremented before or after it gets used in the statement that it is used in.

(d) : :

Refer to Page No.-175, Q.No.-6(iv)

(e) Throw exception

Ans. Refer to Page No.-167, Q.No.-3(a), Dec-03

Q4. (a) How can a library of your own function be created? Create a library to include the function power (x, n) and swap (a, b).

Ans. Library of our own functions is created by storing the header file a nd that header file can be included in any other file.

<u>Lib. H</u>

```
long power (int x, int, n)
[     int i; long result = 1;
      for (i =1; i <=n; i++)
            result * = x;
            return result;
}
void swap (int & a, in sab)
{  int temp;
```

```
    temp = a;
    a = b;
    b = temp;
}
```

(b) What is Reusability? Explain any five factors that influence reusability.

Ans. Reusability: Refer to Page No.-76, Chapter-6

Reusability implies some explicit management of build, packaging, distribution, installation, configuration, deployment, maintenance and upgrade factors. If these issues are not considered, software may appear to be reusable from design point of view, but will not be reused in practice.

Q5. (a) Write a class template using C++ for creating a linked list.

Ans. Class template: Refer to Page No.-118, Q.No.-3

(b) How can objects be passed as arguments to a function? Using this method, write a program for adding two matrices.

Ans. The object can be passed as argument similar to basic data type in a function. e.g.,

matrix sum (matrix, matrix);

Refer to Page No.-29, Q.No.-4

CS-72: C++ AND OBJECT ORIENTED PROGRAMMING
June, 2011

Note: *Question number 1 is* ***compulsory****. Attempt* ***any three*** *from the rest. All examples must be in C++ programming language only.*

Q1. (a) Define a class ACCOUNT that includes following members:
Data Members: Name of Depositor, Account no., Type of A/c, Balance Amount.
Member functions: To assign initial values, deposit amount, withdraw after checking balance, To display name and balance.
Write a program in C++ and test it for 10 Customers.

Ans.
```
#include <iostream.h>
#include <stdio.h>
#include <conio.h>
#include <process.h>
//statement of customer detail....
struct acc_inf
{
char c_name[25];
int acc_no;
float balance;
char acc_type[7];
};
//statement of Class....
class bank
{
struct acc_inf x;
public:
void input( );
void withdrawal(int,float);
void deposit(int,float);
void display(int);
};
//statement of customer information...
void bank::input( )
{
cout<<endl<<" Enter the name of customer:- ";
gets(x.c_name);
cout<<" Enter account no:- ";
cin>>x.acc_no;
```

```
cout<<" Enter opening balance:- ";
cin>>x.balance;
cout<<" Enter acc_type (SAVING/CURRENT):- ";
gets(x.acc_type);
}
//statement of withdrawal function...
void bank::withdrawal(int ac,float money)
{
if(x.acc_no= =ac)
{
if(x.balance-1000>=money)
x.balance -= money;
else
cout<<"Sorry, Insufficient Balance";
}
else
cout<<"** Sorry, Account no. is not found ** ";
}
// Statement of deposit function...
void bank::deposit(int ac,float money)
{
if(ac= =x.acc_no)
x.balance += money;
else
cout<<"Sorry, Account no. is not found...";
}
// Statement of display Function...
void bank::display(int ac)
{
if(ac= =x.acc_no)
{
cout<<"\nYour acc_no is: "<<x.acc_no;
cout<<"\nYour name is: ";
puts(x.c_name);
cout<<"\nYour current balance is: "<<x.balance;
cout<<"\nYour type of account is: "<<x.acc_type;
}
}
//statement of main Function....
main( )
{
```

```
bank obj; //creating object for class bank
int ac;
float money;
int c;
clrscr( );
do
{
clrscr( );
cout<<endl<<"Welcome to Banking System";
cout<<"\n______________________________";
cout<<endl<<endl<<"1: Open New Account of the customer.";
cout<<endl<<"2: Withdrawal the money.";
cout<<endl<<"3: Deposit the money.";
cout<<endl<<"4: Display information about customer.";
cout<<endl<<"5: Quit";
cout<<endl<<"what is your choice: ";
cin>>c;
switch(c)
{
case 1:
obj.input( );
break;
case 2:
cout<<"Enter account no: ";
cin>>ac;
cout<<"enter the money to withdrawal: ";
cin>>money;
obj.withdrawal(ac,money);
break;
case 3:
cout<<"enter acc no: ";
cin>>ac;
cout<<"enter the money to deposit: ";
cin>>money;
obj.deposit(ac,money);
break;
case 4:
cout<<"enter acc no: ";
cin>>ac;
obj.display(ac);
```

```
break;
case 5:
exit(0);
default:
cout<<"Sorry, unable to process.. Try again later";
}
cout<<"Press Enter to continue...";
getch( );
}while(c!=5);
return 0;
}
```

OUTPUT

```
Welcome to Banking System
_______________________________________
1 : Open New Account of the customer.
2 : Withdrawal the money.
3 : Deposit the money.
4 : Display information about customer.
5 : Quit
What is your choice: 1
Enter the name of customer:- GULLY BABA
Enter account no:- 123
Enter opening balance:- 500000
Enter acc_type (SA/CA):- SA
Your new account has created...............................
THANKYOU
Press Enter to continue...........
Welcome to Banking System
_______________________________________
1 : Open New Account of the customer.
2 : Withdrawal the money.
3 : Deposit the money.
4 : Display information about customer.
5 : Quit
What is your choice: 2
Enter account no:- 123
Enter the money to withdrawal:-100000
Press Enter to continue...........
Welcome to Banking System
_______________________________________
1 : Open New Account of the customer.
```

2 : Withdrawal the money.
3 : Deposit the money.
4 : Display information about customer.
5 : Quit
What is your choice: 3
Enter account no:- 123
Enter the money to deposit:-50000
Press Enter to continue...........
Welcome to Banking System

---

1 : Open New Account of the customer.
2 : Withdrawal the money.
3 : Deposit the money.
4 : Display information about customer.
5 : Quit
What is your choice: 4
Enter account no:- 123
Your acc-no is : 123
Your name is : GULLY BABA
Your current balance is: 450000
Your type of account is: SA
Press Enter to Continue...
Welcome to Banking System

---

1 : Open New Account of the customer.
2 : Withdrawal the money.
3 : Deposit the money.
4 : Display information about customer.
5 : Quit
What is your choice: 5

(b) Differentiate between:

(i) Procedural Programming and Object Oriented Programming.

Ans. Refer to Page No.-1, Q.No.-1, Chapter-1

(ii) Data Encapsulation and Inheritance.

Ans. Refer to Page No.-11 [Encapsulation and Data Hiding]

(c) Explain the utility of the friend function, using an appropriate example.

Ans. Refer to Page No.-312, Q.No.-1(e), June-2006

(d) Explain the steps involved in drawing interaction diagram with the help of an example.

Ans. Refer to Page No.-317, Q.No.-4(a), June-2006

Q2. (a) What do you mean by exception Handling? Write a C++ Program that throws an arithmetic exception whenever the Input number is less than zero.

Ans. Refer to Page No.-290, Q.No.-5(b), Dec-2004

```
Class Sample
{
Private:
        int a;
Public:
        enum
        {
        Sample ( );
        Sample (int);
        Void display( );
        };
 Sample :: sample (int x)
        {
        if (x<0)
        throw  (x);
        }
 Void funct(int n)
        {
        try
        {
        Sample obj(n);
        }
        Catch (int k)
        {
        Cout << "Less than zero";
        }
 }
```

(b) What do you mean by Polymorphism? Explain with an example.

Ans. Refer to Page No.-169, Q.No.-5(b), Dec-2003

Q3. (a) How do you use scope resolution operator for accessing global variables? Also discuss its other uses.

Ans. Refer to Page No.-171, Q.No.-6(iv), Dec-2003

(b) What is a Virtual Base Class? Explain with an example.

Ans. Refer to Page No.-84 [Virtual Base Class]

Q4. (a) What is an inline function? Explain with an example and also discuss its limitations.

Ans. Refer to Page No.-58 [Inline function]

(b) Define operator overloading. Explain its advantages.

Ans. Refer to Page No.-72 [Operator Overloading]

Q5. Explain the following with examples:

(a) Input and Output streams

Ans. Refer to Page No.-203, Q.No.-4(b), Dec-2002

(b) Constructor and Destructor

Ans. Refer to Page No.-22 [Constructor] & Page No.-23 [Destructor]

(c) Abstract classes

Ans. Refer to Page No.-85 [Abstract Classes]

(d) Preprocessor directives

Ans. Preprocessor Directives: When the preprocessor encounters this directive, it replaces any occurrence of "identifier" in the rest of the code by "replacement". This replacement can be an expression, a statement, a block of statement etc. The preprocessor does use # defines. Its format is # define identifier replacement.

For example

```
#include <iostream.h>
#define getmax(a, b) [(a)>(b)?(a):(b)] int main( )
{
int x=5, y ;
y=getmax(x, 2);
cout<<y<<end1;
cout<<getmax(7, x)<< end1;
return 0;
}
```

CS-72: C++ AND OBJECT ORIENTED PROGRAMMING
December, 2011

Note: *Question number 1 is* ***compulsory****. Attempt* ***any three*** *from the rest. All examples must be in C++ programming language only.*

Q1. (a) Differentiate between the following:

(i) Class diagram and Interaction diagram.

Ans. Refer to Page No.-349, Q.No.-1(e), June-2008

(ii) Dynamic loading and late binding.

Ans. Refer to Page No.-348, Q.No.-1(c), June-2008

(b) What is function overloading? Write a program in C++ which has a function add that is able to concatenate two strings, if value passed are strings and can perform addition, if values are numbers.

Ans. Refer to Page No.-358, Q.No.-1(a), Dec-2009

(c) Discuss various looping statements provided in C++? Explain their syntax with example.

Ans. There are three loops in C++ which are:

(1) The for Loop: A main function of for loop is to repeat statement while condition remains true.

Ø For loop Contains Initialization, condition and increment in a single line.

Ø It work in following ways:

- Initialization is executed
- Condition is checked. If it is "true" the loop continues otherwise the loop end and statement is skip (not executed).
- Statement is executed.
- Finally Increment/Decrement and go to Step2 "Condition checked".

Syntax:

```
For (Initialization; Condition; Increment)
{
Statement 1;
Statement 2;
.
.
.
Statement n;
}
```

Example:

```
#include <iostream.h>
#include <conio.h>
```

```
void main ( )
{
int i ;
for (i=1; i<=10; i++)
Cout << i<<",";
getch( );
}
```

OUTPUT

1,2,3,4,5,6,7,8,9,10

(2) The While Loop: The functionality of while loop is simply to repeat statement while the condition expression is true.

Syntax:

```
Initialization
While (condition)
{
Statement 1;
.
.
.
Statement n;
Increment;
}
```

Example:

```
#include <iostream.h.>
#include <conio.h>
void main ( ) {
int i ;
i =1;
while (i<=10)
{
cout <<i<<",";
i=i+1;
}
getch( );
}
```

OUTPUT

1,2,3,4,5,6,7,8,9,10

(3) The Do-While Loop: Its functionality is exactly same as while loop, except that condition in the do-while loop is evaluated after the execution of statement instead of before, granting at least one execution of statement even if condition is never fulfilled.

Syntax:

```
Initialization
do
{
Statement 1;
Statement n;
Increment;
}
While (condition);
```

Example:

```
#include <iostream.h>
#include <conio.h>
void main( )
{
int i;
i=1:
do
{
cout<<i<<",";
i=i+1;
}
while (i<=10);
getch( );
}
```

Output:

1,2,3,4,5,6,7,8,9,10

Q2. (a) Write a C++ program to reverse a four digit number.

Ans. Refer to Page No.-341, Q.No.-4(a), June-2007

(b) What do you mean by object oriented programming? How it differs from modular programming?

Ans. Refer to Page No.-350, Q.No.-3(b), June-2008

Q3. (a) Explain the advantages and usage of Macros with an example.

Ans. Refer to Page No.-345, Q.No.-4(b), Dec-2007

(b) What is operator overloading? Overload the '+' operator for adding two complex numbers.

Ans. Refer to Page No.-345, Q.No.-3(a), Dec-2007

Q4. (a) Explain this pointer with an example.

Ans. Refer to Page No.-171, Q.No.-6(ii), Dec-2003

(b) Differentiate between private, public and protected data members of the class using examples.

Ans. Refer to Page No.-22 [Public, Private and Protected Members]

Q5. Explain the following:

(a) Multiple and multilevel inheritance

Ans. Refer to Page No.-81 [Multilevel inheritance] & Page No.-82 [Multiple inheritance]

(b) Base and derived classes

Ans. Base Class: A class can be built as another class that is already defined and it is existing. This existing class is called the Base Class or parent class or Super Class.

Ø A base class is a class that is created with the intention of deriving other classes from it.

Derived Class: The derived class inherits all the properties of Base Class. That is to say that the child class inherits all the member variables and methods of the Base Class.

Ø The child class can have its own member variables and methods.

Syntax for Deriving Derived Class:

Class child Class: Public Base Class

```
{
---
---  } // Body of Child Class
---
}
```

Example:

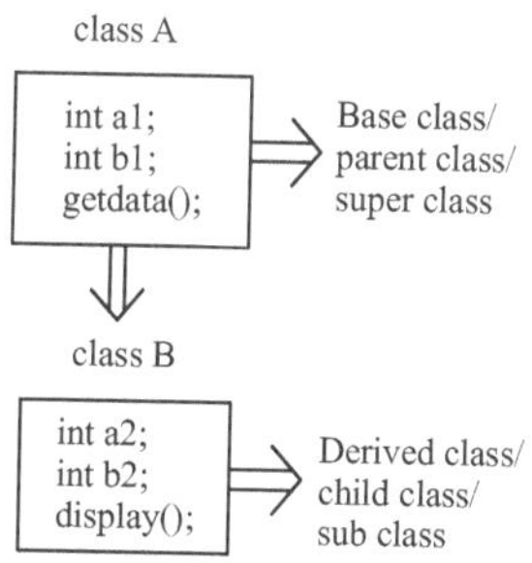

(c) Scope resolution operator

Ans. Refer to Page No.-171, Q.No.-6(iv), Dec-2003

(d) Parameterized constructor

Ans. Refer to Page No.-282, Q.No.-3(a), Dec-2004

CS-72: C++ AND OBJECT ORIENTED PROGRAMMING
June, 2012

Note: *Question number 1 is* **compulsory**. *Attempt* **any three** *questions from the rest. All example must be in C++ programming language only.*

Q1. (a) What is Object Oriented Programming? Explain any three advantages of OOP over Procedure Oriented Programming.

Ans. Refer to Page No.-1, Q.No.-1, Chapter-1

(b) Create a class Employee. Include Emp-no, Emp-name, Basic – Salary, DA, HRA, Conveyance and Medical as data members. Include member functions to accomplish the following:

(i) Accept Emp-no, Emp-name and Basic-Salary from the user.

(ii) Calculate DA as 50 per cent of Basic Salary and HRA as 30 per cent of Basic-Salary.

(iii) Initialise conveyance and Medical to ₹2000 and ₹1000 respectively, whenever on object is created.

(iv) Count the number of objects created.

(v) Display the data of all employees entered and the gross salary computed as sum of the Basic – Salary, DA, HRA, conveyance and Medical.

Write the appropriate main function for the above.

Ans.

```
# include <iostream.h >
class Employee
{
        private:
                int emp-no;
                string emp-name;
                float basic, da, hra, conv, medical;
        Public:
                void input ( );
                float calc ( );
                void display ( );
};
void Employee :: input ( )
{
        cout <<"\n enter emp-no";
        (in>> emp-no;
        cout <<"\n enter employee name";
```

```
        (in>> emp-name;
        cout <<"\n enter basic salary";
        (in>> basic;
}
float Employee :: calc ( )
{
        da = (50*bs)/100;
        hra = (30*bs)/100;
}
Employee :: Employee ( )
{       static int count;
        count ++;
        convey = 2000;
        medical = 1000;
}
void Employee :: display ( )
{
        cout << emp-no;
        cout << emp-name;
        cout <<"\n"<<basic<<", "<<da<<","<<hra
        <<","<<convey<<","<<medical;
        cout <<"Gross Salary"<< (basic + da + hra + convey + medical);
}
void main ( )
{
        Employee e;
        e. input ( );
        e. calc ( );
        e. display ( );
}
```

(c) What are friend functions? Explain two merits and two demerits of using friend functions.

Ans. Refer to Page No.-169, Q.No.-5(a), Dec-2003

Merits:

(i) We can able to access the other class members in our class if, we use friend keyword.

(ii) We CAN access the members without inheriting the class.

Demerits:

(i) Maximum size of the memory will occupied by objects according to the size of friend Members.

(ii) We cant do any run time ploymorphism concepts in those members.

(d) Explain the following with relevant examples:

(i) inline functions

Ans. Refer to Page No.-172[inline function]

(ii) call by reference

Ans. Refer to Page No.-170, Q.No.-5(c), Dec-2003

(iii) break, continue and exit.

Ans. The break statement: The break statement will transfer control to the first statement after the body of the latest for, while, do or switch in which it is present. For example.

```
while (1)
{
        cin >> height;
        if (height > 10000)
        break;
}
cout <<" Reduce Altitude";
```

The continue statement: The continue statement will terminate the current iteration of the while, for or do loop statement;

```
For (I = 0; i<st-strength; ++ i)
{
        if (marks [(i+1)]>=50
        continue;
        else
        // communicate to the student that
        //he has failed
}
```

The exit statement: The exit statement is used to finish or exit the execution of an enclosing loop statement. If the exit statement includes a condition, then the exit from the loop is conditional.

Q2. (a) What is Exception Handling and how is it implemented in C++? Elaborate it with the help of an example.

Ans. Refer to Page No.-167, Q.No.-3(a), Dec-2003

(b) Explain the scope and inheritance of public, private and protected members of a class.

Ans. Refer to Page No.-22, Chapter-3 & Page No.-310, Q.No.-1(d), June-2006.

Q3. (a) What is a default copy constructor and why is it needed? Explain with the help of an example.

Ans. A copy constructor is a special constructor in the C++ programming language for creating a new object as a copy of an existing object. The first argument of such a constructor is a reference to an object of the same type as is being constructed (const or non-const), which might be followed by parameters of any type (all having default values).

Normally the compiler automatically creates a copy constructor for each class (known as a default copy constructor) but for special cases the programmer creates the copy constructor, known as a user-defined copy constructor. In such cases, the compiler does not create one. Hence, there is always one copy constructor that is either defined by the user or by the system.

Now, Refer to Page No.-22[Constructor]

(b) What do you mean by templates? Explain the creation and usage of function templates for executing linear search on an array.

Ans. Refer to Page No.-112, Chapter-7

```
#include<iostream.h>
using namespace std;
template <class T>
void Lsearch(T *a, T item, int n)
{
        int z=0;
        for(int i=0;i<n;i++)
        {
                if(a[i]== item)
                {
                        z=1;
                        cout<<"\n Item found at position = "<<i+1<<"\n\n";
                }
                else
                if(z!=1)
                {
                        z=0;
                }
        }
        if(z==0)
        cout<<"\n Item not found in the list\n\n";
}
void main()
{
```

```
        int iarr[10] = {2,42,56,86,87,99,323,546,767,886};
        double darr[6]= {2.4, 5.53,44.4, 54.45, 65.7,89.54};
        int iele;
        double dele;
        cout<<"\n Elements of Integer Array \n";
        for(int i=0;i<10;i++)
        {
                cout<<" "<<iarr[i]<<" ,";
        }
        cout<<"\n\n Enter an item to be search: ";
        cin>>iele;
        cout<<"\n\n Linear Search Method\n";
        Lsearch(iarr,iele,10);
        cout<<"\n Elements of double Array \n";
        for(int i=0;i<6;i++)
        {
                cout<<" "<<darr[i]<<" ,";
        }
        cout<<"\n\n Enter an item to be search: ";
        cin>>dele;
        cout<<"\n\n Linear Search Method\n";
        Lsearch(darr,dele,6);
        system("pause");
}
```

Q4. Differentiate between the following with the help of examples.
(a) Operator overloading versus function overloading.
Ans. Refer to Page No.-71 & 72, Chapter-5

(b) Static binding Vs. dynamic binding.
Ans. Refer to Page No.-217, Q.No.-4(b), June-2002

Q5. (a) What are Virtual functions? Where are they needed? Are virtual functions inherited? Justify your answer with the help of an example.
Ans. Refer to Page No.-150, Q.No.-5(a), June-2004
The virtual functions allow programmers to declare functions in a base class, which can be defined in each derived class. A pointer to an object of a base class can also point to the objects of its derived classes. In this case, a member function to be invoked depends on the class's object to which the pointer is pointing. When a call to any object is made using the same interface, the function relevant to that object will be selected at run-time.

(b) Explain the various data types used in C++. What are the rules for naming variables in C++.

Ans. Refer to Page No.-339, Q.No.-1(b), June-2007

Rules for Naming C++ Variables

Variable names can consist of:

- Letters
- Digits
- Underscores

Example: "num1" to store the first of 3 numbers

- Variable names cannot start with a digit.

Example: "3integers" is illegal

- Variable names should not start with an underscore.

Example: Avoid the use of variable names like "_number"

- Variable names should consist of 31 or fewer characters to ensure portability.
- Variable names should be descriptive of their use.

Example: "grade" would be a good name to use for a variable that stores a student's test grade.

- Variable names are case sensitive.

Example: "x1" is not the same as "X1"

Keywords such as "int" and "float" cannot be used as variable names.

CS-72: C++ AND OBJECT ORIENTED PROGRAMMING
December, 2012

Note: *Question number **1** is **compulsory**. Attempt **any three** questions from the rest. All examples must be in C++ programming language only.*

Q1. (a) Imagine a publishing company that markets both books and audio-cassettes version of their work. Create a class Publication that stores the title (string) and price (float) of a publication. From this class derive two classes: Book which adds a pagecount (int); and Tape which adds playing time in minutes (float). Each of the three classes should have a function to accept data from the user and a function to display data to the user.

Write a main programme to test the book and tape classes by creating instances of them, asking user to fill in data and then displaying the data.

Ans. Class publication

```
{
        protected:
                string title;
                float price;
        public;
                void input ( );
                void display ( );
};
class book: public publication
{
        protected:
                int page-count;
        public:
                void input ( );
                void display ( );
};
class Tape: public publication
{
        protected:
                int time;
        public:
                void input ( );
                void display ( );
};
void publication :: input ( )
```

```
{
        cout<<"Enter book name";
        cin>>title;
        cout<<"Enter price";
        cin>>price;
}
void publication :: display ( )
{
        cout<<"Name"<<title;
        cout <<"price" <<price;
}
void book :: input ( )
{
        publication :: input ( );
        cout <<"Enter no. of pages";
        cin>> page_count;
}
void book :: display ( )
{
        publication :: display ( );
        cout<<"pages"<<page-count;
}
void Tape :: input ( )
{
        publication :: input ( );
        cout<<"Enter playing time";
        cin>> "time";
        void Tape :: display ( )
        {
                publication :: display ( );
                cout<<"Time" << time;
        }
        void main ( )
        {
                publication p;
                Book b;
                Tape t;
                p.input ( );
                p.display ( );
                b.input ( );
                b.display ( );
                t.input ( );
                t.display ( );
        }
}
```

(b) Explain the difference between inline functions and macros in C++, giving examples of each.

Ans. Refer to Page No.-67, Q.No.-8, Chapter-4

(c) Explain how objects are initialised. Give examples using C++.

Ans. Refer to Page No.-352, Q.No.-1(c), Dec-2008

(d) What is object oriented programming? Explain any five characteristics of object oriented programming languages.

Ans. Refer to Page No.-1, Q.No.-1, Chapter-1

The characteristics of OOP languages are:

- Class definitions – Basic building blocks OOP and a single entity which has data and operations on data together
- Objects – The instances of a class which are used in real functionality – its variables and operations
- Abstraction – Specifying what to do but not how to do; a flexible feature for having a overall view of an object's functionality.
- Encapsulation – Binding data and operations of data together in a single unit – A class adhere this feature
- Inheritance and class hierarchy – Reusability and extension of existing classes Polymorphism – Multiple definitions for a single name - functions with same name with different functionality; saves time in investing many function names Operator and Function overloading
- Generic classes – Class definitions for unspecified data. They are known as container classes. They are flexible and reusable.
- Class libraries – Built-in language specific classes
- Message passing – Objects communicates through invoking methods and sending data to them. This feature of sending and receiving information among objects through function parameters is known as Message Passing.

(e) Define Inheritance. Explain single Inheritance and multiple inheritance with the help of examples.

Ans. Refer to Page No.-76[Inheritance] & Page No.-239, Q.No.-1(d), June-2001

Q2. (a) Write a program in C++ to overload the + = operator to allow the following operation on strings.

S1 + = S2 where S2 is concatenated to S1 and the result is stored in S1.

Ans.
```
/*PROGRAM TO IMPLEMENT STRING CONCATENATION USING
OPERATOR OVERLOADING*/
#include<conio.h>
#include<iostream.h>
#include<stdio.h>
```

```
#include<string.h>
class string_concat
{
        char name[20];
        public:
        void input()
        {
                gets(name);
        }
        void output()
        {
                cout<<name<<endl;
        }
        string_concat operator+(string_concat s2)
        {
                string_concat s;
                strcpy(s.name," ");
                strcat(s.name,strcat(name," "));
                strcat(s.name,s2.name);
                return(s);
        }
};
void main()
{
        string_concat s1,s2,s3;
        clrscr();
        cout<<"Enter first name: ";
        s1.input();
        cout<<"Enter last name: ";
        s2.input();
        cout<<"first name is: ";
        s1.output();
        cout<<"Last name is: ";
        s2.output();
        s3=s1+s2;
        cout<<"Complete name is: ";
        s3.output();
        getch();
}
```

(b) What is function overloading? How is it implemented? Illustrate it with the help of an example.

Ans. Refer to Page No.-71[Function Overloading],

Following example shows implementation of function overloading:

```
#include <iostream.h >
#include <math.h>
#define PI 3.14
using namespace std;
void area(int);
void area(int, int);
void main()
{
        area(5);
        area(2, 5);
        getch();
}
int area(int r)
{
        float area_cir;
        area_cir = PI * r * r;
        cout << "\nArea of circle: " << area_cir;
}
int area(int a, int b)
{
        int area_rect;
        area_rect = a * b;
        cout << "\n\nArea of rectangle: " << area_rect;
}
```

Q3. Differentiate between the following with examples:

(a) Constructors and destructors

Ans. Refer to Page No.-22 & 23

(b) Call-by-value and call-by-reference

Ans. Refer to Page No.-51 & 52

(c) Do-while and while loops

Ans. Refer to Page No.-379

(d) Structures and classes

Ans. Refer to Page No.-18 & 19

Q4. (a) What is dynamic binding? Explain it with the help of an example.

Ans. Refer to Page No.-102, Q.No.-11, Chapter-6

(b) What are virtual functions and pure virtual functions? Explain their utility with the help of an example.

Ans. Refer to Page No.-86[Virtual Functions], Page No.-87[Pure Virtual] and Page No.-386, Q.No.-5(a), June-2012

Q5. (a) What are friend functions? How do they act as bridges between two classes? Explain with the help of an example.

Ans. Refer to Page No.-169, Q.No.-5(c), Dec-2003

A **Friend Function** is a function that can have access to even the private, protected members of a class. This can be an ordinary function or a member of another class. It acts as a bridge between two classes. For example:

```
#include <iostream.h>
class friendcl
{
        private:
        int a,b;
        public:
        friend int sum ( friendcl x);
        void set( int w, int q);
};
void friendcl:: set( int w, int q)
{
        a= w;
        b=q;
}
        int sum (friendcl x)
{
        return x.a + x.b;
}
        int main()
{
        friendcl r;
        r.set(6,7);
        cout << "The sum of the values is::" << sum (r);
        return 0;
}
```

In the above example the class "sum" is a friend function for the class "friendcl". So this can use even the private variables "a,b" of the class "friendcl". The function "sum" is not a member of any class. The "x" is an object of the class "friendcl" function, which is declared in the friend function to pass arguments. Thus, a bridge between two classes, i.e. "sum" and "friendcl" can be established.

(b) Explain this pointer with an example.

Ans. Refer to Page No.-188["This" pointer]